THE MAKING OF RUSSIAN ABSOLUTISM
1613–1801

LONGMAN HISTORY OF RUSSIA

The Making of Russian Absolutism 1613–1801

Second Edition

PAUL DUKES

LONGMAN
London and New York

Longman Group UK Limited,
Longman House, Burnt Mill, Harlow,
Essex CM20 2JE, England
and Associated Companies throughout the world

*Published in the United States of America
by Longman Inc., New York*

© Paul Dukes, 1982, 1990

First published 1982
Second edition 1990
Second impression 1991

British Library Cataloguing in Publication Data

Dukes, Paul, 1934–
The making of Russian absolutism, 1613–1801.– 2nd ed.–
(Longman history of Russia).
1. Russia. Absolutism, history
I. Title
321.60947

ISBN 0-582-00324-5

Library of Congress Cataloging in Publication Data

Dukes, Paul, 1934–
The making of Russian absolutism, 1613–1801 / Paul Dukes. —2nd ed.
p. cm. — (Longman history of Russia)
Includes bibliographical references.
ISBN 0–582–00324–5
1. Soviet Union—Politics and government—1613–1689. 2. Soviet
Union—Politics and government—1689–1800. I. Title. II. Series.
DK114.D84   1990
947'.046—dc20   90-5496
                                                                              CIP

Produced by Longman Group (FE) Ltd
Printed in Hong Kong

Contents

Preface to the First Edition

The principal purpose of this book is to trace the development of the Russian variety of a fairly common European phenomenon, absolutism. It will not therefore consist simply of the story of the Romanovs and their achievements and failures, although some of them, notably Peter the Great and Catherine the Great, will occupy a large place in it because of their roles in the making of this state system. Because of the basic concept, there will also be more concentration on political and social aspects than on economic and cultural. For the same reason, there will be emphasis on Russia in its international setting. A minor theme accompanying the structural metaphor will be the vicissitudes in the history of the Moscow Kremlin.

In most chapters, I have made at least a little use of my own primary researches, but most of the work is a synthesis of the reading and talking, listening and thinking about the subject that I have managed to achieve during the course of twenty years involvement in it. I have tried to acknowledge my most important debts, as well as to give some indications of further reading, in the Notes and Select Bibliography. In addition, I have benefited from the help and advice given in many libraries, especially those at the University of Aberdeen, whose predecessors were already accumulating many of the books that I have been able to consult during the period under consideration.

Unless otherwise stated or implied, dates are given in the Old Style, that is ten days behind New Style in the seventeenth, eleven days in the eighteenth century. The transliteration system used for the most part is modified Library of Congress. The major departures from it are the omission of the diaresis on ё, elimination of all references to hard and soft signs, rendering of final -ii by -y and adoption of aberrant common forms or usages.

The dedication is to my colleagues in the Study Group on Eighteenth-Century Russia; I hope that this will not restrain their criticisms, and that neither they nor others will be inhibited from pointing out the book's errors, misunderstandings and other inadequacies by my acceptance of full responsibility for them.

King's College, Old Aberdeen,   PAUL DUKES
23 April 1981

Preface to the Second Edition

Warm thanks are due to the dedicatees and others, in particular James Forsyth, for their observations which have led to the elimination of typographical and other errors, and to a certain amount of reformulation. On the whole, however, the basic structure has not been changed, and wide difference of viewpoint with at least a few critics will have to remain. I have sought in an extended conclusion to draw attention to some of the general issues confronting the student of Russian absolutism, and in the Notes and Select Bibliography to incorporate at least a little more of the vast range of material available on the subject in English, and to a lesser extent Russian (bearing in mind that most readers might be deterred by too formidable a list of recommendations, and are unlikely to have command of other foreign languages).

King's College, Old Aberdeen,   PAUL DUKES
30 September 1989

List of maps

CHAPTER ONE

Introduction – Reconstruction under the Romanovs: Michael, 1613–1645

Russia was discovered in 1553, and in a manner which recalls the more famous discovery of America in 1492. For, just as the expedition led by Columbus was expected to reach the riches of the Orient by way of the Western route, so the adventurous band under the command of Sir Hugh Willoughby was expected to reach the same goal by sailing east, round the North Cape. A further link between the two routes of exploration was embodied by Sebastian Cabot, earlier renowned for following in the wake of his father John over to the New World, now governor of the group sponsoring this fresh venture. As the voyage turned out, Willoughby and the crews of two of the ships from a fleet of three got lost and were frozen to death somewhere in Lapland in the winter of 1553–54. Meanwhile, perhaps luckier rather than more skilful, Captain Richard Chancellor had sailed the third ship, the *Edward Bonaventure*, into the White Sea and dropped anchor at the mouth of the River Dvina. From there, Chancellor went overland to Moscow at the invitation of Tsar Ivan IV, to whom he presented on arrival a letter from Edward VI of England addressed to 'all kings, princes, rulers, judges, and governours of the earth, and all other having excellent dignitie on the same, in all places under the universall heaven'. Proposing the establishment and development of mutual trade, the letter argued that: 'the God of heaven and earth greatly providing for mankinde, would not that all things should be found in one region, to the ende that one should have neede of another, that by this meanes friendship might be established among all men, and every one seeke to gratifie all'. God's will as interpreted by Edward VI and his advisers was not to be fulfilled in the short or the long run. Nevertheless, although Edward himself was now in fact dead, Ivan IV did respond in a positive manner to his brother monarch's letter, and from this small and somewhat accidental beginning relations between England and Russia were to grow over the next two centuries or so to a level of considerable significance.

The 'discovery' of Russia had occurred at just about the right moment, like most accidents of any significance in history. For, much more than the arrival of Columbus in America, that of Chancellor in Russia was not so much in a land completely unknown as in a land hitherto unheeded. True, consciousness of Muscovy, as the English were first to call the land of the tsars, had previously been greater in areas nearer to it in central Europe, but had certainly also existed even in England. If the first important book on the subject had been Sigismund von Herberstein's *Rerum Moscoviticarum commentarii* first published in Vienna and based on visits in 1517 and 1526, news of the place had certainly percolated to London before the work began to go through seventeen editions between 1549 and 1589, and, if Ivan III had made in 1493 an alliance with Denmark, individuals from the British Isles, especially Scotsmen, were known to be in Muscovy from about that time onwards. And, even before, contacts established during the Kievan period had not been completely forgotten during the years of the Mongol yoke and the establishment of the dominance of Muscovy over other principalities. But now the time was ripe for the further emergence of Russia into the European consciousness. Why was this so, and what kind of civilisation had developed in Russia over the centuries previous to 1553?[1]

The fundamental fact of Russian history, according to V. O. Klyuchevsky, the outstanding pre-revolutionary historian, was colonisation in a boundless plain. This fundamental fact, in Klyuchevsky's view, worked itself out through three successive phases. First, there was Kievan Rus on the River Dnepr. This emerged from an age-old Slavonic culture, which had stabilised in the midst of a number of nomadic peoples in the vast steppe to the north of the Black Sea. Among many external influences were the arrival of mercenaries from Scandinavia and the reception of Christianity from 'East Rome' or Byzantium. The second phase of Russian colonisation, after domestic dissension and the Mongol invasion in the early thirteenth century, took place in the upper regions of the Volga and its tributaries. Here, an appalling climate, poor soil and great forest combined to produce a distinctive social organisation based on the extended family and surmounted by a government of princes. By the late fifteenth century, Moscow had firmly established its supremacy over neighbouring cities, and Ivan III or Great began to call himself 'tsar' (from Caesar). The third phase of colonisation began for Klyuchevsky early in the seventeenth century, at the same time as his book. Before considering the reasons for this demarcation, let us look at Muscovy in the late sixteenth century, at the end of the second phase.

During the reign of Ivan IV, both the Russian conception of world history and Russian participation in it assumed something like clear definition, along with the first establishment of absolutism. Ivan himself, usually known as the Terrible, elaborated a genealogy for the tsars first devised by Ivan III which made them the heirs of Caesar

Augustus and the Byzantine emperors. His negotiations with Habsburg and English monarchs, carried on at the same time as parleys and wars with the Turks and the Tatars of the Crimea and the Volga, put Muscovy firmly into Europe. His grasp on the central government was probably more assured than that of his predecessors, and the influence of that government widened to take in such regions as Novgorod to the west and Kazan and Astrakhan to the east. In the second of these two directions, a Cossack counterpart of the Elizabethan sea-dogs, Yermak extended Russian influence overland into Siberia, and the natural wealth of that vast area began to be exploited in a systematic manner, while, on the other side, Chancellor's first contact soon led to many others and the formation in London of the Russia Company. The trade developed with England was of no small significance, the ships which defeated the Armada being partly furnished with Russian materials, for example. What the English now did, some such as the Germans had already done, and others such as the Dutch were about to do, and, if trade followed the flag, it in turn was followed by further forms of contact, including cultural. Russia was not such a stranger to the great movements of the Renaissance, Reformation and Counter-Reformation as is often supposed, particularly if ecumenical definitions are employed for Orthodoxy to be given its full place in the Christian family. Moreover, in Russia as elsewhere, the waning of the Middle Ages was accompanied by the dawning of a new humanism, and by reformist and apocalyptic movements in the Church.

While the case just put forward in a summary fashion might convince the uninitiated, there are experts in sixteenth-century Russian history who would no doubt consider that its assertion has been too confident. In order to mollify them and indeed in order to redress the balance, some antithesis needs to be advanced. Thus, the self-portrait drawn by Ivan IV was not as appreciated by others as it was by himself. If he could address Elizabeth of England in terms of easy fraternal familiarity, the Virgin Queen in response did not feel her heart warmed by thoughts of the tsar or of his icy kingdom. The general conception of Muscovy even among those who had visited it or subjected it to study was clearly revealed in books and maps to be vague and inaccurate. If Ivan had subdued the Tatars of the Volga, he was not able to contain the Tatars of the Crimea, who still made forays from their Black Sea citadel deep into territories already assimilated by Moscow, while Ivan failed completely in his bid to secure for his state a firm foothold on the Baltic Sea. Even to call sixteenth-century Russia a state is to go too far, perhaps, for Ivan's absolutist or proto-absolutist control was more an aspiration than a reality, as is evident in his weird experiments in state-craft including an arbitrary administrative division — the *oprichnina* — a puppet tsar and multiple matrimony. If commerce could be conducted only with some misunderstandings and failures of communication, how much more were cultural contacts with the outside world no more than imperfect and spasmodic. And the Russian Orthodox Church had to coexist with an old Slavonic culture consisting of pagan belief and folk wisdom at home as well as with Roman Catholicism and Protestantism abroad.

Even Ivan's apparent madness might to some extent be explained by his realisation of the impossibility of accomplishing the tasks that he had necessarily set himself as well as by personal disability. As if to underline the extent of the problems that confronted him, the State such as he had built up fell apart soon after his death in that turbulent period of Russian history known as the Dark Time or Time of Troubles. After this almost complete disintegration, the State began to take shape again and then to expand under a new dynasty, the Romanovs, who were to be intimately associated with the making of Russian absolutism on a firmer and more lasting basis than that achieved by their predecessors.

However, in the fresh foundation, there had to be much use of old materials, real as well as metaphorical, as many of the acts of the seventeenth-century drama were played out against the background of the Moscow fortress-city, the Kremlin, and the scene was to some extent set by the principal players. Let us, as guidebooks used to say, linger a while to dwell on this scene.

Archaeological digs have discovered remains of wooden defences on the raised site on the banks of the River Moscow which date as far back as the eleventh century, but it was not until the late fifteenth century that the headquarters of Muscovite tsardom took on something like their definitive appearance during the reign of Ivan III, or Great. The basic irregularity of contour had already been determined by the natural setting, the lines of the hill and the flow of the River Moscow and a tributary, but now Ivan promoted the erection of over two kilometres of red brick wall around the periphery of the Kremlin's sixty or so acres, as well as the raising of the twenty towers set into it. The most impressive of these is perhaps the Spasskaia or Redeemer Tower leading into the Kremlin from Red Square near St Basil's Cathedral. This was built in 1491, the year before Columbus sailed to America, and was designed by another Italian, Pietro Antonio Solari. Many repairs were done to it in the sixteenth century, and then, characteristically, substantial alterations were made during the reign of the first Romanovs, just a few of many instances of a distinctive stamp being put on their inheritance by the new establishment. Michael ordered clothes to be made to cover the nakedness of statues set into the tower in order to satisfy the standards of modesty of the time. Alexis installed an icon to the Redeemer, thus giving the tower its present name, and at the same time issuing an edict that no man, not even the tsar himself, could pass through the gateway without dismounting from his horse and removing his hat.

The manner in which the Kremlin interior cathedrals and palaces as well as external walls and towers were constructed by Ivan III and his successors was a solid representation of the manner in which the tsars of the sixteenth and seventeenth centuries made their contribution to the formation of Russian absolutism. Of course, in several respects, the imposing structures of the Kremlin constitute too imposing a metaphor for their rule. The vast distances and the intractable climate of Europe's eastern extremity rendered the autocracy an aim rather than an achievement, even when there was no immediate fear of Tatar incursion or foreign war. Nevertheless, the Russia emerging from the ordeal of the Time of Troubles, young and weak like the tsar though it was, already pointed the way forward to the mighty Empire of Peter the Great and Catherine the Great. Indeed, Klyuchevsky went so far as to say that the year 1613 marked the beginning of modern Russian history, and, as a good university professor, he gave reasons for his choice: 'a new dynasty, new and enlarged territorial boundaries, a new class structure with a new ruling class at its head, and new economic developments'. At the same time Klyuchevsky emphasised that the process was not by any means painless:

The policies pursued by the state imposed such strains on society that it was unable to respond; the acquisition of new territories through wars increased the powers of the state, but had an inhibiting effect on the activities of the people. The external successes of this new Russia are reminiscent of a bird, whose wings are useless as it is buffeted about and carried along by a whirlwind.[2]

And so, along with the consolidation of the Romanov succession came the entrenchment of serfdom at the bottom of the social pyramid and the enlistment of a service class at its apex, while the early development of Russian capitalism was inhibited in such a manner that many analysts would deny that it developed at all during the seventeenth century. We will return to these problems of interpretation later; for the moment, let us concentrate on the manner in which Michael Romanov achieved supreme power and then put it to use.

In fact, Michael did not achieve power so much as have it thrust upon him. His elevation came about after long deliberation, with those in a position to make the choice at first agreeing only that they wished to rid Muscovy of foreigners and foreign puppets. Even allies could not be trusted, as a contemporary account by Henry Brereton powerfully illustrated. In his *Newes of the present Miseries of Russia*, he gave the following description of a campaign launched by the Swedes in 1610:

Now must the miseries of Russia be augmented by the coming of this Army compounded of so many Nations, English, French, and Scots. For though they came as a friend, and for their aid, yet who can stay an Army from spoil and rapine, which the unhappy Russian found true in the pursuit of this bloody war, not only on their goods and chattels, but even in their wives and daughters which in all places were made a prostituted prey to the lustful appetite of the soldiers.

Experiences such as this moved one of the new national leaders, Prince Dmitri Pozharsky, to declare in 1612 that 'We do not now need hired people from other states. . . . We ourselves, boyars and nobles. . .serve and fight for the holy, godly churches, and for our Orthodox Christian faith and for our fatherland without pay.'[3] Fervently wishing to see the last of mercenary allies, Pozharsky was in no doubt that the greatest enemies of faith and country were the Catholic Poles. Whoever was elected tsar should not bear the taint of collaboration with them.

Such a bill was not easy to fill, since most of the boyars and nobles had at some point during the many sudden reverses of fortune during the Time of Troubles associated themselves with a cause that could be identified as Polish. The Romanovs were not so much more blameless than other families in this respect as less exceptionable from other points of view. For Prince Pozharsky and his aristocratic associates, there was nobody else from their own class who could satisfy them at the same time as being acceptable to other social forces joining in the work of liberation, especially the Cossacks, who led by Ivan Bolotnikov had just been involved in a vast peasant war.[4] For the top members of Muscovite society, the Romanovs could boast a pedigree extending as far back as the foundation of Kiev as well as experience of the ways of the court and the procedures of administration stretching over the course of several centuries. As for the Cossacks, their own relations with the Poles and their puppet tsars had been far from exemplary, and they were therefore not too much disturbed by the circumstance that Michael's father, Filaret, had been elevated to the patriarchate by one of the puppets, especially since he had then been held in captivity in Poland. Filaret's exile not only aroused sympathy for the Romanov family at a time of patriotic upsurge, but also made Michael, a by no means robust youth of sixteen, appear malleable enough to many who hoped to be influential in the formation of the new regime. And so a *zemsky sobor* or national assembly duly agreed that the whole people should humbly beseech Michael to become their tsar. And this, after he had been discovered in the seclusion of a monastery and after he had made the customary refusals, is what he did, and his coronation ensued in the Kremlin in the summer of 1613.

There has been much discussion among historians concerning the question of whether or not the manner of his elevation to the throne involved Michael in some kind of constitutional contract with his subjects. The formal answer to that question should almost certainly be in the negative, although, at least as much as before, the power of the autocracy rested on the foundation of an informal contract with the boyars and other members of the nobility. Through this alliance more than any other conjuncture there ensued the making of Russian absolutism.

If the new tsar had power thrust on him, his father soon relieved him of the burden. For, six years after the coronation of Michael

Fedorovich, the Patriarch Filaret (formerly Fedor Nikitich Romanov) was released by the Poles from eight years of captivity, and came home to share with his son the title of 'Great Sovereign' but to take over the reins of government exclusively for himself. To satisfy the elaborate protocol of the Russian court, a formal duplication or unison of ceremonial and edict was observed, but nobody, least of all Michael, was in much doubt about who was in real charge of the affairs of state until the death of the Patriarch in 1633.

A contemporary description quoted by John Keep presents Filaret as a man 'of medium height and build' with 'a fair knowledge of the scriptures'; he 'was of an irascible and suspicious temperament, and so imperious that even the tsar was afraid of him'. Keep himself makes a searching appraisal of the Patriarch:

Beneath his ecclesiastical robes there beat the heart of a power-loving boyar. Though personally pious, he had a fondness for luxury, ostentation and ceremonial display. Of autocratic mould, proud and stubborn, his strength of will was not matched by breadth of intellect. It would perhaps be misleading to draw a parallel with his great contemporary, Cardinal Richelieu, whom he resembles in some external respects. Filaret had nothing but disdain for western culture; instead, he drew inspiration from Byzantine traditions of the Russian past. He could be narrow-minded to the point of bigotry. In his concern to safeguard the purity of orthodoxy from contamination by heretical ideas, he attempted to isolate Muscovy behind an ideological curtain which retarded the country's intellectual development. The concept of progress had no place in his thinking. He was, in the literal sense of that overworked word, a 'reactionary', who sought to solve present problems by applying the formulas of a bygone age.[5]

His basic attitude and his skill reinforced by his experiences during the Time of Troubles and his years of imprisonment in Poland, Filaret now turned to their application in his foreign and domestic policy. To take international affairs first, the armistice of Deulino concluded with Poland at the end of 1618 brought about the release of Filaret and then allowed him a breathing-space. Another event of 1618, however, was the notorious Defenestration of Prague which marked the commencement of the Thirty Years War, approximately half of which was an insistent accompaniment to Filaret's pursuit of Muscovite international security. This fundamental purpose, it must be emphasised, required Filaret to concern himself with Asian and European problems simultaneously. For the sake of clarity, I will now concentrate on the west of Muscovy, leaving the south and east as far as we can for separate consideration later — a luxury which Filaret himself, of course, was denied.

In early 1617, the year before Deulino, the Peace of Stolbovo had been concluded with Sweden, Gustavus Adolphus agreeing to lift his siege of Pskov and to give up Novgorod. However, he held on to towns on the Gulf of Finland, thus depriving Russia of a foothold on the Baltic Sea. As for Deulino, this armistice was to last for fourteen and a half years, but the Poles did not give up Smolensk and some adjacent areas occupied by them, and the Polish king's son Wladyslaw did not abandon his claim to the Russian throne. And so while the Time of Troubles could be said to have been brought to an end before Filaret came home to be joint Great Sovereign, erstwhile enemies had deprived Muscovy of a considerable amount of its former territories, while bands of brigands, Cossacks and Tatars all posed considerable threats to domestic peace and stability.

Filaret's prime purpose was to reduce the power of his previous patrons and captors, the Poles, and he sought to do this by exploiting the tensions between them, the Swedes and the Turks in the generally taut international situation brought about by the Thirty Years War. After the Defenestration of Prague in 1618, the Habsburgs aimed at suppressing the movement for Bohemian independence, and could therefore no longer give their full support to the Poles in the drive to the east, or in the conflict with the Swedes that broke out in 1620. At this time, Gustavus Adolphus attempted to involve the Russians in the war, and soon afterwards the Turks also suggested an alliance against the Poles. In the autumn of 1621, Filaret convened a *zemsky sobor*, which expressed its readiness to support an alliance with Sweden, but the Russian forces were hardly in condition to put brave words into any kind of action, and in any case Gustavus Adolphus made peace with Poland after having seized Riga. Meanwhile, the Turks had suffered a reversal against the Poles in a battle at the River Dnestr, and were therefore in no position to press for immediate further campaigns.

The Thirty Years War had obviously only just begun to acquire the duration of time that would later give it a name, but already it had staked a firm claim to being looked upon as the first conflict to involve either directly or indirectly the whole of Europe. Now that the Austrian Habsburgs had restored their kind of order in Bohemia, they could work with their Spanish relations to contain France at the same time as working towards the consolidation of their position on the North Sea to the potential embarrassment of the recently independent Dutch Republic. As a counter to this expansionist policy, Cardinal Richelieu encouraged Christian IV of Denmark, who was also in receipt of subsidies from England and Holland, to carry the fight to Ferdinand II, the Habsburg Emperor, in 1625. Sensitive to the possibility of renewed conflict with the Poles, Filaret helped to prolong the preoccupation of their Habsburg sponsors with the Danish embroilment by giving subsidies to Christian IV in the form of cheap grain when the Anglo-Dutch assistance ran out in 1627. Denmark managed to keep going for a further two years, but its collapse in 1629 appeared to lay the way open for further Habsburg expansion towards the Baltic with consequent dangers for Swedish interests there. Fortunately, Gustavus Adolphus was able to conclude in the same year the truce of Altmark with his relative, Sigismund III of Poland, who still would not risk conflict for fear of leaving his eastern flank exposed to a Russian attack. In the summer of 1630, Gustavus Adolphus sprang to occupy Pomerania, receiving like Christian IV of Denmark before him the support of Richelieu, with subsidies from both France and England soon to follow.

Further assistance, in the shape of cheap grain which could be resold in the booming markets of Western Europe, especially Antwerp, came in increased quantities from Russia. Profits from this source could be even greater for Gustavus Adolphus than they had been for Christian IV, since the embroilment of Sweden with Poland over Pomerania meant a reduction in exports from the Baltic littoral at a time when the necessity of supplying mercenary armies combined with a fresh rise in European prices in general as a result of the import of silver from the New World. These grain subsidies, which were to be continued over a number of years, encouraged Gustavus Adolphus to strike deep into the heart of the Habsburg Empire even before the monetary assistance arrived from Western Europe.

At the same time as receiving this help from Filaret, the Swedish king was negotiating with his Russian counterpart for assistance of a more tangible kind, asking him to follow up the grain with his army. But the aims of the two monarchs did not completely overlap: Gustavus Adolphus wanted the Russians to engage the Poles so that he could continue his campaign in Germany; Filaret would have preferred the Swedes to aim for Warsaw rather than the German principalities so that his projected campaign for the recapture of Smolensk could be achieved the more easily. To entice Gustavus Adolphus, Filaret encouraged him to think of taking for himself the Polish crown in succession to Sigismund. To ease the path of his troops more generally, Filaret made an appeal at the beginning of 1631 to the English, Scots, Danes and Dutch for their support in his fight against the eastern flank of the Habsburg Catholic reaction. At the same time, Sweden signed a treaty with France, which promised further aid. In the spring, plans for a joint attack on Poland were worked out by Swedish and Russian representatives, and this news helped spur on Gustavus Adolphus to greater effort and to more victory. The Swedish monarch's triumph at Breitenfeld was celebrated in Moscow with a salute of cannon and a triumphant parade almost as if it were Stockholm. Meanwhile, further negotiations were carried on with the Turks, with the aim if not of military alliance at least of the restraint by the Sultan of his Crimean Tatar clients from attack on Russia and of the encouragement by him of them to join in the struggle against the Poles.

The actual commencement of the war for Smolensk was delayed not only by the protracted nature of these and other diplomatic activities, but also by the circumstance that the Russian army required several years to gird up its loins for the fight. Weapons and ammunition had to be procured as well as fortresses along the frontier strengthened. And since the army was composed of a heterogeneous mixture of noble levies, Tatar and Cossack detachments and foreign regiments, its assembly and mobilisation constituted a task of unusual complexity. And the money had to be raised through normal and extraordinary taxation channels.

A favourable moment for the inauguration of hostilities occurred in the spring of 1632 with the death of Sigismund III, and the subsequent struggle for the succession among various factions of the Polish-Lithuanian nobility. A *zemsky sobor* in the early summer gave its support, but the attack was delayed by an incursion from the south of the Crimean Tatars, breaking their previous agreements. And a promised plan of campaign from Gustavus Adolphus did not reach Moscow until the late summer. Finally, the army moved forward under the command of the boyar M. B. Shein, who had previously distinguished himself with a defence of Smolensk during the Time of Troubles and was now hoping for even more glory through an attack on the same citadel.

After capturing other towns on the way, Shein and his army moved on Smolensk towards the end of 1632, picking up fortresses as if they were birds' nests, according to one account. Meanwhile, Gustavus Adolphus had been preparing some of his troops for an attack on Poland and an important embassy had set off from Moscow to sign a treaty of alliance with the Swedes. But then, in the hour of his final victory, Gustavus Adolphus was killed, and his army lost much of its drive. As the Swedes adopted a negative attitude towards the question of the alliance, the newly elected Polish king Wladyslaw IV prepared for a counterattack. And the other potential ally of Filaret, the Turkish Sultan, had his hands full with the war against the Persian Shah. After a not completely secure winter siege of Smolensk, Shein subjected the city to a bombardment and attempted to undermine and take it in the early spring of 1633, but the Poles held out and the Russian army grew sick in body and morale as its commanders bickered among themselves. Moreover, encouraged by the Poles, the Crimean Tatars struck deep into the heart of Muscovy, approaching the capital itself, and some of Shein's army melted away to defend their homes, while others took advantage of the general disarray to form partisan bands terrorising Poles and Russians alike.

Towards the end of the summer of 1633, Wladyslaw himself came to Smolensk with a fresh army several thousand strong. Shein now found himself under great pressure, and a Russian relief army could not be properly mobilised because of the Tatar incursion and social disturbance. To cap all the Russian problems, Filaret followed the deaths of Sigismund and Gustavus Adolphus with his own, the arguments among the Russian commanders grew worse and Shein was forced to conclude an armistice at the beginning of 1634. Having handed over his artillery and supplies, and seen about half his mercenaries go over to the other side, Shein left Smolensk with about 8,000 remaining from an army which at the start of the campaign had numbered 35,000. He was soon to pay for his failure with his life. Wladyslaw could not press home his advantage as much as he would have liked; for his part, the orphaned and much troubled Michael was more than ready to bring the war to a formal conclusion. And so the 'perpetual' Peace of Polianovka of summer 1634 left the Poles in possession of Smolensk and the other Russian towns that they had gained from the Time of Troubles. Wladyslaw formally renounced his claim to the Russian throne, and informally pocketed a present of 20,000 roubles.

Freed from the embarrassment of the Smolensk War, Wladyslaw could fix his attention on the Swedes, who in their turn were now under pressure and more than ready to renew the truce with the Poles at Stuhmsdorf in the autumn of 1635, a few months after the Treaty of Prague had brought the Swedish phase of the Thirty Years War to an end. With continued support from anti-Habsburg sources, notably France, the Swedish army could continue to play a part in the remainder of the Thirty Years War which if less spectacular than it had been under Gustavus Adolphus was still of considerable significance. As for the Russians, they still harboured hopes for the recapture of Smolensk and revenge against the Poles, but the insistent probings of the Crimean Tatars forced them to turn their immediate attention to the south.[6]

During the postwar years, 1635 and 1636, the Russian government spent much money and effort on the construction of new defensive lines and fortress towns. It was not until the completion of the Belgorod line in the 1640s, however, that Moscow could feel relatively safe from the Tatar threat. A vigorous colonisation policy accompanied the building process, and hardy frontiersmen reclaimed the land for their farming purposes from the nomads who had been able to call the southern steppe their own for many years before.

Among the wandering peoples, some of whom themselves were becoming more sedentary, were the Don and Dnepr Cossacks, whose loyalty to Moscow, guaranteed by gifts of money and supplies, could be of no small importance to the central government. In 1637, taking advantage of the Turkish Sultan's preoccupation with war against the Shah of Persia, the Cossacks seized the strategically important fortress of Azov. This epic campaign immobilised the Tatars and incensed the Turks, who attempted to make their Crimean clients more attentive to their duties and themselves moved to lay siege to Azov in the summer of 1641, as soon as was practically possible after the war with Persia and another with Venice had been brought to an end. Although many times outnumbered, the Cossacks refused to surrender and managed with great skill and courage to survive continued bombardment and prolonged investment. Faced by the threat of winter, hunger and insurgency among the janissaries, the Turks lifted their siege.

Realising in late 1641 that they could not hold out indefinitely without more aid from Moscow, the Cossacks sent their emissaries to petition Michael to adopt Azov formally and to instal a garrison in it. All too conscious of the thousands of soldiers and roubles that such a step would entail, the tsar and his advisers decided to summon the *zemsky sobor*, which duly met in early 1642. Representatives from the upper classes lost no time in voicing their complaints on all kinds of scores such as bureaucratic delays in government, the depredations wrought by foreign merchants, and the flight of Russian peasants. As far as Azov was concerned, there was some enthusiasm for taking the fortress over, but very little for handing over the necessary wherewithal. Taking such disgruntlement and reluctance into consideration along with their own desire to avoid head-on confrontation with the Turks at such an inauspicious moment, Michael and his boyars decided to instruct the Cossacks to give up Azov, which they duly did later on in 1642.

The capture, defence and surrender of Azov was the most noteworthy of a considerable number of incidents involving Cossacks and Tatars in the vast undulating southern steppe, and chain reactions of various kinds could make themselves felt from the Dnepr to the Volga and back again.[7] We have already noted how wars between Russia and Poland or between Turkey and Persia affected developments throughout the broad space in between. An internal example could be taken from the years 1634–36, when the Nogai hordes of Tatars moved away from the Volga under pressure from the Kalmyks and, after vigorous altercations with the Cossacks on the Don, broke through to join and strengthen their fellow Tatars in the Crimea. Along the Volga during the first half of the seventeenth century, not only Tatars but other tribesmen were at least reducing their internecine strife, and Russians were increasingly infiltrating the region for strategic, commercial and missionary purposes. But violence could flare up at almost any time, and banditry was endemic.[8] Muscovy had not yet penetrated far into the mountain fastnesses of the Caucasus, although beyond the Volga the Bashkirs owed fealty, paid tribute and contributed to frontier defence. Their capital, Ufa, gained importance as a trading centre and staging post en route for Siberia.

If the southern steppe was vast, the wilderness of Siberia was truly immense, and many of the indigenous population saw as little of incomers as their Eskimo and Red Indian cousins in North America. On the other hand, considerable fortunes were already being made out of the fur trade by such families as the Stroganovs, and much income also accrued thereby to the state. If rarely looked on as El Dorado, Siberia was nevertheless a place of mystery and fable: among its fauna and flora was often included the ambiguous *boronets* or 'vegetable lamb', which looked like a lamb but grew like a vegetable, expiring after having consumed whatever was within its reach. And in his diary of a voyage to Russia via the North Cape in 1618, John Tradescant gave the following description of the 'Sammoyets' of the equally mysterious and even more sparsely populated regions around the White Sea:

In my judgment is that people whom the fiction is feigned of that should have no heads, for they have short necks, and commonly wear the clothes over head and shoulders. They use bows and arrows, the men and women be hardly known one from the other, because they all wear clothes like men, and be all clad in skins of beasts packed very curiously together, stockings and all.[9]

While problems to the west and south gave Tsar Michael most concern in the years following his father's death, he could not ignore many which stemmed from the east and north. Similarly, if his relations with Turkey, Poland and Sweden constituted the most important objects of Muscovy's diplomatic activity, states more remote were frequently engaged in negotiations. These included Holland, France, England and Scotland, an incipient friendship between Romanovs and Stuarts already possessing considerable political and economic significance, for example. Michael's personal interest was most apparent perhaps at the end of his reign when in the spring of 1642 he sent a special mission to Denmark to offer the hand of his daughter Irene to the son of Christian IV, Prince Waldemar. The instructions given to the envoys in Moscow must have seemed more than a little strange in Copenhagen: a customary overture to such negotiations, the delivery of a portrait, was to be avoided with the explanation that the taking of portraits could be dangerous for the health of Russian princesses, who in any case were to be viewed whether in the flesh or in effigy by close relatives only. The possibility of Waldemar becoming one of the latter nearly foundered at the beginning over the more serious question of his determination to remain a Lutheran, and when he travelled to Moscow on the understanding that he would not have to convert to Orthodoxy only to find his prospective father-in-law a fervent proselytiser, a stalemate ensued which kept the prince under close house arrest. Deeply disturbed by the likelihood that the match could not be honourably arranged as well as by the death of his two eldest sons, Michael sank into a deep depression from which he never recovered. He collapsed at his name-day service in July 1645, and died soon after appointing his last remaining son as his successor. At the age of sixteen, Alexis was as old as his father had been when elected tsar in 1613, and, although his inheritance was perhaps more secure and not so heavily burdened with all kinds of problems, the reign of the second Romanov nevertheless did not begin in the most auspicious of manners, as we shall see below. For the moment, we must concentrate on further aspects of the making of that inheritance.

The relations of Michael and Filaret with the outside world and with regions being or about to be included in the Russian Empire clearly demonstrated that the Romanovs would be obliged to exercise a vigorous government if they were going to survive and prosper. The boyar duma, the *zemsky sobor*, as well as the central and provincial administration would have to be used in the most expeditious manner possible.

The Time of Troubles had to some extent loosened the strict Muscovite ideas of precedence, and this relaxation enabled the first Romanovs to down-grade some of the old families in favour of their own clients. And so comparative newcomers such as the Cherkasskys, the Saltykovs, the Streshnevs and the Sheremetevs were to be found in the boyar duma along with others whose place was assured by time rather than by proximity to the tsar and his father. Moreover, the informal council known as the boyar duma lost some of its previous functions, such as settlement of land disputes and participation in secret diplomatic discussions, while a smaller advisory body, consisting of four boyars — I. N. Romanov, I. B. Cherkassky, M. B. Shein and B. M. Lykov — was closely consulted on these and other matters of greatest importance.

The greater advisory institution, the *zemsky sobor*, was called together on several occasions between 1613 and 1645. For the first decade of Michael's reign, it was in almost constant session, making no small contribution to the restoration of political and social stability, and to the raising of the taxes vital for this purpose. Although the return of Filaret in 1619 meant a stronger hand on the helm, now that the ship of state was in less stormy waters, the crew began to lose their unanimity of purpose. Cossack and other grave threats were at least for the moment overcome, and so representatives of various groups supporting the government began to complain that their own share of the tax burden was too large.

Having discussed problems of relations with Poland, including that of war, in 1621 and 1622, the *zemsky sobor* was then in recess for a decade after a decade's activity. Pressing problems did not present themselves as much as before either to government or the most powerful social strata. But then, faced in 1632 and 1634 with the Smolensk War and difficulties arising from it, the two great sovereigns decided that it was time for the *zemsky sobor* to be summoned again, the most important item on the agenda remaining as it was before — cash. Petitions emanating from commercial and service sources at about the same time appear to indicate some kind of informal contact between the authorities and their principal social allies as well as some solidification of class consciousness. In the later 1630s, such a process became more apparent as further taxation questions were posed to the *zemsky sobor* as well as others concerning runaway peasants, greedy foreign merchants and the Crimean Tatars.

The last assembly of Michael's reign, in 1642, was specifically connected with the proposal from the Don Cossacks after their seizure of the fortress of Azov that the tsar should take it under his protection. However, as noted above, it quickly broke through its basic frame of reference to consider again the flight of Russian peasants and the avarice of foreign merchants, while some delegates complained about the exactions of officials and the disproportionate nature of tax levies, along with bureaucratic bungling in general.

During the reign of Michael the *zemsky sobor* was useful both to the government and to those members of society represented in it, the upper levels of the clergy, nobility and townsfolk. Some kind of agreement was usually reached about priorities of purpose and means of attaining them, even though this was rarely achieved without much hard bargaining and, indeed, passionate bickering.

The more mundane day-to-day business of administration was carried out in the seventeenth century by *prikazy* or chancelleries, whose number and functions varied according to the needs of a particular time. And so, at the beginning of Michael's reign, there was much activity in the *Razriad* and *Streletsky*, which dealt respectively with the noble cavalry and musketeer infantry. And because of the use being made of Cossacks and mercenaries, two new chancelleries were created — the *Kazachy* and the *Pansky*, the former concentrating on the collection of grain as payment for Cossack and other servicemen, while the latter organised mercenaries and their monetary payments. Meanwhile heavy and light armaments were in turn taken care of by the *Pushkarsky prikaz* and the *Oruzheinaia palata*. From the very beginning, much attention had to be given to the levy of taxes, both regular and extraordinary, and these were handled by a considerable variety of chancelleries. For example, in 1614 a tax called the *piatina* or fifth was placed upon the appropriate portion of the movable property of the payer, and the first collection of it was made the responsibility of the head of the *Posolsky* or Diplomatic *prikaz*. Later collections were entrusted to other chancelleries or specially detailed individuals; for the minting of money, the necessary dispositions were also spread among a number of bodies and people. Finally, as far as the first years of Michael's reign were concerned, *prikazy* were introduced to suppress popular discontent and to provide a safety valve for it — the *Razboinyi* or Brigand and the *Chelobitnyi* or Petition, to supervise the reconstruction of Moscow and other towns, the *prikaz Kamennykh del* or of Masonry; and a couple of *prikazy* for the tsar's personal needs, one for his clothing, the other, the *Aptekarsky* or Apothecary, for his health. Altogether in the years 1613–19, eleven new chancelleries were introduced to join the twenty-two already in existence, and seven of them were retained for the rest of the seventeenth century.

With the return of Filaret in 1619, there was not so much a wholesale reform of the chancelleries as a new and firmer style of leadership. The father Great Sovereign attempted to make less use of the *zemsky sobor* than had the son, but he also had more recourse to the appointment to key positions of trusted associates from the noble class and from the merchant stratum of society. As before, however, *prikazy* were created or altered to fit an evolving situation, especially as far as Muscovy's finances were concerned. Thus, while as before the *prikaz Bolshogo prikhoda* or of Great Revenue remained the most important financial body, the area of its competence was narrowed to Moscow and the south as far as the collection of customs duties was concerned, other areas being taken care of by the *prikaz Kazanskogo dvortsa* or of the Kazan household. The *Novaia chetvert*, a new version of an older administrative body, was created in 1619 to take care of liquor duties in Moscow and the south, as well as of the illegal sale of liquor and tobacco. And in 1622, the *prikaz Bolshoi kazny* or of the Great Exchequer was created to take care of state trade and industry. At about the same time, the *Streletsky prikaz* took over from the aforementioned specially created chancelleries the financial affairs of the Cossacks and mercenaries. However, so important were imported soldiers as trained fighters and as instructors to the Romanovs as they prepared for their showdown with the Poles that the *Inozemnyi* or Foreign *prikaz* was set up in 1624 and remained in existence until the end of the century, and some additional temporary chancelleries connected with mercenaries and other active servicemen were introduced at the beginning of the 1630s in connection with the Smolensk War. Another widely adopted policy from the early 1620s onwards was the creation of temporary chancelleries of investigation, with some special, limited assignment.

The closest associate of Filaret was his nephew and Michael's cousin — the boyar Prince Ivan Borisovich Cherkassky, who was entrusted with the headship of a number of chancelleries until his death in 1642, including the Great Exchequer, the Musketeer, Foreign and Apothecary *prikazy*. While Cherkassky and other confidants directed the individual chancelleries or groups of them, skilled officials of commercial origin were in charge of the actual administration, in the Great Exchequer and elsewhere. After the death of Cherkassky another relative of the Romanovs, Fedor Ivanovich Sheremetev was entrusted in 1643 with the same important chancelleries and another too, the *Novaia chetvert*, until the death of Michael in 1645. During the last years of Michael's reign, only one long-lasting chancellery was created, the *Sibirsky* or Siberian, in 1637. This shared the administration of the eastern regions with the Kazan household. As before, there were a number of temporary creations set up for specific purposes, for example, to deal with Polish prisoners at the end of the Smolensk War, to raise men and money for the defence of the southern frontier, to supervise the construction of the defensive lines to the south and south-east. And temporary chancelleries of investigation continued to be instituted also, to look at the question of townsfolk who had bound themselves to rural landlords among others.[10] Investigations were especially necessary to limit abuses in local government. The tsar is a long way away, and God a long way up, ran a proverb, the truth of which was indicated many times over in the wide spaces of Michael's Muscovy. Essentially, the early Romanovs were attempting to centralise, but the means at their disposal for this purpose were limited, and even the understanding of the purpose was far from complete. As Klyuchevsky wrote of the early seventeenth century:

Centralisation at this time did not mean that all local administrations were subordinated to a single central administration. It meant that one department [i.e. *prikaz* or chancellery] covered a wide range of interests. The analogy is with a village shop which displays those goods in greatest demand, instead of by type. The people agreed with the government's approach, and preferred to deal with one department; they even complained that dealing with a number of departments was tedious, and that they would prefer to deal with only one department so that 'there should be no pointless offence or loss'.[11]

To satisfy such popular prejudice as well as their own aims, the first Romanovs attempted to institute local government by the official known as a *voevoda* or sheriff in an area known as an *uezd* or district. But such a neat and simple aspiration fell foul of a complex series of obstacles, including not only boundless space, insufficient resources and inadequate understanding but also changing needs and considerable variation in environment. For military purposes, especially to the west and south, the districts were often amalgamated into larger units known as *razriady*. The vast crown lands, distributed throughout Muscovy, were kept apart from the basic network of administration. To the north, towards Archangel, the population was mostly peasant without many noble or ecclesiastical landlords. To the east, in Siberia, there were also few landlords, but Bashkirs and other tribesmen. From the west and south there was the almost constant danger of Polish or Tatar attack, although the danger receded as the series of fortified lines was built. To the north-west, around Novgorod, an older administrative division persisted, while in towns in all regions the problems of the sheriff were rather different from what they were in the rural areas. Some functions were not given to the sheriff — customs and excise for example — and a series of local elective or centrally appointed officials were expected to help him exercise his power. The central chancelleries in some instances aspired to control some activities in his district, and, as mentioned before, special investigation chancelleries or deputies were often pointed in his direction. Nevertheless, the job of sheriff was one much sought after by senior military men, as a famous description of an appointee and his retinue by Soloviev graphically illustrates:

The nobleman is happy as he prepares to leave for the town where he is to assume the duties of sheriff — the office is honourable and lucrative. His wife is happy — she, too, will get presents; happy are his children and nephews — the peasant elder after visiting on a holiday father and mother, uncle and aunt, will not fail to pay them his respects; the entire household is happy — housekeepers and servants — they anticipate abundant food; the little children jump in the air — they will not be forgotten; the sheriff's fool, in his elation, talks more nonsense than ever — he will pick up a few scraps. They all are getting ready to move, knowing that the prey will not escape them.[12]

Of course, the extent of the general celebration would depend to a considerable degree on the location and nature of the specific assignment. However, there is no doubt that, having begun its existence in a military manner and in the sixteenth century being found exclusively in border towns, the office of sheriff broadened by the seventeenth century to become almost omnicompetent and omnipresent. The *voevoda* was now responsible for nearly all matters administrative and judicial and supervised many matters financial. His writ ran to include such cases as infringement of the prescriptions of the Orthodox church and display of lack of respect for parental authority. But fundamentally, his job was to see that law and order were maintained, that infringements received condign punishment, and that taxes were paid promptly and in full.

The social system that the central and local administration were intended to uphold made a clear imprint on the army. At the beginning of the seventeenth century the Muscovite fighting force consisted of the various categories of noble servicemen and their levies on the one hand, and professional or semi-professional groups of soldiers such as the *streltsy* or musketeers and the Cossacks on the other. In addition, non-Russians such as Tatars and Bashkirs would often be enlisted for action, too. The noble servicemen received land and money in return for their own performance as cavalry and their provision of a certain number of rank and file. The other constituent parts of the Muscovite army were similarly rewarded with a mixture of land, money and appropriate privileges. The musketeers were expected to be the crack troops and were thus also provided with arms by the state. Having at first tried to put new life into this old arrangement and to dispense with the foreigners who had been the cause of so much of the Time of Troubles, the Romanovs realised as they prepared themselves for the Smolensk War that they would again have to make use of mercenaries. For about half of the noble levies were deemed fit for garrison service only, while a good proportion of the musketeers had to be used for internal defence and were distributed far and wide.

In 1630 the government decided to form military units of the 'new order' — infantry, light and heavy cavalry, after the manner of armies elsewhere in Europe and with the help of officers experienced in them. In April of that year, members of the middle service class without service lands were invited to come to Moscow to enrol as infantry soldiers with 5 roubles a year pay and 3 kopecks a day subsistence allowance, as well as an harquebus, powder and shot. By September only sixty recruits had turned up, foot slogging under foreigners holding no attractions even for impoverished members of a group accustomed to mounted service, and so the government widened its catchment area to include Tatars, Cossacks and any other free volunteers. In such a manner, six regiments were raised by the commencement of the Smolensk War, and two more were compulsorily created during it.

Each regiment was intended to have a complement of 1,600 men and 176 officers all assigned among 8 regiments.

Among the officers, who were preferably foreign, three were of the greatest importance — the Swiss Franz Pentzner, the Scot Alexander Leslie and the Holsteiner Heinrich Von Dam. And among these, the most significant was Leslie, sent to Moscow by Gustavus Adolphus in the summer of 1630 with an entourage of more than sixty, and then sent out again by the Muscovite government to recruit 5,000 troops and purchase appropriate equipment from the Protestant states of Sweden, Denmark, the Netherlands, England and Scotland. The respective heads of state were for the most part receptive to the idea, Charles I issuing appropriate warrants referring to Leslie as 'generall colonel of the forane forces of the Emperour of Russia', and some thousands of troops do indeed appear to have been recruited, but they along with their arms and ammunition involved the Romanovs in vast expense and did not have anything like the desired impact on the outcome of the Smolensk War, partly because of internecine squabbles.

In June 1632 the formation of a cavalry regiment was announced, to consist of 2,000 men of whom over 1,700 had already signed on by the end of the year. And so the government decided to increase the establishment to 2,400, and to add a special company of dragoons to those already in existence. The cavalry was obviously more attractive to servicemen than the infantry, for reasons of pride and tradition, and the attraction was increased by a pay scale of 3 roubles a month for the rider and 2 roubles a year for the upkeep of his mount, along with a carbine, two pistols and armour. Conscripts were joined to volunteers during the Smolensk War to make up a dragoon regiment of 1,600 officers and men. The service conditions for dragoons were even better than those in the cavalry in general, including a horse with 4 roubles a year for its upkeep and equipment, an harquebus or musket and a pike. The dragoon regiment also received its own artillery: 12 small cannon with 24 balls per cannon.

While the Smolensk War saw the beginning of Russia's regular army, the ten regiments of the 'new order' amounted to approximately half only of the 34,500 force led by Shein, and they were demobilised at the war's end. A decree of June 1634 ordered foreign mercenaries to leave, and the unruly manner of their departure increased the already strong ill-feeling towards them. A few officers remained to continue mainly instructional work, and they were granted lands provided they converted to Orthodoxy. Among those who departed only to return later for further service and appropriate rewards was Alexander Leslie, whose descendants may be found in the Soviet Union today. Especially in his case, but to no small extent in others, the mark left by the mercenaries on Muscovy was considerable. The reception by them of estates constituted part of a movement towards what became a pronounced characteristic of the Russian nobility, which was to contain many officers who, by virtue of their commissioned rank, entered the upper class with the landed and other privileges thereunto appertaining. Concepts of family pride and caste honour, although by no means absent from Russian tradition, were given fresh impetus and flavour by clannish Scots and others, who also had an incalculable impact upon the closed Muscovite culture.[13]

To return to the army, its major task after the failure to retake Smolensk, as pointed out previously, was to defend the southern frontier against Tatars sallying forth from their Crimean headquarters. Such military activity necessitated the raising of temporary, seasonal forces rather than regular regiments, and, now that the driving energy of Filaret was no more, the government almost literally took the line of least resistance. Although the leading European experts of the time, the French, were called in for consultation, most of the work, especially when it involved nothing more than cutting down trees or building palisades, keeping watch or even countering Tatar sorties, did not call for an army of the 'new order' or even for the mobilisation of the middle service class that had been the backbone of the old order. Ever mindful of the enormous expense already incurred, Michael and his advisers held themselves aloof from the all too obvious implication of the failure to recapture Smolensk — that wholesale reform of the army, however costly or socially disruptive, could not long be delayed.

If the army needed to be brought into order, the means of paying for it required at least equally urgent attention, for the State finances at the beginning of Michael's reign were in far from good array. Although the members of the various strata of the nobility were acquiring more estates, and although progress was being made generally from a natural to a money economy, the approach by the government to acquiring some share of the proceeds from agriculture and other branches of labour was inefficient and wasteful.

During the seventeenth century there were three principal sources of state income: taxes, both direct and indirect; coinage; and state industry and trade. Among these, direct taxes extracted from the peasants and townspeople were of greatest importance. And while various forms of tribute, especially in furs, extraordinary payments and grain requisitions continued to be made, especially during the early years of Michael's reign and the years of the Smolensk War, by the time of the accession of Alexis a somewhat more regular system had been devised from a cadastral list made on the basis of sown areas — *sokha* (literally plough), a unit evolving over the centuries and varying in size according to quality of land and type of ownership. By and large the estates of the nobility were rated most favourably, followed by those of the church, with the fields of the peasants in the most disadvantageous position, while the crown lands were kept apart. A *sokha* unit was calculated for townspeople, and for those who combined trade with agriculture. Having received many complaints about the out-of-date and unjust nature of many of the lists, the government attempted in the 1620s to institute a new general survey. This could not be carried out either completely or exactly, and many further inspections had to be instituted in response to more petitions. Some improvements were made, but there was still a long way to go, and meanwhile the heaviest burdens continued to fall on the peasants, especially those to the north. Towards the end of Michael's reign a beginning was made towards the apportionment of direct taxes on the basis of households rather than the *sokha*, but the departure was for extraordinary levies only.

Among indirect taxes the most important were customs and excise. These, like the direct taxes, were included in the assessments made on a year-to-year basis, but unlike them, were often farmed out or entrusted to privileged merchants, leading townspeople or even prosperous peasants. As for coinage of money, this was usually done with imported silver coins, which were made into pieces worth 2 roubles. The rouble itself was in existence only as a unit of account, as were other monetary measurements with the exception of the half-kopeck piece. The considerable profits from such mintage were shared among a number of chancelleries of which the most important was the Great Exchequer. This *prikaz* also supervised state industry and trade, in the first of which activities the most important single enterprise was the saltworks at Solikamsk on the Kama River. There were other saltworks, potash factories and fisheries including caviare extraction on the Lower Volga. There are few figures available on state industry and even fewer on state trade, a reflection on their relative insignificance in the state budget, the most important parts of which were made up by direct and indirect taxes.[14]

The state budget was at least to some extent the sum total of the local budgets made up on a year-to-year basis by the sheriffs, who were obliged to submit detailed accounts to central chancelleries. If there were inefficiency and corruption in the capital, their presence was if anything more keenly felt in the provinces. 'Strong men' and their clients could often avoid paying a fair share, while many peasants could rarely avoid paying more than a rightful due. The chain of budgetary command between the sheriffs and other provincial officials on the one hand and those at the centre on the other was not constructed anywhere near as clearly as might be hoped, with everybody trying to extract the maximum amount of revenue for his own pocket. And yet considerable sums of money somehow made their way to the coffers of the chancelleries, whose expenditures were directed mostly towards military ends, between a half and two thirds of the total being spent in this manner.

No budget could have existed without an economy showing at least some signs of recovery from the ravages of the Time of Troubles. During Michael's reign the basic occupation, agriculture, spread from the centre to include at least some of the lands along the Volga, and

Russian migrants helped persuade the local tribesmen increasingly to desert their nomadic pastoral existence for one more settled and at least partly arable. To the north, in an essentially peasant region, the richer did well at the expense of their poorer brethren. Everywhere there were signs of subsistence farming reacting at least a little to the pressure of the market or of state tax collection, and 'industrial' crops such as flax were sometimes grown along with the more basic grains. On the other hand there were times when even the fundamental requirements of subsistence could not be met, and the grain surpluses exported to acquire arms and men or to assist allies were often dearly won. And inevitably peasant indebtedness was combining with state policy to bring ever nearer to Muscovy the wholesale introduction of the institution of serfdom. However, the peasants did not succumb without resistance, of which the two most significant forms were flight and violence, usually localised but at such times as the movement led by Ivan Balashov, which accompanied the later stages of the Smolensk War, growing into full-scale revolt. Localised violence would often be directed against government officials, stewards of the landlords or the landlords themselves.

The landlords fell into several categories, one of the principal divisions being between secular and ecclesiastical, that is between noble and monastic. Even though there were several decrees in existence against the expansion of the holdings of the black clergy (the monastic, officially celibate, as opposed to the white or parish clergy, who were obliged to marry), neither Filaret as Patriarch nor the secular authorities did anything to enforce them, if anything encouraging the cupidity of such institutions as the Troitse-Sergiev Monastery to the north-east of Moscow. As for the nobles, these were divided into three basic strata, the first two from the capital and the third from the provinces. Of these on average, according to land registers of the late 1630s, the top controlled about 520 peasant households each, the middle controlled 34, and the lower 5-6. At about this time the tsar had the most and those closest to him came next, four boyars — I. N. Romanov, F. I. Sheremetev, I. B. Cherkassky and D. M. Pozharsky — each having amassed between 1,000 and 3,000 households. But the new regime was careful to visit its largesse in the shape of court and state lands on the Moscow clients of such people, too. And there was a special attempt to maintain the position of the lower stratum, which approximated to a gentry, and which contained those who have been called the middle service people. The government attempted to preserve the organisation of this declining stratum in its exclusive districts centred on 'towns', but there was too much ambition directed towards the opportunities of the capital and the new lands along the Volga and to the south for such immobility to be maintained. And so, in order to preserve its position at the top of the hierarchical pyramid, the new dynasty had to show flexibility in this direction as well as lenience or forgiveness to those who had fought on the wrong side during the Time of Troubles and acquiescence or even enthusiasm towards the leaders of Volga peoples such as the Tatars and Chuvashes. To satisfy all strata of the coalescing nobility, the conditional service type of land tenure or *pomeste* was gradually becoming merged with the permanent hereditary type known as *votchina*. Also to satisfy the ruling class, the government moved inexorably if gradually closer to the full institution of serfdom. Delay such as there was arose from divisions of attitude within the ranks of the ruling class itself. For example, one of the most important stumbling-blocks was the prescription of the number of years during which a runaway peasant could be returned to his master. The magnates clerical and secular favoured the continuation of these 'fixed years', since the strong landlords were often likely to harbour the runaways of the weak. The nobles to the south also supported continuation; peasant flight often led in their direction, and some of them indeed were themselves fugitives. One of them, a Cossack, went so far in 1624 as not only to threaten those landlords who took back their peasants with attacks on their estates but also to declare that if the tsar supported the policy of return, 'We ourselves will find another tsar'.[15] The Cossacks and other settlers to the south made their feelings known at their annual spring levies in Tula for defence against the Tatars and at the *zemsky sobor* of 1637. On the other hand the middle servicemen passionately opposed the exactions of the 'strong men' around them and the extension of the 'fixed years' even to infinity. At the death of Michael in 1645 the new tsar Alexis was immediately confronted with the conflicting demands of the two sides in this great dispute, but even he did not finally settle it until after a series of social unheavals at least partly connected with it three years later.

These upheavals were also connected with problems confronting merchants and others involved in industry and trade, for although the reign of the first Romanov brought some economic progress, it also led to attendant dislocation and difficulty. A clear indication of this progress was the expansion by over a half of the population of many towns, the number of which now approached 250, according to Soviet calculations. However, there was just one really large town — Moscow — with more than 27,000 households, and only fifteen others with more than 500 households each, among them Pskov and Novgorod to the northwest, Kazan and Astrakhan along the Volga, and Archangel, Vologda and Kholmogory on northern water routes.

The most prominent members of urban society were included in exclusive corporations. In 1613 Michael granted a charter to the so-called 'guests' and the merchants of the 'guest hundred', freeing them from the payment of all taxes and dues and from the control of the sheriffs and chancelleries. Similar privileges were extended to the merchants of the 'cloth hundred'. By 1630 there were 13 guests, 185 members of the guest hundred and 128 members of the cloth hundred. Guests were empowered to travel abroad on trading missions and to possess estates. The merchants in the corporations were entrusted with the management of state trade and industry, customs and excise, their own wealth liable to forfeit in cases of dereliction of duty. Other powerful citizens, usually merchants or manufacturers, conducted the affairs of the towns in often uneasy concert with the officials of the state. Below them, enrolled in organisations reminiscent of communes and guilds were tradesmen and craftsmen, more often than not engaged in the fulfilment of state orders and subject to the control of such chancelleries as those dealing with construction and armaments. Soviet historians, from whom much of this information is taken, are very interested in the division of labour and categories of townspeople. They inform us that, towards the end of Michael's reign, there were in Moscow just under 130 blacksmiths, about 100 furriers and 600 masters in food preparation and distribution. Numbers in other towns would be smaller, although varying considerably according to local specialisation. While craftsmen and traders would often hire labour, the more influential merchants would often exploit a labour force bonded to them.[16]

After the Time of Troubles manufacturing picked up along with other branches of the economy, especially in Moscow, but in other towns and regions too. While the requirements of the court and the state were of outstanding significance, domestic and foreign demand were also playing a not inconsiderable part in the new prosperity. If the tsar and his entourage might want silks and satins, even his meaner subjects would want coarser cloths, particularly since they were no longer making their own where specialisation was on the increase. And if the state wanted cannon and muskets, the successors to Chancellor and the other early venturers wanted items scarcely less vital in sea warfare such as ropes. So, as the looms and foundries of Moscow were attending to orders from on high, other enterprises were responding to demands from below and without. To pursue the example of rope, factories had been established in the north already in the sixteenth century, but now another factory even bigger was set up in Archangel, to help satisfy the needs of the English and the Dutch. As far as heavier industry was concerned, the Urals were beginning their ascent towards prominence as the metallurgical centre of Russia, but a more famous event of the early seventeenth century occurred to the south of Moscow early in 1632 when the Dutch merchant Andrei Vinius secured a ten-year monopoly and several other privileges for the exploitation of ores which he had discovered at Tula, in return for delivery of a fixed quantity of metal to the state. The enterprise took some time to make its way, and Vinius needed the support of other foreign merchants, who by 1648 had taken over from him completely. By this time two other works had been set up in the neighbourhood, and altogether, Tula was providing a considerable amount of metal and other products for purposes domestic and foreign, military and peaceful. The labour force, at first hired, soon followed a fairly inevitable course in the social climate of the times and became obligatorily assigned. A further reflection of contemporary realities was the frequent obligation of town communities to powerful clerical and secular figures, who would make communities under their protection 'white', that is free from taxes and duties. Other urban groups, now under increased burdens, protested vehemently but mostly in vain against these actions of the 'strong men'.

In spite of such inequities and restrictions, towns took several steps ahead along with activities associated with them. In addition to the evidence already presented regarding such development, we may also take a look at the growth of foreign trade. This carried on in several directions, of which the most important were in turn: through Archangel with the countries of Western Europe, especially England and Holland; via Pskov and Novgorod with Sweden and other powers around the Baltic from which Muscovy itself had temporarily been excluded; and by way of Astrakhan on the Lower Volga to the Orient. Among the chief Russian exports were skins and furs, bristles and tallow, flax-seed and hemp, and various kinds of naval stores and low-quality cloth. Imports included metals and metal goods, armaments among them, gold and silver, wines, sugar and spices, paper, glass, dyestuffs, fine fabrics and other luxury items. The state held a monopoly on the export of grains, rhubarb and caviare, and farmed out monopolies on pitch and potash.

At the beginning of Michael's reign the English retained their most-favoured nation status, paying no duties at all, while the Dutch paid half-duty. Gradually, however, the English, who traded mostly with their own goods, lost ground to the Dutch, who acted more as middlemen for items both Western and Eastern, and who managed to win from the English the monopoly on pitch. The rivalry became more intense as the Thirty Years War grew more serious, and the Swedes attempted to direct more of Russia's commerce through the Baltic. Each rival attempted to win over the government with grandiose schemes, and its subjects with promises, percentages and bribes. Although always kept out of the lucrative trade with the Orient, Western merchants managed to insinuate their way deeply into other forbidden territory — the retail trade —, succeeding to such an extent that even an English representative, John Merrick, confessed that foreign merchants were stealing bread from the mouths of their Russian counterparts. A series of petitions from the 'guests' and other Russian merchants finally led after many refusals or half-hearted responses to a complete repeal of the privileges of all foreigners in 1646, just after the death of Michael.[17]

A further reason for this considerable step was the suspicion still strongly levelled by all Russians towards everything and everybody foreign. Trade might be necessary, but it brought with it many infectious and harmful alien influences, including threats to the basis of the

Muscovite state, its Orthodox faith. Indeed, the embodiment of that faith, the church, was under Filaret more than the basis of the state; it was almost coterminous with it. And this was not so much the result of the dual role played by the patriarch as the culmination of centuries of Russian tradition. Yet, as John Keep points out, 'paradoxically, the period that saw the greatest extension of the patriarchal power was also a stage in that process of secularisation and bureaucratisation of the church which was to call forth the schism'.[18]

At his return from exile in Poland in 1619 Filaret discovered that, although most of his flock were as firm as ever in their crude and chauvinistic faith, infiltration of Roman Catholic and Protestant ideas had led at least a few astray towards sceptical questions and even heretical answers. Filaret was not alone among patriarchs in his belief that the faith would best be protected not through subtle theological disputation, which was in any case alien to Orthodoxy, but by the firm assertion of his own personal authority. And so he was quick to send into exile a potential rival Jonah who had kept the patriarchal throne warm for him during his absence, using as his reason the admittance of two Catholics to Orthodoxy without second baptism and convoking a council to give support to his view that 'Latins are the most impure and ferocious of heretics, ... like unto dogs, known to be enemies of God'.[19] Filaret's determined prosecution of this rival was in indicative contrast with his lenient treatment of other senior ecclesiastics to whom he gave advancement in spite of their corrupt morals and questionable devoutness.

As well as putting down rivals and bringing in clients, Filaret also arranged backing for his own power of an institutional kind. In 1625, he arranged with his pliant son the introduction of church lands apart from the state with their own chancelleries and investigatory agencies. Neither those who had taken monastic vows nor the secular or parish priests in the areas placed under Filaret's jurisdiction escaped visits from the patriarch's shadow administration, especially its tax officials.

Not until the end of his life did Filaret allow a chink of light to penetrate the gloom of Orthodoxy with some half-hearted effort in 1632 to develop education. Heresy continued to be rooted out, whether Roman Catholic or Protestant, or perhaps even worse, secular, such as scientific explanation of the movement of the planets. And suspect publication was countered not so much by reliable publication as by no publication at all, Filaret limiting the output of the seven Muscovite printing presses to an average of no more than three titles a year, and withholding from publication well over a hundred manuscripts that had satisfied the minute scrutiny of the censors but did not appease the acute sensitivities of the patriarch. Filaret's successor as Patriarch Joseph permitted the presses to double their annual production but faced no easier a situation. While outside threats from Roman Catholicism and Protestantism by no means disappeared, internal heresy was still detected in many places. As a means of making a re-entry into Muscovy in 1638, Alexander Leslie wrote a letter to tsar Michael warning of the formation of a new Polish knightly order and the threat posed to the Orthodox faithful by the various Papist vows taken by these potential crusaders. His own Protestantism would have been looked on with somewhat less suspicion, but in order to become fully accepted in Muscovy Leslie later had to abjure the faith of his fathers for that of his adoptive fellow-countrymen. In the 1630s an early manifestation of the apocalyptic strain of theology that was to become so pronounced in the reign of Alexis was associated with the name of Kapiton, a hermit hiding away in the north.[20]

Apocalyptic movements could be found throughout Europe at this time, as could the great witch-craze, which also raged in Muscovy. During the Time of Troubles, Boris Godunov had accused the Romanovs of resorting to witchcraft in their attempt to take the throne from him, for example, and then Michael's first wife, who died in 1625, was reported as being a victim of the same kind of malign influence. In 1632 the tsar commanded that merchants in Pskov be prohibited from buying hops from Lithuania, because 'in the Lithuanian towns there are witches who cast spells on hops which are to be brought into our towns so that by means of these hops they can spread plague among the people'.[21] Affecting the popular mind would be stories of witches and other magical phenomena, with the *skomorokhi* or strolling minstrels as broadcasters of all kinds of tales and veiled rumours. These were by no means all subversive, but in a coded manner the minstrels and the peasants too could disseminate allegations concerning the wrongdoings of local officials and even of those on high, and accusations became more explicit at the time of the revolt associated with the Smolensk War and other minor flare-ups. The Romanovs attempted to make their place on the throne secure not only through the suppression of heresy, witchcraft and revolt, but also through the encouragement of patriotic stories and songs often linked to their own name; the tsar himself was a patron of the *skomorokhi*, hiring three of them to dance and entertain generally at his wedding in 1626, for example.[22]

At the death of Michael in 1645 the new dynasty was by no means as secure as it would like to have been. Its official propaganda, like its additions to the walls and buildings of the Kremlin, gave too optimistic a representation of the degree to which the Romanovs had been accepted as true tsars of Muscovy. Yet they were stronger in 1645 than they had been in 1613 at their accession. They needed to be strong to withstand the storms and buffets of the late 1640s that struck Muscovy with as much force as they struck other countries throughout Europe as the Thirty Years War came to an end. That conflict had brought Russia much more than previously into the affairs of the rest of the continent, with many benefits such as helpful alliances and the introduction of new technology, but at the simultaneous cost of greater exposure to foreign influences that were beginning to undermine to an unprecedented extent the introverted culture of medieval times and the lesser ability to hold aloof from international social and political crises.

NOTES

1. T. S. Willan, *The Early History of the Russia Company, 1553–1603* (London and New York, 1956), pp. 4–5. And see articles by S. Baron and others in *History Today* (Aug–Sept. 1986)

2. V. Klyuchevsky, *The Rise of the Romanovs*, trans. Liliana Archibald (London and New York, 1970), pp. 16–17; V. O. Klyuchevsky, *Sochineniia*, vol. 1 (Moscow, 1956), pp. 30–4.

3. A. V. Borodin, *Inozemtsy – ratnye liudi na sluzhbe v moskovskom gosudarstve* (Petrograd, 1916), p. 7.

4. P. Avrich, *Russian Rebels, 1600–1800* (London, 1973), Part I. And see M. Perrie, 'Russian pretenders of the early seventeenth century', *History Today*, February 1981. See also G. E. Orchard 'The election of Michael Romanov, *Slavonic Review*, vol. 67 (1989).

5. J. L. H. Keep, 'The regime of Filaret, 1619–1633', *Slavonic Review*, vol. 38 (1959–60), p. 335.

6. The previous section taken from O. L. Vainshtein, *Rossiia i tridtsatiletniaia voina* (Leningrad, 1947) and B. F. Porshnev, *Tridtsatiletniaia voina i vstuplenie v nee Shvetsii i Moskovskogo gosudarstva* (Moscow, 1976).

7. See A. A. Novoselsky, *Borba Moskovskogo gosudarstva s Tatarami v pervoi polovine XVII veka* (Moscow–Leningrad, 1948).

8. D. Eeckaute, 'Les brigands en Russie du XVIIe au XIXe siècle', *Revue d'histoire moderne et contemporaine*, vol. 12 (1965); J. L. H. Keep, 'Bandits and the law in Muscovy', *Slavonic Review*, vol. 35 (1956–57).

9. S. Konovalov, 'Two documents concerning Anglo-Russian relations in the early seventeenth century', *Oxford Slavonic Papers*, vol. 2 (1951), p. 133.

10. N. V. Ustiugov, 'Evoliutsiia prikaznogo stroia Russkogo gosudarstva v XVIIv.' in N. M. Druzhinin *et al.* (eds), *Absoliutizm v Rossii (XVII–XVIIIvv.)* (Moscow, 1964), pp. 134–54. Robert O.Crummey, *Aristocrats and Servitors; The Boyar Elite in Russia, 1613–1689* (Princeton, NJ, 1983) pp. 26, 158 emphasises Michael's conservatism.

11. Klyuchevsky, *The Rise*, pp. 176–7.

12. Quoted in M. T. Florinsky, *Russia: A History and an Interpretation*, vol. 1 (New York, 1955) p. 270.

13. A. V. Chernov, 'Vooruzhennye sily' in A. A. Novoselsky *et al.* (eds), *Ocherki istorii SSSR: Period feodalizma: XVIIv.* (Moscow, 1955) pp. 439–44; Richard Hellie, *Enserfment and Military Change in Muscovy* (Chicago and London, 1971), pp. 169–72. See also Paul Dukes, 'The Leslie Family in the Swedish period (1630–5) of the Thirty Years War', *European Studies Review*, vol. 12 (1982).

14. Iu. A. Tikhonov, 'Vosstanovlenie khoziaistva' in M. N. Tikhomirov *et al.* (eds), *Istoriia SSSR*, pervaia seriia, vol. 2 (Moscow, 1966) pp. 308–20.

15. Ibid., p. 307.

16. Ibid., pp. 308–9.
17. Ibid., pp. 317–20. See also S. H. Baron, 'Who were the *Gosti?*', *California Slavic Studies*, vol. 7 (1973); and P. Bushkovitch, *The Merchants of Moscow, 1580–1650* (Cambridge, 1980).
18. Keep, *Slavonic Review*, p. 337.
19. Ibid., p. 338.
20. N. A. Smirnov (ed.), *Tserkov v istorii Rossii (IXv.–1917g.)* (Moscow, 1967), pp. 145, 150. And see G. Florovsky and others, 'The problem of Old Russian culture', *Slavic Review*, vols. 21, 22 (1962–3).
21. R. Zguta, 'Witchcraft trials in seventeenth-century Russia', *American Historical Review*, vol. 82 (1977), p. 1194.
22. R. Zguta, *Russian Minstrels: A History of the Skomorokhi* (Oxford, 1978), pp. 56–7. And see generally G. R. Seaman, *History of Russian Music* (Oxford, 1967), vol. 1, Chapters 1–2.

CHAPTER TWO

New foundations: from Alexis to the Regent Sophie, 1645–1689

When Alexis came to power in 1645 the process of recovery from the dislocation of the Time of Troubles was almost complete. No longer did the government live in daily fear of the instant dismemberment of the state at the hands of foreign invaders. Nor did the dynasty suffer from the pressing anxiety that it was about to be usurped by domestic rivals or pretenders, although they still existed. Ascending the throne at the same age as Michael before him, the sixteen-year-old Alexis had less reason than his father for apprehension concerning his capability for playing the part of Great Sovereign. During his long reign, from 1645 to 1676, there were several important developments which should have reduced his trepidation still further. The acquisition of the Ukraine and of Smolensk solved some of the problems of external security as well as contributing to economic and cultural change. The south-west and west became significant regions in the formation of a national market and acted as transmitters of ideas both theological and secular from Poland and beyond. The reform of the Orthodox church and the consequent schism of Old Belief led to a pronounced reduction in its influence on the state, while at least a few individuals received early knowledge of the scientific revolution and of the changes in outlook and approach which accompanied it. The social structure was adapted to the approach of absolutism with the entrenchment of serfdom at the bottom and the coalescence of a new service class at the top. And appropriate changes were made in the *prikazy* and other parts of the administration, which stretched out its insatiable grasp to take in Siberia. However, a catalogue of progressive change such as this runs the danger of suggesting for Alexis a reign much smoother in its course than it actually was. Soon after his accession his throne was shaken by a revolt in Moscow followed by a wave of further disturbances in other towns which must have made Alexis wonder if he would escape the fate being meted out to his brother monarch, Charles I. There were further urban revolts later on in his reign, and, a few years before the end of it, peasant war with the movement led by Stenka Razin at its centre.

Incursions from the south by the Crimean Tatars and Turks and to a lesser extent from the west by the Poles and the Swedes remained a constant threat, the Tatars and Turks made that threat a recurring reality. On the whole, then, rather than saying that Alexis was more secure as tsar than Michael, we might do better to think again of the son as having less cause than his father for extreme insecurity.

After the death of Alexis in 1676 there ensued a thirteen-year period replete with misfortune for his successors, to whom the greatest danger was posed neither by foreign nor domestic opponents of the tsarist regime, but by rival groups of that regime's closest supporters, the principal two of which were gathered around the families of the late tsar's wives, Maria Miloslavsky and Nathalie Naryshkin. Theodore or Fedor, the eldest surviving son and therefore heir of Alexis, was even younger than his father and grandfather at their accession. Only fourteen years old, he was also sickly and reticent, and spent most of the rest of his short life in retirement. Scheming for power behind the scenes continuously, the two leading families and their supporters came out into the open at Theodore's death in 1682, to engage in a struggle deeply affecting the youth of the junior of two surviving sons of Alexis, one from each marriage, Ivan and Peter, who were now declared to be joint tsars. This fragile co-rule of an adolescent who was half-blind and half-witted and a boy who, although clear-sighted and intelligent, was only ten years old, was preserved for her own purposes by their elder sister Sophie, who assumed a regency which was to last until her overthrow in favour of Peter in 1689. While the struggle continued in and around the court, the positive and negative developments which we have discerned taking place during the reign of Alexis both continued, preparing for Peter an inheritance which at once presented him with opportunities for completing the structure of Russian absolutism and confronted him with problems possessing no easy solution.

At his accession, Aleksei or Alexis Mikhailovich (1645–76) was not accepted unanimously as tsar. There were some rather preposterous pretenders, the most famous of them being Timofei Ankidinov, who claimed variously to be the son or grandson of Vasily Shuisky, who had been deposed in 1610 during the Time of Troubles when there were more formidable pretenders and had later in fact died without issue. Ankidinov had a most colourful career, making appearances at the Polish, Turkish, Papal and Swedish courts before being extradited from Holstein and then after torture being quartered in Moscow at the end of 1653.[1] Neither he nor his immediate contemporaries made any significant progress towards supplanting the new tsar. More seriously, people whispered that Alexis was a changeling, who had been placed on the throne by the boyar Boris Ivanovich Morozov.

The new reign began by completing some business left over from the old. Prince Waldemar of Denmark was sent home to his father Christian IV after honourable discharge from house arrest in Moscow.

The 'perpetual' peace of Polianovka was confirmed by the Polish king, Wladyslaw IV, and joint action against the Crimean Tatars was at least discussed, although Wladyslaw in the end held back for fear of alienating the Turks, and the Russians meantime went it alone. Although the international situation was therefore relatively stable, the domestic scene remained unsettled. Morozov appeared to be consolidating his position when in early 1648, just ten days after Alexis married Maria Miloslavsky, the boyar married her sister Anna, but the Miloslavskys were not a popular family, and Morozov had previously tarnished his by no means brilliant reputation by impoverishing his fellow-countrymen at the same time as indulging his own insatiable appetite for self-enrichment. Widespread discontent enveloped even the nobility of the capital and the provinces, who were not happy about some of the personalities in the new administration nor more generally about the arrangements for the recovery of runaway peasants, while merchants were uneasy about the privileges given to foreigners and to some Russians. They were appeased to some extent by the repeal of the foreigners' privileges in 1646. The general populace was especially concerned at the increase in early 1646 of the tax on that most basic commodity salt, and then, when it was abolished at the end of 1647, by the taxes which were introduced to replace it, with extraordinary levies to make up pressing arrears. Government officials were angry about some of them losing their posts and others part of their pay, while the *streltsy* were restless at often receiving their money late.

So it was not surprising that there should be disturbances in a number of towns in the later 1640s, at first in the periphery. Then most significantly trouble arose in Moscow itself, where a special circumstance was the exemption from taxation of the households owned by important clerical and lay figures, up to two-thirds of the total. Local discontent was swollen by that of petitioners from the provinces. On 1 June 1648 a crowd, attempting to approach the tsar with their pleas as he left a church service, was dispersed and some of its members were arrested. The next day, another crowd gathered as the tsar left the Kremlin in religious procession and then again as he returned. Requests for the surrender to them of L. S. Pleshcheev, one of the most unpopular officials, and the release of the prisoners of the previous day were met with the order from Morozov to the *streltsy* to muster for action, but most of them refused to fight for the boyars against the people. And so the boyars themselves were forced to make an appearance, and when they failed in their turn to restore order, the onus fell on the tsar. Icon in hand, Alexis did his best to quell the noise, but in fact it grew. The houses of Morozov and other hated boyars were burned down and their property destroyed; one of them was killed. On 3 June the fire spread, along with the rumour that Morozov's servants had encouraged it as a diversionary measure. Thousands of buildings and more than a few people were consumed by the flames. The crowd gathered on Red

Square and besieged the Kremlin, demanding that Morozov, Pleshcheev and P. T. Trakhaniotov be handed over. The luckless Pleshcheev was called upon to make the supreme sacrifice, meeting a summary end on Red Square. The next day, however, it was soon apparent that the popular blood lust was far from sated. Trakhaniotov was first sent off and then recalled to share the fate of Pleshcheev, and Morozov seemed likely to follow them soon. Luckily for him, the entreaties of Alexis to the crowd on 5 June and his promise to send his mentor into remote exile just managed to sway the uneasy balance. Then, having avoided this last human offering, the tsar and his entourage handed over presents to the crowd, ensuring the loyalty of the *streltsy*, nobles, merchants and officials with money and promises, while the patriarch and his men did their bit by preaching peace and quiet. The fury was at last dying down with the fire, after a final flurry caused by the tsar's reluctance to carry out his promise to send Morozov into exile. With the favourite's departure, the revolt was virtually at an end in Moscow, although there were sequels in other towns, just as there had been preludes in them.

In response to the requests of nobles and merchants, the government meanwhile decided to call a *zemsky sobor*. Some of the elections were stormy, but all was calm enough when the assembly convened in September 1648 in Moscow, where it was to continue its deliberations until January 1649. Between 300 and 350 representatives of the upper classes, divided into two chambers, carried on their work with the assistance of petitions presented to them by various pressure groups. Among the most urgent requests were from townsmen seeking the abolition of urban tax exemptions, and nobles anxious for the restriction of the movement of their peasants into towns and of their illegal departure elsewhere. Envious eyes were cast by both townsmen and nobles in the direction of the estates of the church, which managed to put up a stout and mostly successful defence of its property. In the *Ulozhenie* or Code of Laws drawn up by the end of January 1649, the other wishes of the delegates were answered, with special emphasis being given to the imposition on the peasantry of the full weight of serfdom, and to the extension to the nobility of exclusive rights to land and peasant ownership. For the townsmen, the abolition of tax exemptions was confirmed, but they were not awarded their much desired monopolistic trading rights.

The continued dissatisfaction of the lower orders of rural and urban society was clearly reflected in further revolts taking place in the north-western cities of Pskov and Novgorod in 1650. In Pskov in February a general discontent was exacerbated by the export of grain to Sweden at a time of poor harvest. Although previously promised by the Muscovite government, this transaction was clumsily arranged and aroused local hatreds as well as a general xenophobia, much to the discomfort of the individuals concerned as popular anger reached the point of explosion. In Novgorod in March, when a comparable situation arose, several officials and merchants had to take evasive action against the fury of the people led by the *streltsy*. Novgorod was soon restored to order by government troops, but far from acting as a tranquilliser on the people of Pskov, the news from the other city gave them greater stimulus. A petition to Moscow met with no positive response, and a punitive expedition sent to bring the insurgents back into obedience found it necessary to put Pskov to a three months siege, which the townspeople were enabled to withstand by the widespread support of the local peasantry. Fearing that trouble might arise again in the capital itself, the central government swayed between more energetic repression and negotiated appeasement, a *zemsky sobor* specially assembled to discuss the question supporting the more peaceful approach. Protracted talks in the end accomplished the aim of bringing the Pskov movement to an end, although the local peasants did not fully return to their former obedience until the following year. Then, with Morozov firmly back in power and the metropolitan Nikon making his presence felt as a politically skilful church leader, the central government was now sufficiently secure for a decade or so to devote its major energies to important problems of foreign policy.

The initiative and self-possession which had been shown by the people of Novgorod and even more of Pskov owed something to their medieval independence. Equally, the persistence of the Muscovite leadership in bringing their revived centrifugal tendencies to an end was to an extent in the tradition of Ivan the Great and Ivan the Terrible. Nevertheless, there were also aspects of these urban revolts which were closely linked to mid-seventeenth-century Europe. Throughout the continent regimes in economic and social difficulties had been faced with vast problems of law and order at this time. Such a circumstance was noted at the time by a Muscovite official involved in the Pskov revolt who made the observation that God was permitting even greater disturbances in England and Turkey. When Alexis heard the news of the execution of his brother sovereign Charles I, he took his coolness towards English merchants beyond frigidity, declaring that 'you English have done a great wickedness by killing your sovereign King Charles, for which evil deed you cannot be suffered to remain in the realm of Muscovy'. More than likely he recalled with a shiver his own treatment at the hands of the Moscow crowd in the summer of 1648.[2]

In retrospect the events in Moscow in 1648, in Pskov and Novgorod in 1650 and in other towns as well as rural areas round about the same time were of a sufficient gravity for Russia to deserve inclusion in any discussion of the 'contemporaneous revolutions' of the mid seventeenth century. Such a case is reinforced by the consideration that at this very time the Ukraine was making a bold bid for independence from Poland, a move which would not only affect relations between Poland and Russia but also influence the balance of power relationships throughout eastern and central Europe and even contain implications for the western part of the continent. This international aspect will be considered below, as will economic and cultural developments of a relevant nature. For the moment we may note simply that while the attempt of Charles I to assert his absolutism met with complete failure, elsewhere, in France under Louis XIV, for example, as well as in Russia under Alexis, such a system of government made a comeback after being subjected to a severe threat from a wide range of social dissent. France, it is true, is the outstanding example, rising in strength swiftly enough to dominate Europe up to the beginning of the eighteenth century. In the Russian case, full consolidation had to wait for the reign of Peter the Great, and his immediate predecessors, while never subjected to another Time of Troubles, were confronted by problems of a seriousness rarely if ever experienced by their brother and sister monarchs to the west.

After 1650 there was relative stability for a decade or so, but then came another shock to the capital for a reason isolated by an immigrant Scottish soldier in September 1661. Among the reasons given by Patrick Gordon for his disappointment on arrival in the Russian service was 'the worst of all, the pay small, and in a base copper coin, which passed at four to one of silver'. Less than a year later, in July 1662, Gordon was on the spot for a revolt, the early climax of which he described in the following manner:

The mutineers. . .were about 4 or 5000 men without arms, only some had clubs and sticks, they pretended a redress as to the copper money, salt and other diverse things, papers having been to that purpose placked on in diverse places of the city, and a writer reading a paper before the *Zemsky Dvor*, containing their grievances, with the names of some persons whom they deemed guilty of abuses, inviting all to go to the tsar and seek redress, and the heads of the evil counsellors, so the rabble coming together, some went and robbed the house of a *gost* or alderman called Vasily Shorin, but for the most part went to Kolominskoe, whither being come as his Majesty was in the church, they importunated some of the boyars and courtiers to make their address to the tsar. At last the tsar coming out of the church and getting to horseback they very rudely and with great clamours pressed him to redress their grievances, the tsar and some of the boyars reprehending them for coming in such a tumultuary way and in such numbers told them that their grievances should be redress, that to this end a council should be immediately held, they should only have a little patience. In the meantime, upon their first coming, orders had been sent to two colonels of the *streltsy* to come with their regiments in all haste to Kolominskoe, and the rest were ordered to repress those in Moscow.[3]

Gordon's account of the events of 25 July 1662 accords sufficiently with others for it to be considered reliable enough. Shorin made a getaway, and was rumoured to have gone over to the Poles; this incensed the crowd, and Alexis gave orders for his arrest. But the tsar managed to delay action on the demand that other 'guilty' men be handed over, and, as soon as the *streltsy* arrived, the revolt was suppressed in the most severe fashion. Hundreds were tortured and executed, and hundreds more sent into Siberian exile. The Copper Revolt, as it became known, was accompanied by the special feature of an outbreak of smallpox, but was broadly similar in its origins to the urban disturbances of 1648–50, financial burdens imposed on the populace reaching the point where they became intolerable. The main socio-political differences between the Copper Riot and its predecessors appear to have lain principally in the less variegated nature of its composition and the more thorough degree of its repression. These have been taken as indications of the greater solidarity of the upper classes and self-confidence of the tsarist establishment at the middle of the reign of Alexis as opposed to its beginning.

Even if this were so, there could be no relaxation of the government's vigilance concerning domestic stability, and the participation in the Copper Revolt of peasants on leave from their estates or having run away gave clear testimony to the fact that internal peace was more than a matter of the towns alone. 'Don't pay your dues, run off to the Volga, to the brigands or the boatmen' was a peasant saying of the time, and many more peasants ran away to the periphery than to the centre. Even those who stayed at home aspired to participate in the rough democracy of the Cossacks, it would seem, and, by no means surprisingly therefore, their great hero became one of the Cossack leaders, Stenka or Stepan Timofeevich Razin, whose most famous exploits began in 1667 with a buccaneering expedition into the Caspian. They then continued in 1669 with the seizure of Astrakhan at the mouth of the Volga, and of Tsaritsyn some hundreds of miles up it. By 1670 the pirate band was becoming an army and their raids were being transformed into a plan of campaign. After establishing himself firmly on the Volga, Razin was perhaps already thinking of moving on Moscow itself, and the word spread that he was 'going to Rus to establish the Cossack way there, so that all men will be equal'. One of his proclamations called on 'whoever wants to serve God and the Sovereign and the great Host, as well as Stepan Timofeevich' to join his followers and help 'eliminate the traitors and bloodsuckers of the peasant communes'. A great reversal was inflicted upon the schemes of Razin when his army was severely defeated at Simbirsk on the upper Volga in October 1670, but he and his movement were by no means finished. As an anonymous contemporary English account described the sequel:

Although Stenka was now hindered to pass further, as being beaten, and wounded himself, insomuch that he was constrained to return to his Astrakhan quarters, yet he did much mischief in Russia by his emissaries, who here and there stirred up the people to insurrection. . . Everywhere he promised liberty, and a redemption from the yoke (so he called it) of the boyars or nobles, which he said were the oppressors of the country. In Moscow itself, men began to speak openly in his praise, as if he were a person that sought the public good and liberty of the people; for which cause the great czar was necessitated to make a public example of some to deter the rest.

Razin took advantage of the fact that at the beginning of the year 1670 the tsar's eldest son had died to spread the rumour that the young man was still alive and under his protection. Moreover, Stenka added that he himself had 'come by order of the great czar to put to death all the boyars, nobles, senators, and other great ones, (that were too near his majesty), as enemies and traitors of their country'. By such 'base practices' the 'ignorant people was inflamed to fight furiously, and those of them that were taken prisoners underwent death with a wonderful resolution, as being possessed with the persuasion of dying for a good cause'.

However, suffering reverses on the Don as well as the Volga, Stenka found it necessary to withdraw, and in the spring of 1671, when Astrakhan alone remained loyal to him, he was arrested and handed over to the authorities by some Cossack elders opposed to him. He was taken to Moscow, interrogated and then in June 1671 executed, his head and limbs being stuck up on display and his body thrown to the dogs. The area covered by the revolt was invaded, even Astrakhan surrendering in November. Thousands of his supporters were cruelly put to death, one of the punitive camps appearing as 'the suburbs of hell' in which there were gallows loaded with forty or fifty men at a time, while nearby lay many beheaded and blood-covered — 'Here and there stood some impaled, whereof not a few lived unto the third day, and were heard to speak'.

Razin and many of his supporters were dead, but the name and the deeds both actual and imagined of this most colourful of the leaders of the 'peasant wars' lived on for many years afterwards. The sun and the raven were among the many images used to conjure up the spirit of the folk hero, whom Pushkin called 'the one poetic figure in Russian history' and whom peasants endowed with great magical powers as they developed the 'subversive legend' of Stenka Razin.[4]

In the short run opposition to the government continued in the north among the Old Believers of the Solovetsky Monastery, and to the south in 1673 a Don Cossack follower of Razin styled himself 'Tsarevich Semen Alekseevich' and tried to raise another revolt. On the whole, however, the last five years of the reign of Alexis enjoyed comparative domestic tranquillity. His first wife having died in 1669, Alexis found an attractive replacement in the shape of Nathalie or Natalia Kirillevna Naryshkin, who had been brought up in the household of Artamon Sergeevich Matveev, whose wife was of Scots descent and completely emancipated by the restricted Muscovite standards of the time. The marriage took place in January 1671 and in May of the following year the future Peter the Great was born.

Tsar Alexis, still in his early to middle forties, was by now very much his own man, although closely attached to his entourage. In adulthood he was hardly the very gentle person described in official propaganda, but foreign visitors often spoke highly of his personal qualities even if they too pointed out that he could be cruel as well as kind, just like one of his models, Ivan the Terrible. His devoutness and regular attendance at church services may well have reflected his own piety, but also demonstrated his concern for a rigid observance of good order and military as well as religious discipline. He was working towards something like the ideology developed more fully by his more famous son, whose work he foreshadowed in many other ways too, when he took sick and died at the beginning of the year 1676.

On his deathbed Alexis confirmed as his successor his eldest surviving son, Theodore, fourteen years old and according to most accounts in poor health, so much so according to some of them that he had to be carried at his accession to the throne from his sick-bed. As tsar, Theodore or Fedor Alekseevich (1676–82) made little impact on the development of Muscovy and, although twice married, made no lasting contribution to the continuance of the Romanov dynasty. He had enjoyed the best education available in Russia at the time at the hands of Simeon Polotsky, and is said to have developed, like his father before him, strong literary aspirations. But certainly the major business of government was carried on by a series of favourites. At first, Matveev was exiled to Siberia on a fabricated charge of witchcraft while the Naryshkins, as we shall see, were kept nearer at hand but still away from power. The tsar's in-laws, the Miloslavskys, made a return to the centre of affairs, but by the end of the 1670s had been supplanted by skilful politicians emerging from Theodore's personal attendance. The most capable of these, although not at first dominant, was Vasily Vasilevich Golitsyn, soon to be the outstanding government adviser after the death of Theodore.

This occurred in April 1682, and was soon followed by a bloody coup mastermined by the Miloslavskys and carried out by the *streltsy*, at the conclusion of which the future Peter the Great was declared as joint tsar along with his elder half-brother Ivan, while a Regency was exercised by Peter's half-sister Sofia Alekseevna or Sophie (1682–89). But the course of events in Moscow and the context of developments in the provinces together indicate that more was involved than a simple change of government. The years of Theodore's reign had not been completely free of internal disturbance. In 1679, for example, there was an uprising in Pskov lasting for several months and recalling the troubles of 1650, while discontent flared up in 1677 among the Cossacks of the River Iaik in a manner reminiscent of Razin, and in the spring of 1682 some Don Cossacks set off on an expedition to the Volga in explicit emulation of their famous forerunner. However, fortunately for the new government, there was no realisation of an idea to move on Moscow and to join there with the *streltsy*. Even as it was restricted to the capital, the social movement linked to the change of government was serious enough, as we shall now see. In the beginning, the Naryshkin family managed in conjunction with the Patriarch Ioakim to declare the young Peter the sole successor to Theodore, and then to gather together for its approval an assembly which they tried to dignify with the label of *zemsky sobor*. But the Miloslavsky family and Sophie managed to win over to their side a preponderant number of the *streltsy*, promising them pay and privilege. The *streltsy* invaded the Kremlin and killed most of the Naryshkins and Matveev, who had previously been allowed to return from exile. Some 'boyar' houses around the town were also attacked and plundered, and their owners often killed. The Miloslavskys emerged triumphant in May, with their nephew declared senior tsar and their niece made regent, and this arrangement was given the approval of another so-called *zemsky sobor*. But the new establishment had set itself up on the most shaky of foundations, the support of the *streltsy*, who would in general expect further material rewards with many among them, including their leader Prince Khovansky, wanting to retain and even propagate the spiritual remuneration of Old Belief. Realising the impossibility of such an arrangement, Sophie lured Khovansky away from Moscow and disposed of him in mid September. Then, after lengthy and difficult negotiations with the *streltsy*, she persuaded them to accept a new commander and to pledge their undivided allegiance to her government. Meanwhile, in the summer and autumn of 1682, there were *streltsy* uprisings in a considerable number of towns, and more restlessness among the peasants over significantly wide areas, especially in the south, where the Cossacks were still turbulent, too. In order to bring this disarray to an end, on 13 February 1683 the new government promulgated a decree ordering that all slaves who had taken advantage of the chaos to secure their release or simply to run away should be seized, flogged and turned over to their former masters or sent into permanent Siberian exile. On 21 May another decree ordained that in towns and villages nobody should make any reference to the immediately preceding disturbances on pain of death. But decrees alone could not guarantee domestic peace, and Sophie's Regency suffered from more than its fair share of alarms and excursions.

Apart from the many social problems that confronted her, Sophie was dogged also by the basic insecurity of her personal and constitutional position. She was hovering around the throne rather than on it. She was a woman at a time when even polite society insofar as it existed in Muscovy was sexist to an extreme degree, and was not prepossessing enough to work her feminine wiles. 'The Princess is very ugly', wrote a contemporary visitor Foy de la Neuville. 'She is squat, monstrously fat, has too large a head, and hair on her face, and sores on her legs. She is twenty-five and looks forty'. But another foreigner, who did not arrive in Moscow before the end of her Regency, formed a much better impression of her capabilities, Alexander Gordon writing that she was a princess of great abilities and strong spirit as well as limitless ambition.[5] And she benefited mentally (even probably physically) from her close association with V. V. Golitsyn. As far as the joint rule was concerned, at the time of the confirmatory *zemsky sobor* the Byzantine precedent of Honorius and Arcadius and even the Egyptian precedent of Pharaoh and Joseph were cited, but even then Sophie's Regency was by no means constitutionally sound. As the years went by, Sophie made further attempts to shore up this fragile edifice, notably in 1687 when she tried to strengthen her title from *pravitelnitsa* or regent to *samoderzhitsa* or autocrat. Meanwhile, neither her internal nor foreign policy was meeting with much success, and people of influence were beginning to think again of instituting the rule of an autocrat: not Sophie, but her half-brother the younger tsar, Peter Alekseevich, whose rise to power we shall be looking at more closely in the next chapter.

So far in this chapter we have concentrated on the tsars and their establishments and the principal threats posed to their security from inside their dominions, noting in passing that the urban crisis of 1648–50 and some of the other domestic disturbances were exacerbated by problems of foreign policy. We must now more fully describe the international context of Muscovite history from Alexis to Sophie. While questions arose from all directions during this period, the first pressing problem was posed to the south-west by the Cossacks of the Ukraine, who at the same time as the termination of the Thirty Years War in the Treaty of Westphalia in 1648 under the leadership of Bogdan Khmelnitsky, rose up against their Polish overlords. With their political, social and religious autonomy reduced virtually to nothing, the Cossacks had been waiting for an opportunity to restore their previous freedom and, in a sense paradoxically, to increase the number among them of 'registered' or privileged and paid, and now, supported by the peasantry and allied to the Crimean Tatars, they struck a telling blow on the Polish army. A treaty drawn up with the newly elected king Jan Casimir appeared to be making satisfactory concessions on both major counts, but neither side was prepared to accept that the war had been brought to a successful conclusion and hostilities were resumed in 1649 and again in 1650. This time, their Tatar allies defecting at a key moment, the Cossacks lost and were obliged to accept a much less satisfactory treaty. Realising that his men could not gain all that they sought without assistance, Khmelnitsky increasingly turned to Moscow, asking tsar Alexis for protection. With their own internal problems only recently settled and their full understanding that war with Poland could revive them — conscious also that the centrifugal aspirations of Khmelnitsky by no means dovetailed with their own view of how a region under their protection should be controlled — the Russian authorities made no conclusive move for nearly three years. The war in the Ukraine continued in a somewhat confused manner, with great suffering for the local people, especially the Jews, whom Khmelnitsky persecuted. Finally the Russians made their minds up when Khmelnitsky threatened to return the Cossacks to their former loyalty to the Poles or even to seek the protection of the Turks, and a *zemsky sobor* was convened in

1653 to confirm the government's decision. At the beginning of 1654 the other Cossack leaders came together with Khmelnitsky to swear allegiance to the tsar, and the union between the Ukraine and Muscovy was made official at Pereiaslavl.

But the two sides continued to look upon their amalgamation from different points of view. As C. B. O'Brien[6] put it: 'The Ukraine was determined to exchange one protector for another on its road to independence; the Muscovite regime saw an opportunity to advance its frontier southward.' On the one hand, 'For Khmelnitsky and his followers the treaty provided a military alliance that permitted the Cossacks to preserve their rights, privileges, and freedom of action.' On the other hand, 'The recovery of lands traditionally regarded as "Russian" would greatly compensate Moscow for earlier setbacks in westward expansion and particularly for military losses to Poland and Lithuania.' Moreover, 'the acquisition of Ukrainian lands would also substantially strengthen Orthodoxy and would add an important new element — the Cossack army — to Moscow's fighting forces'.

While the Ukraine and Moscow entered their new close but uneasy relationship, the Poles could not stand idly by. On the contrary, they found a new ally in the Crimean Tatars, and war between the two sides soon broke out. The Russians did extremely well to begin with, taking Smolensk and then besieging Riga, but these successes were at once helped and hindered by Sweden, which was also trying to derive advantage from Poland's weakness in the same area. So from 1656–58 the war with Poland was temporarily suspended and another with Sweden embarked upon inconclusively. At the same time Khmelnitsky held back from fighting as much as possible while carrying on negotiations with a wide range of potential European partners, having gained for himself something of a reputation as 'not less daring, not less experienced in politics than the English Cromwell'.[7] At some junctures even Sweden appeared the most likely of new allies, but Khmelnitsky died while the Russo-Swedish war was still in progress, and the fragile unity of the Cossacks collapsed to be replaced by internecine conflict of a social and religious nature and by a switch of loyalty from the Russian not to the Swedish but to the Polish side and back again. Then, while Yuri, son of Bogdan Khmelnitsky, took the Right Bank Ukraine over to the Poles as war resumed between them and the Russians, the Left Bank Ukraine under Ivan Briukhovetsky adhered to the Muscovite alliance. More than the River Dnepr separated the Cossacks, however, as has just been noted. The 'registered' Cossacks and the elders were at odds with the rank and file, while the Cossacks as a whole diverged in their interests from the leaders of town society who wished to maintain a measure of independence from the control of the chief or hetman and his followers. There were internal divisions among church officials as well, with the lower orders unsympathetic on the whole to the desire of the Kievan metropolitan and his entourage to achieve autonomy for the

Ukrainian church and greater status for themselves. And the majority of the people, the peasantry, were generally dismayed at the ruin brought upon them from inside and outside their localities.

And so, when Briukhovetsky was given the exalted title of boyar and the hand of a Russian princess, and his elders were ennobled, there was great resentment against them among many who had previously given them their support. Turmoil in the Ukraine could not be brought to an end by the armistice of Andrusovo drawn up between the Russians and the Poles in 1667, even though there was a concerted attempt to settle religious, social and political differences in the face of threats to internal security as well as the ever present fears of attack from outside, especially by the Turks and their Crimean Tatar clients to the south. Briukhovetsky actually encouraged the aggressions of the infidel by appealing to the sultan in a desperate effort to shore up his own crumbling position in the face of new pressures from a vigorous hetman of the Right Bank Cossacks, Peter Doroshenko. Briukhovetsky was murdered, Doroshenko reunited the Ukraine and then himself sought the protection of the Turks. Moscow worked hard to break the Left Bank away again, but was then threatened in 1672 by an invasion from Turkey, which also quickly forced Poland to accept a humiliating peace. At this point the Aberdonian Paul Menzies was sent on an important diplomatic mission, travelling to Vienna and then on to Venice in an attempt to arrange a Christian anti-Turkish league before moving on to Rome with a letter from Tsar Alexis urging Pope Clement X to rally Western Europe to this cause.[8] This mission met with little success, and little consolation was afforded Muscovy by the return to its side in 1676 of Doroshenko.

At the death of Alexis, Russia was in danger of following Poland in defeat against Turkey, which was to invade the Ukraine in the following summer of 1677. Alexis had led his troops into battle, had attempted to win election to the Polish throne and had used an insult to his title as a reason for embarking upon war with the Swedes. But much of the actual conduct of foreign affairs had been in the hands of such men as A. L. Ordyn-Nashchokin, who gave high priority to the settlement of the Baltic question but was forced by circumstances to devote more attention to problems of Poland and the Ukraine. These were by no means settled when the new administration was forced to direct its attention to the south. Before we do likewise, we should underline the importance to Russian development of the assimilation of the Ukraine, which although incomplete at the death of Alexis had reached the point of no return. From an economic and cultural point of view, the takeover of the south-west was of great significance; as far as political and strategic considerations are concerned, its importance was also great. Russia had moved a giant step forward towards establishing itself permanently upon the Black Sea and placing itself where it could take a close interest in proceedings in Central Europe. Tragic and outrageous though the whole process understandably appears to Ukrainian nationalists, it was not categorically different from that taking place as absolutism laid its foundations throughout Europe. As C. B. O'Brien[9] rightly observed:

There is little justification for regarding Moscow's policy as deceptive or sinister. The tsar's approach to the problem would have been well understood by Richelieu or Mazarin, as it was by the German Emperor Leopold I, the Great Elector Frederick William, and Louis XIV. If ambiguities existed concerning the nature of the Moscow–Ukrainian union, these dated from Bogdan Khmelnitsky's time, and he and his advisers must share responsibility for them. Moscow had simply extended its jurisdiction over an area that was Orthodox, that was portrayed by the tsars as traditionally 'Russian', and that had solicited Muscovite protection from foreign enemies.

Nor, whatever the protestations of Russian, Soviet and some Western historians, was there any greater element of the deceptive or sinister about the Turkish invasion of 1677, which was also a response to a by no means exceptional expansionist impulse. The Turkish army was directed towards Kiev and then Chigirin, the political centre of the Ukraine, which however managed to withstand a fearful siege long enough for a Russian army to arrive to drive the Turks back, and again in 1678, with a considerable technical contribution from Patrick Gordon, who arranged for the fortress to be blown up at the final evacuation. Numerically inferior but superior in training and in morale, the Russian army continued to manage to hold the Turks at bay while diplomats strove for alliances with Poland and Austria against the common enemy. Nothing came of the negotiations, and in the end the Russians were left with no alternative but to make a separate peace. The Treaty of Bakhchisarai of 1681 kept the Left Bank Ukraine and Kiev in Russian hands in return for giving up the lower Dnepr and paying the Crimean Tatar khan an annual tribute.

Theodore's main contribution to these proceedings had been prayers of supplication and thanksgiving. His sister Sophie was rather more active after her assumption of the regency at his death in 1682, especially in close association with her principal adviser V. V. Golitsyn, even though they too were as much caught up in events as their predecessors and as little able to implement preconceived designs. The first problem for the new regime was recognition, for which purpose formal correspondence in the name of the two young joint tsars was carried on with a number of fellow heads of state. The most enthusiastic welcome to the arrival on the throne of the young pair was given by those who saw gain accruing to themselves from Russia's affiliation with either of two coalitions, one against Sweden, one against Turkey. Although acquisition of the foothold on the Baltic that war with Sweden might have brought remained a long-term ambition for Russia, the government was soon obliged to give its major consideration to the south, for war broke out between Turkey and Austria in 1682 and in the summer of 1683, as Vienna was put to siege, Christendom appeared to be under the age-old threat from the Muslim invaders. The siege was relieved with the assistance of an army led by the King of Poland, by now Jan Sobieski, and the possibility of an anti-Turkish coalition appeared to be strong. But mutual suspicion between the Poles and the Russians meant that lengthy negotiations came to nothing, and little more progress was made in negotiations between the Russians and the Austrians, even though the Habsburg emissaries already talked of Turkey as 'an incurably sick man' which could be 'converted into a corpse' and held out the tempting prospect of the Black Sea beckoning the Russians and the Red Sea waiting impatiently to embrace them — 'All Greece and Asia await you'.[10]

At the beginning of 1684 V. V. Golitsyn asked for the views of Patrick Gordon concerning a war against Turkey, and the canny Scot duly set out the pros and cons, nine of each. The youth of the tsars could be a problem, but successful wars had been embarked upon during the minority of such monarchs as Henry V of England and Queen Christina of Sweden. Moreover, while the dual rule meant that the state was divided into factions and there was 'nonconcordance, jealousies and dissensions among the nobility breeding confusion, and irresolution in counsels', war could nevertheless be embarked upon if there was wide agreement and good leadership. And if there was 'scarcity of money and want of treasure which are the nerves of war' (a phrase incidentally very similar to one used later by Peter the Great), enough could be found if there was a real necessity for it. A further problem was the 'discontents, disobedience and unwillingness of the soldiery and commonalty', but their disagreements among themselves and the imposition of discipline from above could combine to keep them acquiescent enough. And if there was a general want of inclination to war, especially 'in the grandees and councillors', 'hopes of honour, fame and riches will move some, and fear of punishment, disrespect and loss will drive others', and rewards should be given to military personnel only. As for the Turks and Tatars, they might keep the peace, and then they might not. It might be irreligious and unlawful for the Russians to break the peace, but the Turks and Tatars were already guilty of infringements and threats. And what about the Poles? In this case, neighbours would aways be a problem, and the Poles might even be mollified if they saw the Russians taking the Christian cause upon themselves; if not, there would be good reason for any further war embarked upon against them. Finally, peace brought plenty and profit, pleasure and ease, but there could not always be peace, and it would be dangerous to keep the Cossacks unoccupied and 'to let your soldiers and people grow out of use of arms, when all your neighbours are so busy using them'.[11]

Weighing up the advice of Gordon no doubt and also taking their own counsel, Golitsyn and the government made no move until, after further negotiations with the Poles, a Treaty of Eternal Peace confirming the terms of Andrusovo nearly twenty years before was signed in Moscow in the spring of 1686. Among the commitments made by Russia in return for concessions by Poland was the launching of a war against the Crimean Tatars. Although continued discussions with other European powers came to nothing and the great anti-Turkish crusade was still much more an aspiration than a reality, Turkey was involved in a war with Poland, Austria and Venice and Golitsyn duly led a campaign to the Crimea in 1687. This was a failure, partly because the Cossacks made no more than a half-hearted movement in support, but was loyally celebrated by Sophie. A second campaign in 1689 led to no more success, even though the Cossacks were more active. Sophie talked of 'incredible victories', but this time widespread dissatisfaction led to the coup in favour of Peter, the younger tsar.

A remote accompaniment to the Crimean campaigns, themselves exotic enough from a Western point of view, were engagements in the infinitely more remote valley of the River Amur against China. These came as the culmination of a Russian interest in the region that had been developed in the sixteenth and early seventeenth centuries by adventurers, hunters and traders, especially in furs, and grown considerably in the reigns of Alexis and Theodore, when forts were set up at Argunskii, Albazin and Nerchinsk. However, at about the same time that Europe was experiencing its mid-century crisis, China was also in turmoil from which emerged a new, powerful dynasty with special interests in the north. The Manchus were not happy with the Russian presence in the Amur, and sent several reconnoitring expeditions to find out exactly where the Russians were and what they were doing. At this time the primary Russian interest in the area undoubtedly remained trade, as several diplomatic missions to Peking attempted to make clear. But arguments over the niceties of ceremonial as well as deeper misunderstanding made it impossible for any accommodation to be reached. At the end of 1683 the Chinese government ordered the Russians to leave the Amur. Although Golitsyn had grandiose ideas for the settlement of Siberia, even he was not prepared to argue that any military effort could at that time be made by the central government to protect these far-flung outposts. In 1685, after a short siege, Albazin was abandoned by the Russians and then destroyed by the Chinese. The Russians returned and began to rebuild the fort in the early autumn and had nearly completed their work by the summer of 1686, when the Chinese returned in larger numbers than before. A second siege was resisted with great courage but much loss. By now diplomatic contacts were being resumed between the two sides, and a plenipotentiary ambassador arriving in the area in early 1687 had been instructed at his departure from Moscow about a year earlier to end the dispute without bloodshed even if considerable concessions had to be made. More procedural wrangles as well as radically different basic postures meant more delay, and then the negotiations themselves were embarked upon but at times seemed to be breaking down. Jesuits acted as intermediaries, and made a significant contribution to the composition of the final treaty, as was clearly reflected in the circumstance that the authoritative text was that in Latin rather than that in Russian or Manchu. Generally speaking the Treaty of Nerchinsk of August 1689 removed the Russians from the valley of the River Amur and expressed the belief that commercial relations between them and the Chinese could now flourish in an amicable manner, while tacitly signifying the mutual political recognition of the two signatories. Although heavily criticised by some historians for its humiliating concessions, the treaty fell far short of the initial Chinese demands that the Russians withdraw beyond Lake Baikal and abandon the fortress and the littoral of the Sea of Okhotsk. With the government's top priorities being given to the Black Sea and its hinterland, there was no possibility of a sufficient show of force to protect Albazin and the other outposts of the nascent empire along the Amur.[12]

Elsewhere in Siberia, however, with no opponent of anything like comparable strength, the Russians were pushing on throughout the second half of the seventeenth century. The Pacific coast was first reached at the end of the 1630s and Okhotsk founded in 1647. Further to the north soon after this the Bering Strait was discovered, although access to the Pacific Ocean from the Arctic Sea was inhibited by the 'Stone Nose', or 'Impassable Nose' which became a prominent feature of early maps of the extreme north-east of the Eurasian continent.

Kamchatka was not penetrated before the end of the century, and altogether New or Eastern Siberia was not a focus for much activity before the reign of Peter the Great, or even later. Elsewhere in the vast open spaces, although there were probably no more than 100,000 Russians, the river and portage routes were well travelled in the search for furs and other riches, the 200,000 or so indigenous inhabitants offering only fitful if occasionally ferocious opposition, as well as more welcome tribute. Conditions for those involved in Siberian expeditions were graphically described by the Archpriest Avvakum:

And in winter we would live in fir cones, and sometimes God would send mare's flesh, and sometimes we found the bones of stinking carcasses of wild beasts left by the wolves, and what had not been eaten up by the wolves that did we eat; and some would eat frozen wolves and foxes — in truth, any filth that they could lay their hands on.[13]

This revolting description then becomes unrepeatable.

However, by the late seventeenth century life in Siberia was by no means just a matter of dangerous pioneering expeditions. An integrated administrative system centred on Tobolsk on the River Ob was being built up for the collection of *iasak* or tribute, and the maintenance of law and order. To the west of the Urals a similar process of incorporation was under way. The nomadic Kalmyks took an oath of loyalty to Tsar Alexis in 1655 and confirmed it in later years. These skilful horsemen became usually trustworthy allies for the Russians in their struggle against the Crimean Tatars and their patrons the Turks. But the wanderings of the Kalmyks impinged upon territories which had come to be considered as theirs by the Bashkirs, and the resulting tensions along with the exactions of the tsarist government led to a large-scale Bashkir uprising in the years 1662–64. By and large the central government was able to manage its relations with these peoples of the trans-Volgan steppe through a mixture of appeasement of the leaders, pacification by missionaries and suppression by the army, although there was never any widespread elimination of the indigenous peoples on either side of the Urals. Meanwhile, contacts with the peoples of Central Asia were at this time no more than tenuous and occasional, consisting mostly of commercial dealings and the odd raid.

In order to police Siberia as well as the more central provinces and to conduct its larger-scale military activities to the west and south, the government had to continue the process of the modernisation of the army embarked upon in the reign of Michael, and the changes needed to be quantitative as well as qualitative. At the time of the Smolensk War in the early 1630s, as we have seen, approximately 34,500 men comprised the Muscovite army; fifty years later, the complement could be variously assessed at from 160 to 200,000 or more. For as long as possible the government made use of what Richard Hellie has called the 'middle service class' and its old-fashioned cavalry, attempting to improve its preparedness both material and moral, and realising that any immediate wholesale change would bring with it a potentially dangerous amount of social dislocation. But in the wars against Poland and Sweden, both fully conversant with the new ways of waging war, it became increasingly necessary to abandon medieval feudal levies, and the various strata of the nobility were therefore obliged to an even greater extent to enrol in modern cavalry or infantry regiments. Patrick Gordon tells us that on 28 October 1688, for example, orders were to be sent out for 'all the Gentlemen, officers, horsemen, lancers, soldiers and all the military persons' to appear at a general rendezvous 'with a warning that whosoever should not appear at the last term, their lands should be taken from them for their Majesties'. Thus, their commitment to the ownership of their estates and serfs acted as a restraint upon the noble servicemen as they were forced in the end to change their time-honoured manner of contributing to the Muscovite war effort. As for the musketeers, the *streltsy*, a vital component of the army in the sixteenth century, their numbers grew to 55,000 by 1681, but their importance diminished as they were relegated more and more to garrison duties and never more than a third and often less than a third of them were employed in wars against external enemies. With no such stake as the noble servicemen in the prosperity of the established order, many of them turned to Old Belief and to civil disobedience, even revolt, as is also described in the pages of Patrick Gordon's diary.[14]

Gordon himself and a number of other mercenaries tended now to train and to command units in the reformed army rather than to comprise them as had been the case at the time of the Smolensk War. Gordon was very surprised on his arrival in Moscow in 1661 to be asked to demonstrate arms drill, asserting that this was in his view the least qualification for an officer, but duly obliged with a demonstration when told that even the best colonel coming into Muscovy must prove his proficiency in this regard. Nearer the beginning of the reign in 1647 a military manual was published in Russian after its translation from the German, *Kriegskunst zu Fuss* (to give the short title, by Johann Jacobi von Wallhausen and first appearing in Oppenheim in 1615) now becoming *Uchenie i khitrost ratnogo stroeniia pekhotnykh liudei (The Drill and Strategy of the Military Formation of Foot Soldiers)*, another indication of the modernisation of the Russian army. By the end of the reign of Alexis this process had reached a stage at which three-quarters or more of the armed forces were organised in so-called 'foreign units' — cavalry, dragoons, hussars, infantry. Even the most important group of irregulars, the Cossacks, found themselves increasingly brought into the new forms of organisation, which was acceptable to some if it brought rewards in material goods and status, but irked others to the point that they were prepared to bite the hand that was attempting to feed them.

Of course, although the formation of a modern army had begun in the reign of Michael and was carried several stages further during the reigns of Alexis and his successors, there was some way to go in organisation, training and equipment before the process neared anything like completion, and Peter the Great had a significant part to play in this respect. This was much more the case as far as the navy was concerned, although even in this junior Muscovite service the work of the tsar carpenter was at least foreshadowed. Ships would not be necessary in any great numbers until Russia had access to the sea, but in 1667 Alexis decreed that a small fleet should be constructed for the purpose of patrolling Muscovy's main artery of communication, the Volga. Built with the assistance of Dutch masters, the principal ship, the *Orel* or *Eagle*, was launched near Kolomna on the Oka, a Volga tributary, in 1669 and sent down almost immediately to Astrakhan at the Volga's mouth. Another ship was built there in the following year, but after his seizure of the city Razin destroyed both it and the *Orel*. Although there was some talk and even a little action concerning further naval activity during the regency of Sophie, mostly instigated by V. V. Golitsyn, the next real step forward occurred during the early years of the independent reign of Peter the Great, on the Don, the White Sea and then the Baltic.[15]

If the navy could not flourish while Russia was still landlocked, the army remained the chief concern for Alexis and his successors as it had been for Michael. Therefore, in conjunction with the regularisation of the army there developed a regularisation of the state apparatus as a whole, as we shall now see. A key moment was the drawing up of the *Ulozhenie* or Code of 1649, although generally speaking, the dual process of regularisation was gradual rather than abrupt; Alexis and his children subjected the inheritance of the Romanovs to evolutionary change rather than to drastic overhaul.

Thus, although no longer the power in the land that it had been, the boyar duma remained in existence down to the end of the century, discussing questions not only of legislation but also of internal and foreign policy, and with a considerable representation from the various strata of the Muscovite nobility. Yet, like his father before him, Alexis tended to lean for advice most heavily on those to whom he could give his full trust rather than those who were in the duma by right. He therefore made much use of an informal privy council and of such individuals as B. I. Morozov, F. I. Sheremetev, I. D. Miloslavsky (his and Morozov's father-in-law) and N. I. Odoevsky, each of whom in turn was in control of the most important *prikazy*.

The *zemsky sobor*, which had been in frequent session during the reign of Michael, reached the height of its influence soon after the accession of Alexis. But, in a sense, what had been 'a social moral authority, supporting a still uncertain governmental power' now became a rubber stamp for a governmental power that had now firmly established itself, and its later meetings tended to be somewhat empty formalities.[16] While this process reflected primarily the growing self-confidence of absolutism, it did not necessarily mean the loss of self-confidence on the part of the most powerful members of society, but rather that now that their basic anxieties and wishes had been taken care of in the Code of 1649, they had no need for further noisy demonstrations of fear and desire. The entrenchment of serfdom gave a firm foundation to the security of the service class, which had now an even greater stake in the completion of the making of absolutism, which was in any case a socio-political system rather than the rule of one as described in convenient legal fiction.

We will return to the Code of 1649 and its implications after completing this survey of the formal structure of government from the accession of Alexis to the overthrow of the Regent Sophie. To turn to the *prikazy* or chancelleries, they, like the boyar duma and the *zemsky sobor*, were taken over as bequeathed by Michael and then subjected to certain alterations. These at first involved the traditional practice of creating temporary chancelleries to take care of immediate pressing needs. Thus, in the first decade or so, a number of *prikazy* were set up to deal with matters arising from the acquisition of the Ukraine and the associated wars with Poland and Sweden; only one of these, the *Reitarsky* or Cavalry Chancellery, concerned with regiments of the new formation including the infantry, remained in existence down to the end of the century. Other temporary chancelleries set up in the reign of Alexis were directed at solving the problems posed by the Kalmyk people, the Code of 1649 and the degrees and title of the new ruling dynasty.

The most important of the more lasting chancelleries introduced during the reign of Alexis was the *Tainyi* or Secret *prikaz* first instituted in 1654 and described with customary flair by Klyuchevsky:

Its title was more sinister than its function. It had nothing to do with secret police, but managed the Tsar's field sports. Tsar Alexis was a passionate falconer, and this department was in charge of two hundred falconers and gerfalconers, more than 3,000 falcons, gerfalcons, hawks and as many as 100,000 dovecots for feeding and training purposes. This kindly but parsimonious Tsar made this department responsible for a range of personal household, as well as general state, business. His personal, as well as diplomatic and military, correspondence was conducted by this Department, which was put in charge of the Tsar's numerous properties, the Imperial salt and fishing industries, the business of his well-loved Sava Storozhesky Monastery, and distributed the Tsar's alms. When Tsar Alexis wanted to intervene directly in government, initiate new measures, such as mining or granite quarrying, he issued personal directives through the Department of Secret Affairs. It therefore became his Privy Chancellery, and was the government's own particular instrument for surveillance, acting apart from the boyar duma which was responsible for general control.[17]

Arguably, Klyuchevsky was in this evocative picture somewhat generous to Alexis and at least a little unfair to his chancellery; while the tsar was not necessarily so kindly, his administration was perhaps not quite as confused. Although it would no doubt be wrong to suggest a uniformly smooth movement towards the completion of the administrative edifice of absolutism, the workings of the Secret Chancellery and a rearrangement of the financial *prikazy*, demonstrated that Alexis and his entourage were developing an interest in government that transcended their own personal concerns, even though both these government departments were abolished soon after the death of Alexis.

Rearrangement of the *prikazy* was continued by the new establishment of Theodore, in which the most important figure was I. M. Miloslavsky. Although, again, there must be no exaggeration of the degree of good order and bureaucratic discipline, the attempt was certainly made to concentrate all matters concerning the landed property of the nobility in the *Pomestnyi* or Estates Chancellery and to extend the area of competence of the *Razboinyi* or Brigand Chancellery to cover the whole of Muscovy. The Cannon was merged with the Cavalry Chancellery, and some of the administrative bodies known as *chetverti* were merged with the Diplomatic and Musketeer Chancelleries. Most significantly, many important financial activities were brought together, first under the personal direction of Miloslavsky and his associates, then under the institutional control of the Great Exchequer, with which the Great Revenue, *Novaia chetvert* and the financial affairs of other *chetverti* were merged.

However, at the beginning of the regency of Sophie, in which the dominant figure was V. V. Golitsyn, the government realised that after losing fiscal authority the *chetverti* could no longer control the activities of the local authorities in the areas under their jurisdiction nor meet current expenditures including the salaries of their own officials, and so, except for customs and excise, their financial powers were restored to them. By this time there were about forty chancelleries altogether, and the process of rationalisation as to function and region had at the very least been inaugurated and brought some fresh procedures into the hide-bound world of the officials of old Muscovy.[18]

The most important of these officials were members of the nobility, whose efficiency was restricted not only by red tape but also by blue blood, for the system of appointment to places according to family known as *mestnichestvo* was still in existence until the very end of the reign of Theodore. In its day this system had arguably been of use to the government as it reconciled proud independent princes and others to their centralisation and subordination, but by now it had become no more than a vehicle for often empty aristocratic pretensions. A contemporary, G. K. Kotoshikhin, savagely caricatured the conduct of a noble who refused to sit below another of equal rank at the tsar's table:

And if he is forcibly seated, he will not remain seated below the other but tries to break loose from the table; and he is restrained and persuaded not to incur the tsar's wrath and to be obedient. But he cries, 'The tsar can have my head cut off if he wants, but I still won't sit below him', and slides under the table; and the tsar orders him to be removed and sent to prison, or forbids him to be admitted into his presence until ordered. And afterwards, for his disobedience, he is deprived of his rank...and then he regains his old rank through service.[19]

Kotoshikhin, an undersecretary at the Diplomatic Chancellery who supplied the Swedes with secret information in 1663 and who then ran away in the following year to Stockholm, has often been criticised for slandering his native land, but may be more seriously faulted for concentrating on court etiquette, ambassadorial protocol and other ceremony at the expense of more important aspects of the lives of the tsar and his advisers. On the question of *mestnichestvo*, however, he turns his failing to satirical advantage. Undoubtedly wrangling for place, at least in this medieval manner, could not be reconciled with the achievement of the task of modernisation upon which the early Romanovs, however fitfully and selectively, had embarked. In this case, as in so many others, the primary impetus came from a military direction, to be precise from a commission on army reform which sat during the reign of Theodore under the chairmanship of V. V.

Golitsyn. Golitsyn himself would have liked to have implemented a wider programme of reform, but in the face of the opposition of some churchmen and many boyars, he was perhaps lucky to achieve even as much as the abolition of *mestnichestvo* and the partial introduction of a new system of gradation.[20]

Kotoshikhin made a point of wide implications when he talked of the noble who had lost rank regaining it through service. For service was catching up with blood as a means of achieving rank, although it was not to overtake it until the reign of Peter the Great. Whether in the army or the chancelleries, boyars and those of lesser rank were all being called upon to make their contribution to the state's security and welfare. This characteristic affected local government as much as central, the *voevoda* or sheriff who remained the key figure almost invariably being a man of mature years, who had usually participated in several campaigns. If anything, this official became more important during the later part of the seventeenth century than he had been at the beginning, since the number of *razriady* or amalgamations of districts grew in the border regions and then nearer the centre. To the south, once the fortified line based on Belgorod with an associated *razriad* was completed, another was begun to the south west with its capital at Sevsk. These were still very much frontier lands, with a frequent necessity for preparation of defence against marauding Crimean Tatars or against threatening attacks from the Poles, and the military emphasis on the sheriff's work was heaviest in them. Because of their remoteness and newness, these *razriady* also afforded the greatest opportunities for corruption, which were often taken. To the west a *razriad* was formed after the official conclusion of the union with the Ukraine in 1654 around Smolensk, in which town Alexander Leslie, Thomas Dalyell and Paul Menzies were a remarkable series of trusted Scottish governors, all collaborating with the local *voevoda*. To the north-west, another *razriad* was formed in about 1656 at the time of the war with Sweden in the neighbourhood of Novgorod, the old Russian town with its own distinctive form of government not completely submerged for all its incorporation into the general body of Muscovy. And to the east, guarding the Volga marches, the Kazan *razriad* which earlier on in the century had included Siberia within its purview was now more narrowly directed from a centre not at Kazan but Simbirsk to its south. To the north, as before, there was little fear of invasion, but special problems for the sheriffs because of the strong traditions of peasant self-government. From 1680 *razriady* were apparently formed around Vladimir, Tambov and even Moscow. Altogether these new administrative divisions succeeded in suppressing much of what was left of centrifugal medieval autonomy and pointing the way forward to Peter the Great's formation of *gubernii* or provinces.[21]

Meanwhile the underpinnings of local and central government were strengthened by the introduction of serfdom in 1649 which enabled

Peter to complete the process of the construction of absolutism, just as the emancipation of 1861 brought serfdom to an end and thus led in the direction of absolutism's demolition. Here we encounter the apparent paradox that the process of modernisation, in which during the seventeenth and eighteenth centuries the absolutist regime was to play a positive part, was aided by the introduction of a system of forced labour such as the rest of the modernising world had already given up. The paradox is resolved somewhat when we realise that although *krepostnoe pravo* is usually translated as serf right or law and *krepostnichestvo* as serfdom, translation by itself does not make what was introduced into Muscovy in 1649 the same as what had been removed from other parts of Europe some years before. Russian serfdom was the consequence of the necessity of the states of Eastern Europe to look inwards for modernising resources at a time when the states of Western Europe were looking outwards; the Habsburgs and the Hohenzollerns faced a similar problem to that of the Romanovs, and made a similar response. Serfdom in the east of the continent from the middle of the seventeenth to the middle of the nineteenth century is in several important respects the equivalent of slavery in the Atlantic world.[22]

This is not to deny that the most characteristic social feature of Russian absolutism possessed its own peculiarities; as well as external pressures there were also strong internal impulses towards the introduction of serfdom. There has been a vast amount of historical discussion as far as Russia's own version of the institution is concerned, with the arguments concerning its introduction in 1649 falling into two groups, one concentrating on action from above, the other on action from below. To the first group, the state felt a growing need to exploit its human resources as much as possible as it succeeded in exerting its absolutist grasp; to the second group, the peasants brought their misfortune upon themselves in the sense that their indebtedness to noble landowners forced them to obligate themselves for increasing lengths of time which could in the end lead only to temporary arrangements becoming permanent. Such obligation would be welcomed by the noble landowners who were attempting to make the most of their estates in conditions of labour shortage. If we go on to recall that the absolutist state was a socio-political amalgam dependent on the co-operation of the greatest landowner, the tsar, with the greater, great and lesser landowners comprising the nobility, we realise that in the making of serfdom action from below and action from above were not alternative to each other but complementary. Such a conjuncture becomes all the clearer when we return to the actual circumstances of the final introduction of serfdom, the *zemsky sobor* which convened in September 1648 and the *Ulozhenie* or Code that it produced by January 1649, the urgency of the business bringing about its speedy completion.

In the *sobor* there were approximately 350 participants including 14 from the higher clergy, 40 boyars and other high-ranking nobles, and 153 from the provincial nobility. The embryonic third estate was represented by 3 'guests', 27 from the Moscow *streltsy* regiments and militia hundreds, and 79 from the town population in general. The social origin of 20 or so others is unknown, although there are known to have been no delegates from the peasantry, Siberia or the lower Volga. As for the actual workings of the *sobor*, it was divided into two houses according to rank and was much influenced by the petitions that it received from both noble and urban groups. Other sources for the Code of 1649 were the Muscovite laws and codes already in existence, Byzantine and especially Lithuanian precedents, the Lithuanian Statute of 1588 constituting not only a useful guide but also, albeit in adapted form, the origin of many of the clauses. Although the Code as finally produced was a hasty and somewhat careless piece of work inferior to many of its models and, although there is much truth in Klyuchevsky's assertion that its survival until 1833 'should not be interpreted as proof of its merits, but as an indication that Russia could do without a respectable collection of laws', it did deliver rough justice for the groups attending the *zemsky sobor*. This, in its turn, meant an injustice that was much rougher for those groups who were not represented at the assembly. So when the Code's preface stated that its principal purpose was 'to make the administration of justice in all cases equal for men of all ranks, from the higher to the lowest', it did not contain within its purview those men without rank outside society who were now in effect to be designated not so much human beings as possessions. And even those within the pale of rank could not agree on what constituted justice for all of them, and there were many squabbles during the composition of the Code between and even within the various groups who were often united only in their realisation that persons of property would have very little legal protection if they could not accommodate their differences in the face of the major threat posed by non-persons of no property.[23]

The Code as finally ratified consisted of 25 chapters: 1–9 on state law; 10–15 on judicial procedure; 16–20 on property; 21–22 on criminal law; and 23–25 on the *streltsy*, Cossack and taverns. Under the first heading Orthodoxy and tsarism were protected by the death penalty for blasphemy or treason and its near equivalent, the knout, for less serious misbehaviour in church or at court. The second section's most significant chapter was number 11, abolishing the 'forbidden years' during which runaway peasants could not be recaptured and binding them forever to their masters. The second section also contained punishments for offences to the honour of individuals ranging from the patriarch and the boyars to the peasants; these entailed fines and floggings for the most part. Although respect was shown to the dignity of the patriarch by placing him top of the list, his power and that of the church in general tended to be weakened in relation to the secular branch of government, and this tendency was emphasised by the creation of the Monastery Chancellery, which was to deal not only with litigation involving churchmen but also with administration of church lands. The secular ascendancy was also marked in chapters 16–20, number 19 ordering all church settlements in Moscow and other towns to be taken over by the state with their inhabitants losing their tax exemptions. In such measures the framers of the Code were probably thinking of the pretensions of the past Patriarch Filaret; they also quite possibly stimulated the pretensions of the future Patriarch Nikon.

Many of the clauses of chapters 16–20 were directed at reinforcement of the property rights of the boyars and other nobles, with some looking after the more important members of the third estate. Generally speaking, landowners were now given confirmation of their rights to two forms of property, the *votchina* or unrestricted hereditary estate and the *pomeste* or estate dependent on state service. Chapter 20 dealt with slaves as such, a dying social stratum; the serfs, it will be recalled, still retained an independent legal existence even though in fact their predicament was akin to slavery. Chapter 19 was concerned with the tax-payers of the towns who had been agitating for some time for more equitable distribution of the fiscal burden and were now satisfied by the abolition of previous exemptions for all households and groups of households except those of the sovereign. But the town taxpayers were not forced into uniform mould; gradations among them were fully recognised by the Code, especially for the 'guests' and even more for the renowned and influential Stroganov family. Certain inequalities were also recognised in Chapters 21 and 22 dealing with criminal law, although the most powerful impression conveyed by them is of the flogging, torture, mutilation and death awaiting anybody deemed guilty of transgressing the state's harsh laws. There was little protection for the innocent, although the circumstances that even informers were knouted on the rack or burned with fire if they refused to make public testimony or if the accused refused to confess must have discouraged idle denunciation. Chapters 23–25 dealt with subjects not easily considered earlier, the *streltsy*, the Cossacks and taverns.

The principal features of the Code, then, were the supportive regularisation of the position of those comparatively few fortunate people who were not bound by legal slavery or the virtual slavery of serfdom, and the extension of tight controls to lower to the most abject level the position of the vast majority of the inhabitants of Muscovy. Further points of some importance were the relative decline in the status of the clergy, the clear confirmation of differential treatment for persons of rank, and the persistent threat to any individual stepping out of line of severe and merciless punishment. Such was the social foundation of Russian absolutism.

From the social we now turn to the at least equally important economic foundation. Absolutism could not prosper without adequate income, and the government continued to give as much attention as before to the gruesome task of extracting as much money as possible from the people. We have already seen how from Alexis to Sophie there was some administrative rearrangement to improve the efficiency of this extraction, but the process remained roughly the same as before with the *voevody* and other local government officials striving to collect enough for their own cut and a satisfactory return to the central coffers. The first general state budget was probably drawn up in 1679 and it was certainly in this year that the basis of direct taxation was fully changed from the unit known as the *sokha* based on land to the household. This reform appears to have been of some benefit to the tax collectors but none to the taxpayers. The equally important indirect taxes were standardised in 1653 with a uniform sales levy of 5 per cent per rouble being placed on commercial transactions. The necessity to augment the income from the traditional second source, coinage, led to much social dislocation culminating in the Copper Revolt in 1662, after which the government had to proceed more warily with debasements. A third source of state income remained trade and industry. Samuel Collins, doctor to tsar Alexis, deemed his illustrious patient to be 'The chief Merchant in all the Empire' and he was an important industrialist as well, reserving unto himself like his father before him a large part of these allied activities in salt, potash and caviare, for example.[24]

Among foreigners Muscovy at this time had a considerable reputation for economic potential and performance. 'For Aliment, necessary for the subsistence of Man,' wrote one, 'Muscovy produces so good, and in that quantity, that it yields not to the best country in Europe.' Another asserted that 'Russia if taken in general is better stored with tame Cattle and Wild beasts than any Country in Europe, or as some believe, in the whole World.' Gold and other mineral deposits were widely believed to be substantial, and of the human resources, a third visitor remarked that the people as a whole showed 'cleverness and shrewdness' in their commerce and that the merchants in particular were 'shrewd and eager for profit'. Such statistics as are available go at least some way towards supporting such observations, and encourage Soviet historians in the wake of Lenin to talk of the seventeenth century as the period when a national market and a bourgeoisie began their formation.[25]

This phenomenon would have been observed most clearly along the river systems connecting sources of supply with markets and markets one with another. Mother Volga and her children provided many of the most important links. Vast amounts of salt were carried down the Kama or up the Volga itself, with something like 25,000 long-suffering boatmen being engaged in this branch of transport alone. Iron came down the Ufa, grain down the Viatka and the luxuries of the Orient as well as fish came up from Astrakhan, several months steady pull from Moscow. To the north, the Sukhona-Northern Dvina route led to Archangel, Muscovy's principal entrepot for the trade with the West. In the late seventeenth century imports included luxury items made from precious metals and stones, from fine textiles and the grape; goods of increasing daily use such as dyestuffs, paper, hats, pins and needles, sugar and spices; and varied necessities such as arms and other metal goods, medical supplies and fish. Exports consisted of skins and furs, and pitch and potash, hides and tallow, flax and hemp, masts, a certain amount of cloth and all too much grain. There were further lines of commercial communication along the Oka to the Ukraine where the Dnepr could lead either down to the Black Sea or up to the much-fought-for city of Smolensk from which portage could be arranged to the Western Dvina. Directly from Moscow to Smolensk and also through the once great trading cities of Pskov and Novgorod there were further routes to the West overland or via the Baltic.

Government commercial policy might be described as a crude kind of mercantilism, the necessity for English, Dutch and other foreign intermediaries being realised but much regretted both by the government and Muscovite merchants. In the late 1640s, therefore, there was much pressure for restrictions of the English activities in particular, one of many petitions on the subject including in 1646 the argument that 'English trading people are all not close to Charles and have separated from him and have been fighting with him already for four years'. The Muscovite troubles of 1648 and the execution of the English king in 1649 added to difficulties which were to a considerable extent purely commercial, and so after nearly a century of continuous connection, Anglo-Russian commercial links were temporarily severed. A little later the New Commercial Regulations of 1667 prohibited the involvement of foreign merchants in retail trade and imposed high tariffs on their goods.[26]

The most important Muscovite entrepreneurs remained in the latter part of the seventeenth century as they had been in its earlier part, the *gosti* or 'guests', while the Stroganovs were almost in a class by themselves. The most important guest was G. L. Nikitinov, who dealt in wool cloth, fish and salt, had his own private fleet on the Volga and owned about a quarter as much as all the other guests put together. Beneath them were a varied number and nature of merchants in Moscow and the other towns, with even peasants being known to have dealt at least occasionally in such foreign wares as 'English cloth'[27] and a wide range of domestic items. Industry continued to develop on the base laid during the reign of Michael, one calculation attributing the commencement of three-tenths of the factories existing in the eighteenth century to its predecessor. Nevertheless, the most typical economic pursuit of the Russian people during the period from Alexis to Sophie was agriculture of a most primitive kind for a bare subsistence return. We must not forget the everyday and omnipresent humdrum tediousness of the lives of probably more than 15,000,000 peasants when considering the economy or indeed the culture of Muscovy, to which we must now move on.

For historians of Western Europe the second half of the seventeenth century is the period when, among other developments, the scientific revolution and the establishment of reason were achieved by a handful of outstanding individuals and a beginning was made to their wider appreciation by at least a highly educated stratum of society. Meanwhile the bulk of the population remained indifferent to these new departures, immersed in culture that was a mixture of a simple Christian faith and a persistent pagan superstition, throwing off their inertness no more than intermittently in a fever of ignorant fanaticism, more notably perhaps in the great witch craze.

This, as we have already noted in Chapter 1, had its counterpart in Russia during the Time of Troubles and the reign of Michael Romanov. A new and greater upsurge appears to have occurred soon after the accession of Alexis, who at the end of the year 1648 sent a decree to the *voevoda* of Belgorod complaining that there were many wizards and witches abroad in town and country enchanting many people and achieving baleful influence over the sick and the young in particular. During the next few years the black arts were practised throughout many districts, including those in the Ukraine and others bordering on Poland. A considerable number of condemned offenders were burned at the stake, and although it appears from the surviving trial records that cases could involve domestic squabbles and personal grudges, as well as such circumstances as tavern keepers denouncing their rivals and sick guests accusing their hosts, inflated claims of sexual prowess or charges of rape, there was also an undoubted element of primitive medicine on the one hand and of mass mania on the other. N. Ia. Novombergsky,[28] who edited many of the relevant records for publication, estimated — 'that witchcraft trials proceeded in Russia with as much cruelty as those in the West and that the government authorities in the Muscovite state were involved in these trials no less than in Catholic or Protestant countries'. The difference between East and West, in Novombergsky's view expressed in 1906, lay in the scale of the activity rather than its nature. The explanation for a smaller amount of witchcraft among the Orthodox Russians could be found first in — 'the absence of demonology', which he defines as 'the religious and philosophical teaching about witches developed in the West in the context of scholasticism under the influence of the legacy of classical antiquity'; secondly, in the presence of 'certain elements of heathenism in the Christianity of the Church still not eliminated in our own day.'

Some seventy years later, accepting much of what Novombergsky concluded, Russell Zguta[29] points out that among the Eastern Slavs — 'the intellectual rationale for witchcraft was predicated on a pantheistic concept of the universe rather than a demonological one', and so the Russian witch 'could be tried and punished, much like the English witch, for the secular crime of malign sorcery — but not for heresy'. Zguta concludes by underlining the irony that the Russian tradition of dual belief that the Orthodox Church was often attempting to eliminate 'may have counteracted the fear of witchcraft among the people and the readiness of officials to prosecute, helping Russia escape all of the horror, the excess, and the ignominy of a full-scale witch craze'.

If at the end of the 1640s and at other times Russia was to avoid the worst of the witch craze, it was to suffer at least its fair share of social disturbance accompanying the contemporaneous establishment of the secular absolutist state which followed the Schism in the Russian Orthodox Church, to which we must now turn. Evaluating this highly significant rupture, Michael Cherniavsky[30] provides two related insights of great value. First, expectation of the end did not appear to be so much in evidence at moments of mortal danger to society such as the Time of Troubles as at a period when society seemed to be going through a crisis of fundamental readjustment such as that at present under consideration. Second:

It is surely not pure coincidence that the Spanish inquisition reached its heights not during the Middle Ages but during the secularization of the Spanish state in the seventeenth century; that the rigid laws of Religious Conformity were imposed in England, in the seventeenth century, by a secular-minded government; that the German Reformation, completed politically by the Thirty Years' War, produced the curious theological principle *Cuius regio, eius religio*; and that the revocation of the Edict of Nantes took place at the end of the seventeenth century, under Louis XIV, whose secular concern was expressed in the slogan engraved on some of his medallions, again expressing a curious theology: *Un roi, une foi, une loi*.

All these parallels possessed their own peculiarities, as would another not mentioned by Cherniavsky, the Covenanter movement in Scotland and the opposition to it,[31] and as would the Schism itself. However, if demonology was less developed in Russia than elsewhere, the announcement there by opponents of the reform of the apocalypse and the commencement of the reign of Antichrist was at least as passionate as in most parts of Europe, while the extreme response of self-immolation was made to an extent far greater than throughout the rest of the continent. As for the establishment side, so to speak, a sweeping reform of the church was followed by the downfall of the overweening reformer, the Patriarch Nikon, and the consequent decline of the power of the church in general. As in many other spheres of the national life, Tsar Alexis in his ecclesiastical policy prepared the way for the completion of the assertion of autocratic power by his son, the future Peter the Great.

We cannot here enter into the niceties of doctrine that constituted the ostensible reason for the Schism. In any case, it would be impossible even for the most devout readers of today to appreciate fully how the number of alleluias sung and genuflections made at certain moments in its services or the number of fingers used in making the sign of the cross or the nature of the letters employed in the spelling of the name of Jesus could contribute to a great split even in a church much concerned with ceremony and ritual. More comprehensible, beyond the ambition of Nikon who became Patriarch in 1652, is the necessity that arose to amend old texts and practices as fresh breezes swept in from the West, and especially after the Union with the Ukraine in 1654 made it necessary for theologians from both sides to discuss the manner in which they could bring together their two systems of dogma. To begin with Alexis supported Nikon, but increasingly resented the Patriarch's interference in matters which did not directly concern him such as foreign policy, as well as his overbearing manner in general. And so there was a personal break between the two highest men in the country as well as a different kind of Schism at a lower level. Nikon was sent into exile after a Church Council in 1666, while his former friend, later leader of the Schismatics or Old Believers, Avvakum, was burnt at the stake in 1681. Then Alexis and his successors managed without difficulty to maintain their superiority over both factions of the Orthodox Church. Church leaders fought a stout rearguard action on behalf of their former wide influence while retaining and even expanding their vast properties, but the eyes of the nobility were already jealously focussed on the lands of the clergy and their respect for the cloth was certainly in decline. Patrick Gordon tells us how there was in October 1688, a year in which toleration was to some extent recognised in England, an informal indication of a comparable latitudinarianism in Russia where there was 'a great council, nothing concluded, where the Patriarch inveighed against me and said that their arms could not prosper nor have any good of progress for said he a heretic hath the best people in our Empire under his command, but he was taken up smartly by all the nobility, and even laughed at'.

And certain individuals from the nobility would be prepared to resist such obscurantist pronouncements as curses on those who loved geometry and censure on those who studied Latin. V. V. Golitsyn, A. S. Matveev and A. L. Ordyn-Nashchokin were among those with libraries containing works not only in Latin but also in modern foreign languages with at least implications of geometry. Simeon Polotsky, who had been made tutor to the tsar's children at an earlier date, moved on in 1666 to take charge of a theological school, a sure indication that the reform espoused by Nikon did not fall along with himself. Then in 1682 another such institution was opened in Moscow under one of Polotsky's pupils, to be merged in 1687 with yet another to form the Slavono-Greek-Latin Academy. Polotsky himself was able to combine a number of roles including that of poet laureate. Generally speaking there was much discussion of new ideas in private behind locked doors by at least a few consenting adults.

As for the tsars, Alexis began as a man of deep piety. At his first wedding in 1648 there were three days of Orthodox intonation, and no sign of the *skomorokhi* who had helped celebrate his father's nuptials in 1626. Then, in December 1648, under the influence of a reformist group close to him known as the Zealots of Piety (of which the future enemies Nikon and Avvakum were both members) Alexis decreed that these celebrants of old pagan rites should be suppressed, and so the minstrels passed from the village squares as well as from the court.[32] The tsar's second marriage in 1672 to the partially Westernised Natalia Naryshkin increased the pace of his own Westernisation; theatre and ballet came to his palaces and European order to his gardens. But even Alexis had to tread carefully, acknowledging the prejudices of his people as well as the persistence of some of his own piety in a decree of 1675 forbidding the cutting of hair and clothes in the foreign manner that his most famous son was to introduce by force a quarter century later. His less famous son and immediate successor Theodore was devout but, with Simeon Polotsky as a tutor, also aware of the world beyond Orthodox ritual, commissioning the painting of portraits and the printing of engravings.[33]

The majority of his subjects would shrink away from such outlandish practices and join with Avvakum in condemning the new style that seemed to be creeping even into icons with the presentation of Christ as a beer-bellied, red-faced German. As already intimated, a simple, rigid faith accompanied often by an elaborate set of superstitions and almost invariably by a profound distrust of everything foreign and all foreigners occupied the outlook of most Russians at this time. Ignorance could be seen as an advantage, a contemporary having remarked in the 1660s upon its great depth in Russia and gone on to declare: 'And indeed experience doth teach us this truth, that Seditions and Revolutions have not been anywhere near so frequent as in Commonweals where Learning was commonly in great esteem, and even when it triumphed most.'[34] However, the summary account made in this chapter has shown clearly enough that Russia at this time was no stranger to 'Seditions and Revolutions', while another contemporary had proclaimed in the 1640s that Russia's domestic upsets could be seen as part of a wider movement:

to take all nations in a lump, I think God almighty hath a quarrel lately with all mankind, and given the reins to the ill spirit to compass the whole earth; for within these twelve years there have been the strangest revolutions, and horridest things happened not only in *Europe*, but all the world over, that have befallen mankind, I dare boldly say, since *Adam* fell, in so short a revolution of time. . . .I will begin with the hottest parts, with Africa. . . .The *Tartar* broke over the 400 miled wall, and rushed into the heart of *China*. . . .The great *Turk* hath been lately strangled in the seraglio. . . .The Emperor of *Muscovia* going in a solemn procession upon the *Sabbath* day, the rabble broke in, knocked down and cut in pieces divers of his chiefest counsellors, favourites, and officers before his face; and dragging their bodies to the mercatplace, their heads were chopped off, into vessels of hot water, and so set upon poles to burn more bright before the court-gate. In Naples, a common fruiterer hath raised such an insurrection. . . .*Catalonia* and *Portugal* have quite revolted from Spain. . . .knocks have been betwixt the Pope and *Parma*: the *Pole* and the *Cossacks* are hard at it, *Venice* wrestleth with the *Turk*. . .[35]

And so on, even before the Civil War had come to a climax in England and Scotland with the execution of Charles I. What could be discerned already in the 1640s should be clear enough to us now. The world discovered in the previous century had already shrunk sufficiently for comparable events to take place simultaneously in its several parts, and in a manner which is becoming more clearly revealed to have been interconnected as historians embark upon their own voyages of discovery in our own time. True, such connections would not always have appeared clearly to the tsars and their establishments ensconced in the Kremlin and other residences of a sometimes outward-looking but often introverted Muscovy.

NOTES

1. See P. Longworth's contribution on Timofei Ankidinov in J. L. Wieczynski (ed.), *The Modern Encyclopedia of Russian and Soviet History*, vol. 2 (Gulf Breeze, Florida, 1976). And see generally Philip Longworth, *Alexis: Tsar of All the Russias* (London, 1984).
2. P. Dukes, *October and the World: Perspectives on the Russian Revolution* (London, 1979), p. 18. See also D. H. Miller (ed.), 'Popular protests and urban violence in 1648 in Muscovy', *Soviet Studies in History* vol. 17 (1978).
3. 'The Diary of Patrick Gordon', located in the Central Military-Historical Archive, Moscow, 9 September 1661, 25 July 1662.
4. P. Avrich, *Russian Rebels 1600–1800* (London, 1973), pp. 53, 89; A. G. Mankov, *Zapiski inostrantsev o vosstanii Stepana Razina* (Leningrad, 1968), pp. 97–8, 109–10. And see P. Longworth, 'The subversive legend of Stenka Razin', *Rossiia: Russia: Studi e ricerche a cura di Vittorio Strada*, vol. 2 (1975).
5. Foy de la Neuville and Alexander Gordon quoted in Baroness S. Buxhoeveden, *A Cavalier in Muscovy* (London, 1932), pp. 256–7.
6. C. B. O'Brien, *Muscovy and the Ukraine: From the Pereiaslavl Agreement to the Truce of Andrusovo, 1654–1667*, University of California Publications in History, vol. 74 (Berkeley and Los Angeles, 1963), pp. 26–7. On Khmelnitsky's treatment of the Jews, see entry on him in *Evreiskaia Entsiklopediia*.
7. The contemporary Pierre Chevalier quoted in O'Brien, *Muscovy*, p. 34. This section also taken from V. Picheta, 'Vneshniaia politika Rossii pri tsare Aleksee Mikhailoviche' in V. V. Kallash (ed.), *Tri veka*, vol. 2 (Moscow, 1912).
8. See N. V. Charykov, *Posolstvo v Rim i sluzhba v Moskve Pavla Meneziia, 1637–1694* (St Petersburg, 1906).

9. O'Brien, *Muscovy and the Ukraine*, p. 131.

10. Ibid., pp. 92–4.

11. 'The Diary of Patrick Gordon', 16 January 1684. See L. A. J. Hughes, *Prince Vasily Golitsyn: A Seventeenth-Century Russian between East and West* (Newtonville, MA, 1984).

12. C. B. O'Brien, *Russia under Two Tsars, 1682–1689: The Regency of Sophia Alekseevna*, University of California Publications in History, vol. 42 (Berkeley and Los Angeles, 1952), pp. 105–22; and see also M. Mancall, *Russia and China: Their Diplomatic Relations to 1728* (Cambridge, Mass., 1971).

13. 'The life of Archpriest Avvakum by himself' in S. A. Zenkovsky, *Medieval Russia's Epics, Chronicles and Tales* (New York, 1963), p. 338. On Siberia, see D. M. Lebedev and V. I. Grekov, 'Geographical exploration by the Russians' in H. R. Friis (ed.), *The Pacific Basin: A History of its Geographical Exploration* (New York, 1967); R. H. Fisher, *The Russian Fur Trade, 1550–1700*, University of California Publications in History, vol. 31 (Berkeley and Los Angeles, 1943).

14. R. Hellie, *Enserfment and Military Change in Muscovy* (Chicago and London, 1971); T. Esper, 'Military self-sufficiency and weapons technology in Muscovite Russia', *Slavic Review*, vol. 28 (1969).

15. There is an interesting description of naval manoeuvres on the White Sea in Patrick Gordon, 'The Diary', May–July 1694.

16. A. E. Presniakov, 'Moskovskoe gosudarstvo pervoi poloviny XVII veka' in V. V. Kallash, *Tri veka*, vol. 1 Moscow, 1912, p. 54. And see two stimulating articles by J. L. H. Keep, 'The decline of the zemsky sobor', *Slavonic Review*, vol. 36 (1957–58); 'The Muscovite elite and the approach to pluralism', *Slavonic Review*, vol. 48 (1969–70).

17. V. Klyuchevsky, *The Rise of the Romanovs*, trans. Liliana Archibald (London and New York, 1970), pp. 183–4. The Savva Storozhevsky Monastery was at Zvenigorod.

18. N. V. Ustiugov, 'Evoliutsiia prikaznogo stroia Russkogo gosudarstva v XVIIv.', in N. M. Druzhinin *et al.* (eds), *Absoliutizm v Rossii (XVII–XVIII vv.)* (Moscow, 1964), pp. 154–67. A somewhat more optimistic view is taken by Borivoj Plavsic, 'Seventeenth-century chanceries and their staffs', W. McK. Pintner and D. K. Rowney eds., *Russian Officialdom: The Bureaucratization of Russian Society from the Seventeenth to the Twentieth Century* (London, 1980).

19. B. P. Uroff, *Grigorii Karpovich Kotoshikhin, On Russia in the Reign of Alexis Mikhailovich: An annotated translation*, Columbia University PhD 1970, University Microfilms, pp. 101–2. For the original, see A. E. Pennington (ed.), *O Rossii v Carstvovanie Alekseja Mixajlovica by Grigorij Kotośixin* (Oxford, 1980). For an alternative analysis, see J. M. Letiche and B. Dmytryshyn (ed.), *Russian Statecraft: The Politika of Iurii Krizhanich* (Oxford, 1985).

20. M. Ia. Volkov, 'Ob otmene mestnichestva v Rossii', *Istoriia* SSSR, no. 2 (1977); S. O. Shmidt, 'Mestnichestvo i absoliutizm: postanovka voprosa' in his *Stanovlenie rossiiskogo samoderzhavstva* (Moscow, 1973).

21. A. V. Chernov, 'Vooruzhennye sily' in A. A. Novoselsky *et al.* (eds), *Ocherki istorii SSSR: Period feodalizma: XVIIv.* (Moscow, 1955), pp. 449–50.

22. See P. Dukes, 'Catherine II's Enlightened Absolutism and the Problem of Serfdom' in W. E. Butler (ed.), *Russian Law: Historical and Political Perspectives* (Leyden, 1977).

23. Klyuchevsky, *The Rise*, p. 171; S. V. Rozhdestvensky, 'Sobornoe ulozhenie 1649 goda' in Kallash, *Tri veka*, vol. 1; G. Vernadsky, *The Tsardom of Muscovy, 1547–1682* (New Haven and London, 1969), pp. 394–411.

24. S. Collins, *The Present State of Russia* (London, 1671), p. 60; S. M. Troitsky, 'Finansovaia politika russkogo absoliutizma vo vtoroi polovine XVII–XVIIIvv.' in N. M. Druzhinin et al. (eds), *Absoliutizm v Rossii (XVII–XVIIIvv.)* (Moscow, 1964), pp. 281–4.

25. Guy Miege, *A Relation of Three Embassies from His Sacred Majestie Charles II to the Grand Duke of Muscovie...*(London, 1669), p. 30; John Struys, *The Perilous and Most Unhappy Voyages...* (London, 1683), p. 136; S. H. Baron (trans. ed. and intro.), *The Travels of Olearius in Seventeenth-Century Russia* (Stamford, 1967), pp. 139, 159, 160.

26. A. A. Preobrazhensky, 'Vnutrenniaia politika pravitelstva v 40–60–kh godakh XVIIv. i klassovaia borba', in L. G. Beskrovny and others (eds), *Istoriia SSSR, pervaia seriia*, vol. 3 (Moscow, 1967) pp. 59–62; F. N. Rodin, *Burlachestvo v Rossii: istoriko–sotsiologicheskii ocherk* (Moscow, 1975), pp. 30–36.

27. V.A. Illanov, 'Zapadnoe vliianie v Moskovskom gosudarstve' in Kallash, *Tri veka*, vol. 2, p. 38.

28. N. Ia. Novombergsky, *Koldovstvo v Moskovskoi Rusi XVIIogo stoletiia (Materialy po istorii meditsiny v Rossii)*, vol. 3 (St Petersburg, 1906), p. xxxii.

29. R. Zguta, 'Witchcraft trials in seventeenth-century Russia', *American Historical Review*, vol. 82 (1977), pp. 1206–7.

30. M. Cherniavsky, 'The Old Believers and the New Religion', *Slavic Review*, vol. 25 (1966), p. 39. See also N. Lupinin, *Religious Revolt in the Seventeenth Century: the Schism of the Russian Church* (Princeton, NJ, 1984).

31. C. B. H. Cant, 'The Archpriest Avvakum and his Scottish contemporaries', *Slavonic Review*, vol. 27 (1948–9). For a convenient comparative consideration, see Geoffrey Parker (ed.), 'The European witchcraze revisited', *History Today*, November 1980 and February 1981.

32. R. Zguta, *Russian Minstrels: A History of the Skomorokhi* (Oxford, 1978), pp. 57–65. See also H. W. Dewey and K. B. Stevens, 'Muscovites at play: recreation in pre-Petrine Russia', *Canadian-American Slavic Studies*, vol. 13 (1979).

33. V. Nechaev, 'Malorussko-polskoe vliianie v Moskve i russkaia shkola XVII veka' in Kallash, *Tri veka*, vol. 2, pp. 67–93; L. A. J. Hughes, 'Western European graphic material as a source for Moscow baroque architecture', *Slavonic Review*, vol. 55 (1977); P. Longworth, 'Tsar Alexis goes to war', *History Today*, January 1981; L. R. Lewitter, 'Poland, the Ukraine and Russia in the seventeenth century', *Slavonic Review*, vol. 27 (1948–49).

34. Miege, *A Relation*, p. 64.

35. James Howell, *Familar Letters on Important Subjects, wrote from...1618 to 1650* (10th edn), (Aberdeen, 1753), pp. 411–12.

CHAPTER THREE

The new structure: Peter the Great, 1689–1725

The most renowned part of the making of Russian absolutism is that associated with Peter the Great. One of his early publicists put forward a view of the tsar reformer pulling uphill single-handed while millions dragged down, thus contributing to an image of the man that persists widely today. For example, an American art critic looking at 'Treasures from the Kremlin' in the Metropolitan Museum of Art in New York writes: 'Through Peter the Great the country moved from the Medieval world to the Age of Enlightenment in a single, painful move.'[1] In fact the movement associated with Peter the Great, while undoubtedly painful, was also complex and several-sided. If he did indeed open the 'Window on the West', the questions must still be asked: what kind of window, from what manner of building, and on to which aspects of the West? and how did Peter's movement relate to others before him and after? For his proclamation of the Russian Empire at the end of the Northern War was both a culmination and a beginning, an arrival and a departure.

This was in 1721, when Peter was nearly fifty years old, and only four years or so from his death. His might was not widely recognised before 1721, and he served a long apprenticeship before becoming a master tsar. His life and his reign both commenced without much intimation of future 'greatness', and with quite a few pointers towards a different appraisal or to no appraisal at all. And so we must give considerable attention to the early years, to those before 1698, when the shape of things to come was first clearly adumbrated after Peter's return from his first visit to the West, and before 1696, when he himself declared that he had begun state service in earnest after the taking of Azov, and even before 1689, when the opportunity was initially presented to him to assume command with the fall of the Regent Sophie.

Sophie, it will be recalled, was Peter's step-sister, the product of the first marriage of Tsar Alexis to Maria Miloslavsky, as were Theodore and Ivan V, Peter's co-ruler until his death in 1696. The second marriage of Tsar Alexis, it will also be recalled, was to Natalia Naryshkin, the daughter of an hitherto obscure noble family being brought up in the westernised household of Artamon Matveev, whose wife was descended from the Scottish family of Hamilton. Peter was born on 30 May 1672, and much celebration followed, and promotion for members of the Naryshkin family, too. The baby prince was precocious, learning to walk by the age of six months, and giving early evidence of enjoying all the comforts and benefits of the station in life to which he had been called. After the unexpected death of Alexis in 1676 the Miloslavskys were back in power as part of Theodore's entourage; the Naryshkins were sent into retirement and Matveev was banished. But Peter and his mother were kept only three miles from the centre of Moscow, at Preobrazhenskoe, which had been one of the favourite residences of Alexis, and life along the banks of the River Iauza was almost certainly more congenial than it would have been in the Kremlin. Here the young tsarevich no doubt played his first games of soldiers, as well as receiving his first lessons. Among his early tutors may well have been the Aberdonian Paul Menzies, although the first official appointment was Nikita Zotov, who duly attempted to instil the first foundations of reading and writing with the customary use of Holy Scripture. Characteristically, Peter never became much good at writing, but he learned many texts and was fond of quoting them in later life. Similarly, he soon acquired a taste for church singing, which he was also to indulge frequently in adulthood. And so the childhood years of the future Peter the Great were passed, as far as we can tell, in as agreeable a manner as the circumstances of the time would allow. Intelligent child that he was, however, he must have acquired some inkling of possible dangers for somebody in a position such as his, and they were certainly visited upon him in full measure immediately after the death of Theodore in the spring of 1682.

The Naryshkin clan were quick to seize this opportunity of nominating Peter as successor, and gathered an assembly to confirm the appointment. But the Miloslavskys, who had been ousted before the death of Theodore and were led by Sophie, won over the *streltsy* and with their help eliminated the Naryshkin threat. Several of the young tsar's relatives and Artamon Matveev were butchered, some accounts having the bloody incidents taking place before the very eyes of Peter and his mother. A further assembly, as we have seen above, declared the institution of a joint rule, with Ivan V as senior tsar and Peter as his junior. Big sister, who had been pulling the strings behind the scenes, now stepped out into the open to accept the regency until her young brothers came of age. Peter and his mother were sent back to Preobrazhenskoe; the nightmare of Sophie's coup always with them, they resumed as normal a life as possible. The young tsar's war games now became more serious and he developed his taste and talent for leadership along with a number of princes and commoners, Russian and foreign, while his keen if disordered curiosity concerning the wider world was satisfied in some fashion by the more educated members of this variegated crew. A Dutchman Franz Timmerman helped Peter study arithmetic and geometry, ballistics and fortification and was with him when he found an old English boat, 'The Father of the Russian Fleet'. The leading Russian member of Peter's entourage became the 'ignorant, nearly illiterate, but alert and jovial bombardier', as Klyuchevsky described him, 'Alesha' Menshikov; while another important foreigner was the 'staid, punctilious old mercenary' General Patrick Gordon, whose diary gives a good picture of the young tsar's continuing education, and of the series of events in the summer of 1689 which led to the downfall of Sophie.[2] At the beginning of that year Peter married Evdokie Lopukhin, a modest girl of good family chosen by his mother. The probability that the young tsar would soon have an heir contributed to the tension between him and his step-sister. By the beginning of August, for this and other reasons, the point of crisis was reached.

Hearing the news that the *streltsy* were coming to Preobrazhenskoe to kill the Naryshkins and perhaps himself, according to Patrick Gordon,[3] Peter:

got from his bed in great haste without putting on his boots and to the stable where causing to saddle a horse went to the next wood whither his clothes and habit were brought to him, and having dressed himself with such as were ready in great haste rode to the Monastery of the Holy Trinity whither he arrived in the sixth hour of the day very weary, being brought into a room he immediately threw himself upon a bed and fell a-weeping bitterly ...

Gordon was among those quick to rally to the young tsar's side, and the affair was soon resolved in Peter's favour. Sophie was confined to a nunnery, and her close associates were executed or exiled. Power had passed to the Naryshkins, and Peter returned to ever more serious war games at Preobrazhenskoe and wilder revelries in the German Settlement, his closest companion now becoming the Swiss adventurer Franz Lefort, assessed by Klyuchevsky[4] as 'an adept at organising banquets with plenty of drink, music, and dancing partners', but soon appointed both General and Admiral. In 1694 there were naval manoeuvres off Archangel; the death of his mother in February had caused the young tsar great grief but not impeded his plans of preparation. In 1695 the army moved from its many dress rehearsals to its first performance, yet another in the line of attempts to take Azov; like its immediate predecessors, it failed. But after the death of Ivan V at the beginning of 1696 had made him sole ruler, Peter went on a second campaign to Azov, this time successful. A triumphal entry into Moscow in October, with General Gordon at the head and Peter following characteristically dressed as a captain in the suite of Admiral Lefort, marked for many the real beginning of the tsar's personal conduct of his government.

In a similarly transparent incognito Peter took his first trip to the West in the spring of 1697, as Peter Mikhailov, in a Great Embassy of some two hundred and fifty in number headed by Lefort. The official purpose was to work towards a Christian crusade against the Muslim Turks, but as much and as unofficially as possible the tsar busied himself with the mastery of Western technology, especially navigation and shipbuilding. He demonstrated to the surprised inhabitants of Amsterdam, London and elsewhere an omnivorous interest in almost everything under the sun from strong drink to matters of theology, but appears to have been more at his ease in shipyards than in palaces. He and his entourage wrecked the house of the diarist John Evelyn, whose servant described the visiting Russians as 'right nasty', and there are many anecdotes about the disgusting manners of the wild men from the East. But Gilbert Burnet, Bishop of Salisbury, was among those to give a somewhat more positive verdict:

I waited on him, and was ordered, both by the King and the Archbishop and the Bishops, to attend upon him, and to offer such Informations of our Religion and Constitution, as he was willing to receive: I had good interpreters so I had much free discourse with him ... he was, indeed, resolved to encourage learning, and to polish his people by sending some of them to travel in other countries, and to draw strangers to come and live among them. He seemed apprehensive still of his sister's intrigues. There is a mixture both of passion and severity in his temper. He is resolute, but understands little of war, and seems not at all inquisitive that way. After I had seen him often, and had conversed much with him, I could not but adore the depth of the providence of God, that had raised up such a furious man to so absolute an authority over so great a part of the world.

In a letter of March 1698 the same 'Sarum' wrote of Peter: 'he has a degree of knowledge I did not think him capable of, he had read the Scriptures carefully. He hearkened to no part of what I told him more attentively than when I explained the authority that the Christian Emperors assumed in matters of religion and the supremacy of our Kings.'[5]

During the course of the following quarter-century or so, as he built up Russian absolutism, the tsar was to develop many of the interests noted by Burnet, and at least one preoccupation that was not revealed to the bishop, that of war.

Hoping to call in at Venice and elsewhere on his way back from London, Peter was disturbed to learn soon after he reached Vienna in July 1698 about a fresh revolt of the *streltsy*; this appeared to confirm the worst about Sophie's continuing interest in the recapture of power. In fact, she does not appear to have been actively implicated, although many of the *streltsy* wanted to have her back in place of her brother, along with the old ways that he was rejecting and that she would protect. Discussions with Emperor Leopold concerning policies to be adopted towards the Turks, more by now of peace rather than war, had to be curtailed, although Peter was confident enough that order had been restored in Moscow to stop off in Warsaw for conversations with King Augustus, again on Turkey but also leading towards joint action on Sweden. Back in Moscow by September, the Tsar took a keen interest in the bloody completion of the suppression of the *streltsy*, being especially anxious to confirm by torture of the insurgents his suspicions of Sophie's involvement. Very little hard evidence was forthcoming, but Sophie was nevertheless forced to take the veil and kept in strict seclusion for the rest of her life.[6] Peter proceeded to confirm the worst fears of the conservative *streltsy*, forcing the pace of the introduction of reform. By the end of the seventeenth century, the end of Muscovy had been signalled by the notorious cutting of the beards and banishing of the kaftans. Innovations, to be discussed below, had been made in the armed forces and government, and in foreign policy. Time itself was made to recognise the grandiose ideas for change that the Tsar had developed during the Great Embassy, as the calendar was adapted for the year to begin on 1 January rather than 1 September and to be numbered from the birth of Christ rather than the supposed creation of the world.

By 1 January 1700, however, time had taken toll of Peter's personal life. The two great supports of his adolescence, Franz Lefort and Patrick Gordon, were dead, and relations with his wife had cooled to the point that she too had been packed off to her convent and her son, the Tsarevich Alexis, entrusted to Peter's sister Natalia at Preobrazhenskoe. Not that Peter was to be without sleeping or drinking companions during the effective part of his reign. A mistress, Anna Mons, was given a fine house and estate soon after the banishment of Evdokie, but then dismissed when a liaison was suspected with the Prussian Ambassador. Among later mistresses, Marie Hamilton of Scottish descent was executed for infanticide and Catherine, a peasant girl from Livonia, became second Empress. The tsar was never without a bedmate, but not a contented sleeper, as Alexander, another member of the Gordon family, pointed out: not only did he suffer from 'frequent convulsive distortions of his head and countenance', but:

To prevent a surprise, or any attempt on his life he would never lie alone: when he was not with the Empress or other companion, he ordered one of his chamberlains . . . to sleep with him; which was an uncomfortable situation to them, as he was very angry if they awakened him; and in his sleep he often grasped them very hard.[7]

As for the drinking, there were more than enough surviving members of the tsar's exclusive men's club which had first been founded in the early 1690s, 'The Most Drunken Council of Fools and Jesters'. The elaborate ritual of insult to the church and other crowned heads and of worship for Venus as well as Bacchus continued with ingenious additions from Peter himself up to the end of the Great Northern War and beyond, his closest collaborator being Menshikov. While it is difficult not to agree with M. S. Anderson that the 'brutal grossness' of the Council's activities 'reflects a dark side of Peter's character which it is difficult for the historian to explore', James Cracraft puts forward the persuasive view that the Council's perverse merriment should be interpreted as a 'possibly tragic flaw' on the part of the tsar, as a persistent and insensitive tendency 'to regard those who were thereby offended as obstinate children who would not see that most things western or new were better than most things Russian or old, that in Russia radical reform had become urgently necessary.' Some force must also be recognised in the argument of Reinhard Wittram that there could also have been 'a rational political purpose' in the shape of an attack on the ways of the Patriarch and the old-style court.[8] Certainly, too, The Most Drunken Council gave Peter and his companions much needed respite from the most pressing problems of the reign, chief of which was the necessity for victory in the Great Northern War.

Although this long-lasting and large-scale conflict needs to be seen as the culmination of a traditional Russian policy, it possessed from the beginning and retained both elements of personal whim and wider significance. For example, it started at an opportune time when Western Europe was preoccupied with the preliminaries of the War of the Spanish Succession, even though an Anglo-Dutch fleet combined a bombardment of Copenhagen with a Swedish advance on their capital which forced the Danes to withdraw from the Great Northern War at the very moment that the Russians were joining it. And among the official reasons given for the Russian entry in August 1700 were insults supposedly visited upon Peter in Riga en route for Holland nearly two and a half years previously. At that time, we must recall, the tsar was intent on the formation of a Christian alliance against the heathen Turk, and now peace with the Porte had to be concluded before the attack could be made on the Swedes.

Peter was initially hoping that his operations would be concerted with his allies, the Danish king, who had first started the war against Sweden, and the Polish king, acting in his capacity as Elector of Saxony. But he was unfortunately ignorant of the Danish capitulation and the withdrawal of the Saxon forces from an attack on Riga when early in October 1700 he led an army of about 35,000 men to besiege the Baltic fortress of Narva. The dashing young Swedish King Charles XII, whose information about the progress of the war in other regions was up to date, made a characteristically bold attack on the Russians with a considerably smaller force in November, and under cover of a snowstorm inflicted a humiliating defeat. Characteristically too, however, Charles did not press home his huge advantage. After contemplating and indeed planning an advance into Russia during the winter months, he moved instead during the summer of 1701 against Augustus II of Poland, and became enmeshed in the complex throes of the domestic rivalries of the proud and powerful Polish noble families, some of whom saw the Russians and even their own Saxon king as a greater threat to their pre-eminence than Charles XII and his invading Swedish army. Peter was given a breathing-space in which to gather together the shattered remains of his armed forces and to reinforce them with new blood and fresh materials, including cannon from melted-down church bells.

Assisting Augustus II with men and money, Peter soon moved back to the Baltic. In the summer of 1702 his troops seized the Swedish fortress where the River Neva joins Lake Ladoga, and by the spring of 1703 the Neva had been cleared to its mouth, where the beginning of the construction of the Peter and Paul fortress in May marked the foundation of the great city of St. Petersburg. Further successes along the Baltic coast were accompanied by treaties with Poland – Lithuania. A Russian army under General George Ogilvy moved into Poland at the end of 1705 to relieve pressure on Augustus II, whose Polish throne was in grave danger from a Swedish client, although the British and Dutch would not have wanted Charles XII to oust him from Saxony and diplomatic activity as a whole was acting against any great shifts in the Eastern European balance of power. Ogilvy's army fulfilled its primary purpose, but enjoyed no great success and moved in the spring of 1706 towards Kiev. Already troubled by a Bashkir revolt in the Urals which had broken out in 1705 and now by a mutiny of the *streltsy* and others in Astrakhan at the mouth of the Volga in 1706, as well as by a general discontent brought about by demands made on his people for money and services, Peter could not be at all confident of what the next years would bring. Worse was to follow in 1707 as the news leaked out that Augustus II had been forced in the summer of 1706 to renounce his Polish throne in favour of Stanislaus Leszcynski, the client of Charles XII, and attempts by Russian negotiators to achieve closer relations with Great Britain and France had failed. Peter worked with the idea of securing the Polish throne for a candidate under his own protection, but came to realise as a Swedish attack threatened that Russia was on its own.

Energetic preparations were made for the defence of the fatherland. Peasants in a 200-verst strip along the frontier were obliged to hide their provisions and forage, and fortifications were strengthened, especially on roads and in towns. The reformed army, now 135,000 in number, was deployed to await the attack of Swedish forces totalling just over 50,000. Throughout 1708 there were all kinds of discomfort and deprivation for the Swedes during a long hot summer, as a result of which Charles XII decided to abandon his original plan for an advance on Moscow and to turn to the south, where he expected help from the hetman of the Ukraine Ivan Mazepa and possibly from the Turkish Sublime Porte as well. Already Peter had been severely embarrassed in the south by the peasant war under the leadership of the Don Cossack Kondraty Bulavin which had broken out in the autumn of 1707 and not been brought to an end before the summer of 1708. But then in the late summer the Swedes suffered a significant defeat at Lesnaia in White Russia. With his arrival in the Ukraine and Mazepa's adherence to his cause, Charles XII had hopes for better fortunes, but Cossack support was not nearly as forthcoming as expected, and the ensuing winter was as cold as the previous summer had been hot. In the spring of 1709 the Swedish forces laid siege to the important communications centre of Poltava situated on a tributary of the River Dnepr to the east of Kiev. In July a Russian army twice their size joined them in a great decisive battle, at the end of which a wounded Charles fled and a triumphant Peter invited the captured Swedish generals for celebratory drinks, toasting them as the teachers of the Russians after so revolutionary a graduation.

Poltava was not only a reason for domestic celebration, but also the cause of Russia's wider recognition throughout Europe. Denmark rejoined the war, and Prussia promised to do so at the end of the War of the Spanish Succession. Augustus II, now in a subservient position, was restored to the Polish throne, and the tsarevich Alexis gained as a wife the Princess Charlotte of Wolfenbüttel, whose erstwhile reluctant father now turned enthusiastic. Confident, although inconclusive, negotiations were carried on with Great Britain, France and Turkey. Meanwhile, Russian forces consolidated their foothold on the Baltic, taking over the rest of Estonia and Livonia, to the general satisfaction of the local population. The German barons were happy to loose themselves from the control of the Swedes, the merchants saw huge possibilities as middlemen of international commerce, and even the peasants believed that release from the depredations of successive invading armies would lead to some improvement in their miserable predicament.

Everything appeared to be going Russia's way when trouble arose from an unexpected if traditional quarter, Turkey. The King of Sweden and the khan of the Crimean Tatars encouraged the fears and ambitions of a sufficient number of Turkish ruling circles for war to be declared in the autumn of 1710. Western European powers, especially France, also welcomed this new step, and even Peter and his advisers were not at first too downhearted. Here was an opportunity to achieve further consolidation on the Black Sea to accompany that on the Baltic, and several different Balkan Christian groups promised their firm support against the encroachments of the infidel oppressors. So, rather than biding their time and waiting for the other side to move, the Russians decided on this occasion to carry the attack to the Turkish dominions in the spring of 1711. But their hearts were not so high, as Balkan assistance failed for the most part to materialise and the summer heat gave emphasis to their lack of supplies; then they positively sank when the Russian army of just under 45,000 found itself surrounded on the banks of the River Prut by an enemy host nearly 130,000 strong. Peter almost immediately decided to sue for peace, instructing his representatives to accept any condition except slavery, and was immensely relieved when he discovered that the Turkish terms, although onerous, fell short of the worst, too short for Charles XII, who was anxious to lead a sortie to take his rival prisoner. By the terms of the Prut agreement, Russia had to give up Azov and its other holdings on the Black Sea as well as its diplomatic representation in Constantinople, to guarantee Charles XII safe passage back to Sweden, and to withdraw from Poland. Peter led his armies back to the north, leaving behind some high-ranking officials as hostages and further arguments among the Turks and their allies, these leading to two more declarations of war before the Treaty of Adrianople in 1713 confirmed the agreement made at the Prut. Relations with Turkey never resumed the stability implied by the rapprochement made just before the commencement of the Great Northern War, although towards the end of it, in 1720, an official Russian diplomatic presence was restored.

The considerable setback of the Prut apart, the major aims of Peter and his advisers proceeded after Poltava in a smooth enough manner. Already in possession of the Baltic littoral from Vyborg in Finland to Riga in Livonia, they now concentrated on obtaining satisfactory terms of peace from Charles XII, who was still hoping with the aid of his Turkish ally or the Western powers to regain what he had lost. From 1712 to 1714, while they continued some activity on the southern shore in concert with their Saxon and Danish allies, the Russians concentrated their attention on Finland. A development dear to Peter's heart was the contribution made to continuing successes by his ever-growing navy: in the summer of 1714 it defeated its Swedish counterpart at Cape Gangut (Hankö) off the tip of Finland, and then went on to seize the important enemy base in the Aland Islands.

On the other side of the Baltic Sea nothing appeared to be succeeding like success, as the number of Russia's friends was growing. In June 1714 Russia signed a treaty with Prussia, and in October 1715 with Hanover, the Elector of which had newly become King of Great Britain, a conjuncture holding out hopes of even greater support for the Northern Alliance. But Russia's new friends were not disinterested. Prussia wanted to acquire the Baltic port of Stettin (Szczecin) and Hanover wanted to acquire the cities of Bremen and Verden to the north of its own eponymous capital. Moreover, both as Elector and King, George was suspicious of Russia's growing hold on the Baltic and its all-important ship-building resources, from masts to tar, and of its possible support for the Jacobite movement. Suspicion grew to alarm in the spring of 1716 as Peter moved into Mecklenburg, the Duchy near to Denmark, solidified a treaty with the marriage of his niece to its ruler, and from his new base planned an invasion of Sweden, considered the construction of a canal straight across to the North Sea, and even appeared to be stretching his greedy hands out towards Copenhagen and the Sound. Owing largely to Danish and British dilatoriness, Peter called off the invasion of Sweden, in the autumn of 1716, and now found his former allies turning against him, even considering an attack on the Russians rather than the Swedes. Faced by almost general hostility, a treaty of friendship concluded with France and Prussia in the summer of 1717 his only insecure guarantor, Peter withdrew his troops from Mecklenburg in the same season.

France had previously been the principal ally of Sweden, so Charles XII now found himself in a weaker position in that quarter. On the other hand, in something like a diplomatic revolution, Russia's erstwhile allies were now if anything giving their support to its enemy. But the internal situation of Sweden was less satisfactory than the international, long years of war against an enemy with greater resources having brought its economic position, even its social stability, to a level that was dangerously low. And so, with hunger threatening his people and their disgruntlement mounting before him, Charles XII decided to call a halt to his conflict with Russia, while contemplating the possibility of taking the diplomatic revolution a stage further through an alliance with his most powerful former adversary against the lesser ones. Negotiations opened on the Aland Islands in the spring of 1718, and proceeded satisfactorily. Charles was to recognise Peter's conquest of his former possessions from Riga to Vyborg, although he was to get back Finland and most of Karelia, and to receive, as an equivalent for his losses to Russia, an army of 20,000 to help him win back those to Hanover and Denmark. Internal dissension in Sweden accompanied and to some extent caused by international uneasiness led to a delay in the conclusion of the treaty, and the delay was extended by the hesitation and then at the end of 1718 the sudden death of Charles XII, killed almost certainly by the enemy but just possibly by one of his own men while attacking a Danish fortress in Norway.

Power passed to his sister Ulrika Eleonora, who along with her husband Frederick of Hesse was a strong supporter of an alliance with Great Britain, duly concluded in the summer of 1719, and who therefore recalled the Swedish delegation from the Aland Islands in September. By now the British fleet under Admiral Norris, which had previously been sent over to transport the Russian troops to invade Sweden, was patrolling the Baltic to protect it, with orders to annihilate the upstart Russian fleet. But the shallow draught Russian galleys evaded their opponents and several amphibious operations were launched on the Swedish coast, one of them allowing the Cossacks to penetrate to within a couple of miles of Stockholm itself. And in the summer of 1720 the Russian fleet recorded a further significant victory over its Swedish counterpart, just off the Aland Islands. Preoccupied with the domestic crisis of the South Sea Bubble, and conscious of the fact that the projected anti-Russian coalition could not now be formed, since Peter had agreed with Frederick William I of Prussia in February to respect Polish neutrality (and by implication each other), the British government pressed the Swedes to resume peace negotiations, with France happy to mediate. Representatives of the two sides met in the late winter of 1720–21 at Nystad in Finland, yet agreement was not reached before the late summer and several more Russian sorties on the Swedish coast, one of the principal stumbling-blocks being Peter's desire to promote the candidacy of Charles Frederick of Holstein for the Swedish throne, presently occupied by Frederick of Hesse, since 1720 Frederick I. And so among the final terms was a promise from Peter not to interfere in Swedish domestic politics, as well as another to pay Sweden a sum to the value of about one and a half million roubles, and a third to allow Sweden to purchase annually a fixed quantity of grain duty free from her former Baltic provinces. Russia's gains were essentially the same as drawn up at the Aland Congress, the Baltic littoral from Riga to Vyborg, plus certain offshore islands, notably Oesel and Dago (Saaremaa and Hiiumaa). The Russians agreed to observe the rights and privileges of the cities, guilds, corporations and churches in the ceded provinces. The contracting parties also agreed to let bygones be bygones, and succeeded in this regard sufficiently for a treaty of mutual defence to be signed in 1724.

The Treaty of Nystad was 'by no means a dictated peace' but nevertheless 'a magnificent victory' for Russia, in Florinsky's estimation. Great celebrations were justifiably held, and with equal appropriateness, Peter talked of the twenty-one years of war constituting a cruel but finally triumphant educational experience. He may from time to time have been bogged down in unnecessary family affairs; even after Nystad, he did not forget the candidacy of Charles Frederick of Holstein for the Swedish throne, becoming his protector and offering him the hand of his daughter Anna. Florinsky is particularly scornful of such entanglements.

Nothing may appear less worthy of attention than the record of alliances between ungainly Russian princesses and obscure German princelets. These alliances, however, enmeshed Peter and Russia in a network of dynastic jealousies and intrigues, made the tsar the ardent champion of some of Europe's most unworthy princes in their petty quarrels, complicated the international situation, delayed for probably several years the termination of the Northern War, and introduced into the political life of Russia a nefarious element . . . [with] pernicious effects . . .

But possibly there were reasons of state in Peter's management of the marriages of Russian princesses: his own candidate on the Swedish throne could reduce the risk of further threat from that quarter; a connection with the Duke of Mecklenburg could provide a springboard for an attack on Sweden, and possibly too a starting-point for an exit to the North Sea.[9]

This grandiose project may be used as evidence of Peter's long-term ambition for Russia to gain European hegemony. And if his policies towards Asia are taken into consideration, a case can be made for saying he dreamed of Russian influence throughout the world. Although embassies sent to China in 1692 and 1719 came to very little, if anything, and no attempt could be made to redress the disadvantageous terms of the Treaty of Nerchinsk of 1689, a series of expeditions through and around Siberia were commissioned, culminating in the arrival at the Strait that bears his name by the Dane Vitus Bering just after Peter's death. But most activity occurred in or near what we are accustomed to call Central Asia. An expedition was sent in 1714 to the upper reaches of the River Irtysh, the principal tributary of the Ob, with instructions to look for gold and suitable sites for fortresses. Encountering fierce opposition from the Kalmyks, it turned back before its mission was completely accomplished, although it did begin the construction of the fortress of Omsk. Then, in 1716–17, another expedition was sent to the ancient cities beyond the Aral Sea with the aim of establishing a protectorate over the Khan of Khiva and friendship with the Emir of Bukhara. A force some 6,000 strong was annihilated with their leader by the fierce men of Khiva.

Probes into Siberia and beyond the Aral Sea were exploratory for the most part. But involvement in Persian affairs was a necessary concomitant of the Great Northern War, since any weakness in Transcaucasia or to the south of the Caspian Sea might be exploited by the Turks in a manner jeopardising Russia's already fragile southern security. An emissary from St Petersburg in 1715, A. P. Volynsky, went to Persia with the task personally formulated for him by Peter of investigating the internal condition of the country, the location of routes through it to India, and the possibility of acquiring a monopoly in the silk trade for Russia. Volynsky was quickly convinced of the instability of the Sephevid dynasty, reporting that another Alexander the Great could not add to the parlous situation and that a small detachment of Russian troops would be able to take over the country without difficulty. He concluded a commercial treaty with the Shah, who granted Russian merchants the right to carry on their activities throughout Persia and to negotiate there for unlimited quantities of raw silk. A few years later in 1721–22 the Shah was overthrown by a revolt of the Afghans, who installed their own leader in the capital Isfahan, while around the Caspian littoral there were uprisings in Dagestan and Shirvan looking for support to Turkey. In their turn other peoples in the Transcaucasian region, especially the Georgians and Armenians, sought protection from Russia. This appeal, and the seizure of the goods of Russian merchants in the town of Shemakha by some Dagestanis coupled with the end of the Great Northern War, persuaded Peter to launch a campaign over the Caspian in the spring of 1722, achieving considerable success along the western and southern littoral. In the spring of 1723 Turkey declared war on Persia, invaded Georgia and took Tbilisi, the capital. In September Russia concluded an agreement with the son of the previous Shah of Persia giving him military assistance in return for considerable concessions on the Caspian. Now war threatened again between Russia and Turkey, which was being stirred up by the British ambassador, but in 1724, with the mediation of the French ambassador, peace was restored with a recognition of a frontier between the possessions of the two powers.

After Peter's death, as we shall see in the next chapter, Russia's hold on the Caspian was very much reduced, and it was not until the reign of Catherine the Great that pretensions in that direction were revived and assuaged. The gains on the Baltic were, however, of a different nature, being retained until the Revolution of 1917. And so Peter's foreign policy can certainly be called a success, even though it began with disaster, came to a somewhat inconclusive end, and was conducted at enormous expense, both financially and socially. Not only was the Window on the West opened: the Russian Empire now stood firmly among the leading ranks of the European powers, however reluctant they were to admit it. Shafirov, one of Peter's leading diplomats, observed to a French colleague in late 1721:

We know very well that the greater part of our neighbours view very unfavourably the good position in which it has pleased God to place us; that they would be delighted should an occasion present itself to imprison us once more in our earlier obscurity and that if they seek our alliance it is rather through fear and hate than through feelings of friendship.[10]

Yet they did seek the Russian alliance, and Shafirov himself was among the first to develop the concept of a less anarchic and more amicable approach to relations between the states of Europe. And in a practical sense such an approach was facilitated by the increasing use made of such people as Shafirov, who were by the standards of the time professional diplomats. Peter was represented by more than twenty of such ambassadors and consuls, and maintained a permanent diplomatic presence in every European capital of importance. However much the Habsburgs in particular might resent Peter's adoption in 1721 of the title of Emperor, just as their forebears had not been happy with the assumption by Ivan III and Ivan IV of the title of Caesar, of which 'tsar' is the Russian rendition, they and their haughty fellow royal families would have to admit that bestriding the Eurasian continent as it did from the Pacific to the Baltic, this Empire held its title by a more than adequate basic qualification, possession of a vast amount of territory, in addition to its recent demonstration of an almost commensurate armed strength.

As Pushkin said, the entry of Russia into the top ranks of the great powers was like the launching of a ship, accompanied by the knocking of axes and the roaring of cannon. And not only the economic and military aspects of life were affected – all branches of public and many of private activity were subjected to considerable pressure which often resulted in adaptations by no means all of a comfortable kind. To begin with Peter's own closest concern, the armed forces, no example affords clearer illustration of the aphorism that they more than any other institution reflect the nature of society as a whole.

In the beginning there was the partially modernised army described in earlier chapters, and then the military fun and games of Peter's childhood, leading on to the formation of the Preobrazhensky and Semenovsky guards regiments, which saw early action against the *streltsy* whom they were supplanting as well as the Azov campaigns. A large-scale reorganisation of the army began in 1698, on a mixed conscript and volunteer basis, and 27 infantry and 2 dragoon regiments were formed from a total of something over 30,000 men. The recruiting system developed over the first decade of the eighteenth century, and by the end of the reign nearly 285,000 men had been inducted in this manner. Every twenty peasant households had to produce one young serviceman at each intake, with commensurate arrangements for the towns, and there were many runaways both from the rural and urban areas. In spite of problems such as these, the modern basis for the army obviously had many advantages over the medieval feudal levy and the more recent mercenary import. Recovering from the disaster of Narva, the infantry grew to 52 regiments and the cavalry to 33 by 1708, and after Poltava these two major branches of the army were stabilised at about 42 (including 2 regiments of guards and 5 of grenadiers) and 33 (including 3 grenadier and 30 fusilier) respectively, with additional regiments for local garrison duties. The number of infantry regiments was increased again in 1720 to 51, while the cavalry figure remained at 33, and artillery and hussar regiments were more completely incorporated in the army establishment, which was now to reach a grand total of about 130,000 men. By about the end of the reign the number of garrison troops had grown to just under 70,000, in addition to which there were about 6,000 enrolled in the *landmilitsiia*, a kind of home guard, and the irregular Cossack regiments and formations from the nationalities reaching a grand total of over 100,000 men.

In battle the aim was flexible use of line tactics and manoeuvrability, with emphasis on attack employing both the bayonet and the fierce cry of 'ura!' In order to obtain the necessary supplies industry had to be developed to produce everything from the bayonet and smooth-bore handgun to mortars and cannon, as well as uniforms and victuals. As much progress as possible was made towards standardisation, and towards the wide introduction of training and drill. Several instruction books were written, notably the Military Manual of 1716, which was divided into three parts describing in turn: the composition and structure of the army, with the rights and duties of the higher officers and the bases of service in the field; military discipline and justice, as applicable to the various ranks, with the worst penalties for treason and desertion; preparation and tactics. Peter, who took a keen personal interest in the Manual and other such works, gave considerable emphasis to the raising of the level of the army's morale and education. 'Each commander and soldier,' said one of the injunctions of the time, 'is obliged and bound to rescue his comrade from the enemy, to defend the artillery, and to protect his banner and standard if possible as if honour and life itself.' In education, as we shall see below, most attention was given to the officer class.[11]

The officers came near to forming a class in the literal sense since, although more than 80 per cent of them began service in the ranks, less than 15 per cent of them were from commoner origins. These percentages are taken from the establishment of the army at about the end of the Great Northern War, when the number of mercenaries had been reduced in the field regiments to approximately 280 out of 2,250 officers, about one-eighth of the total as opposed to one-third in 1711, itself a reduction in the proportion from the earlier years of Peter's reign. To reinforce this downward trend a decree issued in 1720 ordered newly immigrant officers to be sent back to the country of their origin, another in 1721 restricted the commissioned ranks in the artillery to Russians only, and a further edict of 1722 laid down the ruling that foreign officers still in Russian service should occupy ranks lower than their Russian counterparts, which would surely be a discouragement to them from staying in Russia for the rest of their lives. Thus, by the end of the reign, the army was almost completely led by indigenous nobles, a circumstance that could by then only improve military efficiency and the cohesion of the ruling class. Similarly, the enlistment of the peasants promoted the entrenchment of serfdom, while Cossacks and tribesmen were in this way further subjected to the process of assimilation.[12]

Not only society was very much affected by the reorganisation of the army, so was government too. Early changes in the *prikaz* system culminated in 1706 in the appointment as administrative controller of the military commissariat. The creation of the Senate in 1711 meant further adjustments, of which the last and most important was the introduction in 1717 of the War College, whose first president was Peter's close associate A. D. Menshikov. While this was to be the comprehensive ruling body, armies in the field retained their initiative, the commander-in-chief making use of consultative military councils.

The army was developed during Peter's time on a foundation which he himself attributed to his father Alexis, and which, as we have seen, may more accurately be placed in the reign of his grandfather Michael. As far as the navy was concerned, it could certainly not be called Russia's senior service, for its roots did not stretch far back into the seventeenth century. Although the necessity for its creation occurred to Ivan the Terrible after the arrival in Moscow of Richard Chancellor and his shipmates, neither he nor any of his immediate successors was able to do anything of practical significance towards the implementation of the idea. On the other hand, it is not true to say that there was no precedent at all for the navy whose construction is usually exclusively ascribed to the tsar carpenter. Before his apprenticeship was served, Russian ships had already sailed such mighty rivers as the Don and Volga and such seas as the White and the Baltic, and such statesmen as A. L. Ordyn-Nashchokin had already embarked upon projects that he was to complete, as again he himself was to acknowledge.

Nevertheless, there was nothing like the planning nor the extent of the execution that Peter achieved after the first experiments in the campaigns against Azov and the manoeuvres from Archangel. Even by the spring of 1698 the Russian fleet consisted of over fifty ships, and at least some Russians had become experienced with some immigrant assistance in the art of navigation before the Great Embassy set off to make arrangements for the training of Russians abroad and the importation of more foreign experts. The labours of 'Peter Mikhailov' and his associates in the shipyards of Amsterdam and London and their enrolment of local specialists both constituted important steps forward, but the most powerful impetus for rapid expansion came from the Great Northern War. In the first decade of the eighteenth century over 6¼ million roubles were spent on the construction at Admiralty quay in St Petersburg and at the fortified island of Kronstadt of a Baltic fleet of nearly fifty ships. After a short pause during the campaign of the Prut, a renewed spate of shipbuilding took place around the Baltic and at Archangel on the White Sea while purchases were made abroad to enable the fleet to approach a target set by the tsar at about two hundred capital ships, not to mention auxiliaries and galleys. The important part played by the Baltic fleet in the Great Northern War has already been referred to above, as have the operations of its Caspian counterpart in the campaigns of the early 1720s.

As with the army, there were problems of preparing a sufficient number of officers and men for the navy, and a considerable quantity of foreigners were enrolled while special educational measures were taken: large numbers of recruits had to be pressed into service to sail the ships and to row the galleys; and special manuals were published, notably in 1720 and 1722, of regulations on training, navigation and discipline including the order that 'All Russian ships must not lower their flags, pennants and topsails before anybody on pain of loss of life.' Administrative developments culminated in the creation in 1718 of the Admiralty College under F. M. Apraksin to control a navy which towards the end of Peter's reign stood at 32 ships of the line carrying between 50 and 96 cannon, 16 frigates, 85 galley and sundry others in the Baltic fleet and the not inconsiderable remnants of the Caspian fleet used on the Persian campaigns, with a total human complement of about 28,000 officers and men.[13]

This was towards the end of Peter's reign. We must now return to its beginning to consider the development of the administration in general. By 1699 there were 44 *prikazy* at the centre, while the *voevoda* reigned supreme in the provinces. The process of rationalisation of the central bureaucracy carried on by the early Romanovs was continued by Peter, although he also introduced some new chancelleries which followed Muscovite practice as well as the new foreign ways. Outstanding among these was the Preobrazhensky *prikaz*, first set up in 1689 to deal with the affairs of the Preobrazhensky and Semenovsky Guards regiments. Soon it acquired more jobs such as the levy of recruits,the maintenance of law and order in Moscow, the collection of the tobacco duty and the supervision of aspects of the work of some court estates. From 1697 onwards it was to take care of political crimes throughout the empire, differing from previous *prikazy* in the comprehensiveness of its sphere of competence. Because of such distinguished service as its vigorous mopping up after the Astrakhan and Bulavin revolts, the Preobrazhensky *prikaz* was retained to carry on the good work after the introduction of the colleges. Back at the turn of the century other changes occurred in the chancelleries, several being set up to look after military and naval affairs, while the *streletsky prikaz* was weakened and had its name changed.

Town and provincial government were affected by two decrees of 1699. They first attempted to carry out earlier promises of relieving the commercial classes of the oppressive control of the *voevoda*. This had caused merchants and others a lot of trouble and the state considerable arrears in revenue. And so the bourgeoisie of the capital was to select from its midst *burmistry* – or burgomasters – to run their financial and judicial affairs and to replace the eight *prikazy* which had previously shared these functions. The second decree dealt with provincial towns. These were now to be given the option of electing their own officials, and thus of freeing themselves also from the depredations of the *voevoda*. There was one condition: they would have to pay double taxes. Understandably enough, then, while thanking the government for its offer, most towns declined it, giving as an excuse poverty, poor harvests and fires. Changing its tack, the government now said that the towns would be obliged to reform their government in the prescribed manner, but without the double taxes. Another change was in the functions assigned to the new officials. While they were at first to be principally judicial, they were later designated to be mainly financial, helping the government to pay for the Great Northern War. Such an arrangement helped to weaken the *prikaz* system, and yet even the new town government was shown up as inadequate as new demands were placed upon it and revolts broke out in Astrakhan and on the Don.

Hence the first of Peter's wholesale reforms of local government, which was introduced in the years 1708 to 1710. The whole country was divided into eight large provinces: Moscow, Ingermanland (later St Petersburg), Kiev, Smolensk, Kazan, Azov, Archangel and Siberia. All of these except Moscow contained part of the empire's frontiers, and they were all assigned to some of Peter's close associates, who as governors had comprehensive powers in the huge areas under their jurisdiction. The governor had, among other duties, to supervise the arrest of runaways, the levy of recruits, the supply of the regiments stationed in his province, the collection of taxes and preservation of law and order. Yet another blow was struck at the *prikazy* and many of

81

them now transferred their business to the provinces. At the same time the town reforms of 1699 were rescinded, and the *voevoda* regained his control over municipal government. Provisions for the election of the *voevoda's* assistants by the nobility seem to have come to little, and so the seventeenth-century system of local administration was to a large extent restored.

Meanwhile, at the centre, the boyar duma was moribund and a Privy Council officially subordinated to the duma but manned by eight of Peter's associates took charge of the most important state business. And then, on 22 February 1711, the Senate was set up to take care of such matters while the tsar was away on the campaign of the Prut. At first envisaged as a substitute for the absent sovereign, the Senate soon became a permanent body and its nine members officially the most important bureaucrats. Or at least, the Senators were at the top of the government's structure; but none of them was an intimate of the tsar and at the same time as they were nominated, another group of supervisory officials had been created by him. These were the fiscals, headed by the *ober-fiskal*, who was responsible to the Senate and commanded a network of agents throughout the empire. At their various levels, the *ober-fiskal* and his subordinates were to see that the administration gave just decisions, did not take bribes or misappropriate funds. They were given financial incentives to bring wrongdoers before the Senate, and were not to suffer if those whom they charged turned out to be innocent. Encouraged in this manner, the fiscals did not hesitate to accuse even the highest in the land, including Senators, competing for work with the Preobrazhensky *prikaz*. Thus, as throughout the eighteenth century, it was difficult to answer that all-important question so succinctly put by Lenin, who dominates whom?

As St Petersburg emerged from the swamps, Peter gave considerable attention to the completion of his new admininistrative edifice; of prime necessity were institutions intermediate between the Senate and the provinces. The idea of introducing colleges at this level had perhaps first occurred to the tsar in England when one 'pious and learned Francis Lee, M.D.' had submitted a paper to him on this subject at his own request in 1698. Other, more significant suggestions came from the great Leibniz in the early years of the eithteenth century. By 1715 the basic design of the colleges was clearly worked out in Peter's head, and a Silesian baron named Johann Luberas and a civil servant from Holstein named Heinrich Fick helped Peter to develop it. Both of them submitted projects based on their study of bureaucratic practices throughout Europe, and Fick went on a special mission of investigation to Sweden while Luberas recruited in Western Europe nearly 150 men to serve in the projected colleges. This number was made up to what was considered necessary by adding Baltic Germans and Swedish prisoners of war, both of which groups should have had some experience of the German spirit and the Swedish model that were to be closely followed.

There were twelve drafts of their general regulations, nine of them amended by Peter himself, before the final arrangement in 1720 of eleven of them, falling into three principal groups. The top three colleges, War, Admiralty and Foreign Affairs, were all created in 1718. Apart from its obvious duties, the Admiralty college was to look after sail and gun manufacture, and forests. Another three colleges were to concern themselves with financial affairs: the State Revenue, State Control and State Expenditure colleges. The second of these was abolished in 1722, and its duties transferred to the Senate. A third group of three colleges was to deal with trade and industry: the Mines, Manufactures and Commerce colleges. The Mines college was assigned the supervision of mines, money mintage and prospecting; and given provincial departments in Moscow, Kazan, Nerchinsk, Siberia and Perm. The Manufactures college received as its chief task the care of all other large-scale industry, and to help it carry this out was given further functions connected with the labour force and the police. The Commerce college was to concentrate on foreign trade. Two other colleges were instituted: Justice and Estates. The first had no clear sphere of competence, because law and administration were not yet completely separated in practice, but was to control many aspects of provincial government. The Estates college was to settle land questions and arguments for the noble landlords. To begin with all college presidents were to be members of the Senate, but when the colleges were subordinated to the Senate in 1721 all the presidents except for the top three were replaced. In general the colleges were an advance on the *prikazy* because of their clearer terms of reference, their coverage of the whole empire and their uniform personnel. Each college was controlled, in theory at least, by eleven members comprising a president, vice-president, foreign adviser, four counsellors and four assessors. They were supposed to reach their decisions by majority vote, but because of the weight of tradition and the presence of fiscals, this procedure appears not to have been followed to any extent.

Peter's reform of the central government was completed by the introduction of some officials and bodies to supervise and assist the Senate and colleges. The most important of these was the Procurator-General, an official directly responsible to the tsar, representing him at the Senate, heading the secret network of fiscals and a newly established body of public procurators, and replacing earlier supervisors of the Senate such as an inspector-general and guards officers. The first Procurator-General, Pavel Iaguzhinsky, appointed in 1722, was thought to be the most powerful man in the empire after Peter, and this was suggested in the decree creating the office by the instruction that he should be 'the sovereign's eye'. Of the offices attached to the Senate, the two most important were the Heraldmaster's, which was to conduct the affairs of the nobility, and the Requestmaster's, which was to receive petitions sent to the tsar.

For all these changes and improvements, central government was still confused and inefficient. This can be suggested by a list of the Senate's business on two sample days towards the end of the reign, when its authority had risen by the appointment to it of such highly placed men as Field Marshal Menshikov and Admiral Apraksin, Chancellor Golovkin and Vice Chancellor Shafirov. On 10 November 1721 the Senate considered a school for civil servants, the governorship of Kazan, the Table of Ranks, canals, the road to Moscow, supervision of *voevodas* and nobles, supplies and materials for the Admiralty, ways of marking trees and the distribution of dead generals' estates. On 12 August 1724 the Senate looked at the progress of the Ladoga canal, estimates of state income and expenditure, the income of the admiralty court, a list of schismatics, and the income from monastic estates. Delay in decisions by the Senate was common from the first. According to Vasily Zotov, its inspector-general, only one case had been decided in the year before his appointment in 1715, and only three cases in the three years after. The settlement of one case per year was not a very distinguished record for the empire's highest judicial body.

At the lower judicial and general administrative level Peter introduced in 1718 his second comprehensive reform of local government, masterminded by Fick and based on the model of Sweden. The basic provinces of the first such reform of 1708–10 were now to be retained, but their number increased from eight to twelve, and their subordinate units rearranged in counties subject to *voevodas* and districts controlled by land commissars. A further series of functions and officials stayed mainly on paper. It was hoped that the physical, mental and moral well-being of the people at large would be taken care of, but there was an insufficient supply of finance, expertise and good intention for grandiose dreams to be realised, barely enough of such commodities for the most elementary demands of security and tax collection to be met. And so, as the bureaucratic idyll was forgotten, a new local unit, the regimental district, was created, and the collection of the all-important poll-tax entrusted to the military units quartered in the provinces working together with commissars who were to be elected from the ranks of the landlords.

In a similar manner intricate schemes of town government were never realised, Fick and his fellows once again drawing up blueprints from Swedish and German models for the realisation of which there were simply not enough of the requisite materials. After some preliminaries following on the earlier reforms of 1699, a *glavnyi magistrat* or Chief Magistracy, virtually a college of municipal affairs, was set up in 1721. As the plan unfolded, the most important urban dwellers were to be divided into three main groups or guilds with appropriate rights and responsibilities, but again complex instructions soon became dead letters, and in 1727, as we shall see, towns were subordinated to the state organs of local government and the *glavnyi magistrat* was abolished, as were many of the Petrine ideas for the provincial administration as a whole.[14]

Some progress had been made during the reign, and the acquisition of the Baltic provinces, like that of the Ukraine before it, was to have important implications for the future of Russian government. But bureaucratic performance could not outstrip the imperatives that were inherent in the underlying social structure; over 95 per cent of the taxpaying population were peasants, and nearly a half of these belonged to the noble landlords. Another feudal estate, the church, owned rather less than a quarter of the peasantry, and a fifth of the people were the property of the state. Well under a tenth of the total were court peasants, and the balance was made up of various minor groups. Of course, there were all kinds of peasants within these broad categories, rich and poor, hard-working and idle, intelligent and stupid, content or at least resigned to their fate and discontent or openly rebellious, and although the bulk of the population was to be found near the centre, peasants of each official and unofficial kind could be found in all regions of the empire. State peasants, however, were mostly located in the outer provinces, Siberia, Kazan and Astrakhan accounting for about half of them, Kiev and Azov for more than a quarter, and Archangel and Nizhny Novgorod for much of the remainder. This distribution was the result of the somewhat loose definition of the state peasantry, which tended to include all those not subsumed under any other category. Some peasants would also be clustered in the periphery, having fled from their masters and often being prepared to join the bands of brigands which formed in the frontier areas as the Cossacks had formed before them. Because of peasant flight and brigandage, it was difficult to make an accurate calculation of peasant numbers. This difficulty was compounded by the inefficiency and corruption of both officials and serfowners. Menshikov, Peter's close associate, for example, is known to have concealed whole villages from the government inspectors. 'We all steal,' confessed Iaguzhinsky, the highest official in the land, 'the sole difference is that some do it on a bigger scale and in a more conspicuous manner than others.'[15]

While the dues that the peasant paid and the services that he rendered varied according to the category of his landlord and the area in which he lived, the money and work that the state demanded of him often caused him most concern and sweat during the reign of Peter the Great. Continual war made tremendous demands on available manpower; between 1699 and 1714 more than 330,000 men were mobilised. Town and canal construction took people away from their homes, too; between 1704 and 1707, about 30,000 workers were assembled annually for the construction of Azov and another fortress. St Petersburg was insatiable in its early years, 20,000 peasants being brought to it every year from 1712 to 1715, for example. A group of monastery peasants in the north west had to send workers for construction projects in Novgorod and St Petersburg, to help with ship-building, to make saddlebows for dragoons' horses, to send timber and charcoal to a state munitions works, to provide food and forage and supply thousands of horses and carts.

With conditions such as these, peasant flight naturally became a great problem, and a whole row of decrees aimed at its reduction. Fines and severe punishment were proclaimed for concealment of runaways, but the problem grew rather than diminished. Some exceptions were made for those working in factories or living in the province of St Petersburg, for example, but in 1724 a decree was introduced commanding all those peasants leaving their village to have with them a passport; thus it was hoped to regularise a most confused situation.[16]

The government, to give it its due, did make a few attempts at alleviating the unhappy lot of the people. In 1721 a decree was passed condemning the piecemeal sale of peasants 'like cattle', which caused much grief through the break-up of families. In a new law code the Senate was to see to it that serfs were sold only in families; but such a code was not imposed. Another decree of 1719 threatened the confiscation of a cruel landlord's estate. This was as difficult to apply in practice as another of 1713, which said that the government would knout disobedient peasants at the request of the landlords, who were no longer to mete out such severe punishment themselves.[17]

In a basically peasant state like Russia at the beginning of the eighteenth century the landed nobility was the dominant class. Nevertheless the bourgeoisie made a significant advance in self-awareness and organisation during the reign of Peter the Great. The government made a considerable contribution to this development, as has been pointed out above. The outstanding spokesman of the rising middle class was Ivan Pososhkov, who wanted it to be given the exclusive right to trade, among other concessions.

The official town population at the first revision was little more than 3 per cent of the total, distributed among some 330 towns, with only 30 of these having 2,000 and above in their official community. The biggest town, Moscow, possessed 13,673 souls; its male population would be considerably bigger than this, however, because of the nobles, government officials, priests and foreigners living there on the one hand, and the peasants coming in to the old capital at least seasonally on the other. At the other end of the scale, there were some small garrison towns which had no official town population at all. We can safely say, then, that 3 per cent is probably too low for the actual urban population at the time of the first revision. Like the peasants, burghers were burdened with the poll tax and other payments, and with even more onerous services of one kind and another. Some of these, it must be conceded, however, were for the townspeople's own protection. Field Marshal Sheremetev wrote to Peter's secretary in 1718, 'Moscow is a hotbed of brigandage, everything is devastated, the number of lawbreakers is multiplying, and executions never stop.' In one day in 1722 24 brigands were capitally punished in St Petersburg.[18] In conditions such as these it was entirely necessary that honest townsfolk should take their turn at preserving as much of the peace as possible. Even in the capitals, then, urban life could hardly be called gracious at this time, even though a series of harsh laws attempted to make it so.

Just as the bourgeoisie became more clearly identified during the reign of Peter the Great, so did the nobility. Of central importance to this development was the Table of Ranks of 1722. Unlike some of the other reforms, this one was quite carefully prepared. Its comprehensive applicability to all nobles was preceded by a reform in rank applied first to individuals only, and then, in 1712, to commissioned officers in the army. At this time Peter was to some extent still following the old Muscovite practice of honouring blood before rank. (Even the Table itself has clear traces of such an attitude.) Next, Peter moved towards the careful preparation of the decree that could be called the keystone of Russian absolutism.

The principal collaborator on this project was A. L. Osterman, the son of a Lutheran pastor from Westphalia who had studied at Jena University and who knew Latin, Dutch and French as well as German and Russian. He had been in Russian service since about 1711 and had been involved mostly in diplomatic business before being appointed in 1718 to the Russian delegation at the Aland Congress which was to lead towards the Treaty of Nystad in 1721. In March 1719, according to James Jefferyes, our man in St Petersburg, Osterman travelled to Aland soon after Baron Mardefeld, the Prussian envoy, with whom he was to share a house built at the tsar's expense.[19] Here and elsewhere Osterman was in a position to carry on conversations concerning not only the termination of the Northern War but also the internal reforms in the administration recently carried out by many of the negotiating parties. And so, when the Aland Congress broke up in the summer of 1719, Osterman was very much in a position to accept a new task entrusted to him by Peter in the autumn of that year, the preparation of a draft of what was to become the Table of Ranks. At the same time as continuing to work towards the peace, Osterman busied himself with this additional assignment throughout the year 1720. By January 1721 he had prepared an 'Announcement about Ranks' and fourteen *punkty* or points of explanation.

Osterman took as the basis for his classification the ranks of the court establishment and gave them precedence over those from the civil service as was customary up to that time. While most of the court ranks listed by him had German titles, thirty-four out of the total of forty-four were already in use in Russia from the end of the seventeenth or beginning of the eighteenth century. The remainder were taken from two sources, the regulations drawn up in 1699 by Frederick III

Elector of Brandenburg and the arrangements made by him after he had become Frederick I of Prussia in 1705. Most of the civil ranks, over 90 per cent of them in fact, were likewise in use in Russia by early 1719, but Osterman did take some of them from recent foreign sources, in this case Scandinavian (Charles XI of Sweden's disposition of 1696 and Christian V of Denmark's dating from 1699). From the first of these two enactments, Osterman also took the first 5 of his points of explanation, and from the second, *punkty* 6, 8–10 and 12. To *punkt* 1, concerned with punishments for those demanding ranks higher than those to which they were entitled, Osterman added the phrases 'in public assemblies' and 'as when good friends and neighbours come together'. Here he was probably following the prescriptions of Peter the Great's decree of 1718 concerning the manner in which social gatherings should be held. *Punkty* 2–5, concerned with the monarch's confirmation of titles and ranks and with punishments for crimes, were adopted by Osterman without significant alteration, as were 6, 8 and 9, dealing with the ranks to be carried by women, and again linked in a general manner with Peter's policy of 'Europeanisation'. In *punkt* 10, Osterman attributed hereditary peerage to the top six ranks as opposed to Christian V's three, such doubling constituting in S. M. Troitsky's view 'a logical development of the bureaucratic principle of seniority, the idea of service to the monarch'[20] and at the same time reflecting the guiding bases of the Prussian system. *Punkt* 12 gave the tsar's family precedence over others, while *punkt* 13 talked of the need to check the authenticity of noble families. *Punkt* 7 gave rank to anybody of whatever social origin with the necessary qualifications, an arrangement comparable to those obtaining in Prussia, Sweden and Denmark and in harmony with some previous Russian legislation, such as the decree of 1712 making nobles of all commissioned officers. *Punkt* 11 gave anybody holding two positions the rank connected with the higher of them, and *punkt* 14 asserted that each rank should have the equipage and livery appropriate to it.

In January 1721 Peter himself worked over the draft of the 'Announcement about Ranks' that Osterman had presented to him, making several changes including one of title, *Gosudarstvennyi shtat* or 'State Establishment', which clearly indicated the tsar's general attitude. While Osterman had ignored the armed forces, placed the court first and the civil service second, Peter brought in the army and navy making use of their regulations of 1714 and 1720 respectively,[21] placed them first, the civil service second and the court third. Guards and artillery ranks were to be one higher than the others from the armed forces, while civil service ranks were to be one or two lower than them. The *ober-geroldmeister* or Heraldmaster was transferred from the court column to the civil, a reflection of the tsar's view of the nobility as cadres for service rather than adornments for palaces. Of Osterman's 14 *punkty*, Peter left four alone – 2, 4, 6 and 14 – and made literary changes only to a further five – 3, 7, 11–13. More significant alterations were made by him to *punkty* 1, 5, 8, 9 and 10, while he omitted from Osterman's preamble all reference to the imitative nature of the project and added to it some typical threats to bureaucrats failing to give it full implementation. To *punkt* 1 Peter added threats of punishment to those avoiding service and to *punkt* 5 warnings of loss of rank for those publicly punished or dishonoured. He rearranged *punkty* 8 and 9 so that the womenfolk of military ranks might be given precedence over civil and court, while changing the number of ranks that would receive hereditary nobility in *punkt* 10 from six to eight. Finally he added an important appendix to *punkt* 13: all commissioned officers, *praporshchik* or ensigns and above, from rank 1 to 14, would be hereditary nobles, while the civil and court officials of rank 9 to 14 would be nobles for life only.

In February 1721 Peter gave the amended draft for discussion to the Senate, the War and Admiralty colleges. The Senate accepted Peter's recommendation of the superiority of ranks in the armed forces without demur, pointing out that 'the arrangement made for military and naval ranks is comparable to that made by sovereigns, especially the French, as an ancient and autocratic king'.[22] The Senators compared the Russian draft not only with its nearest equivalents in France, but also with those in Prussia, Sweden, Denmark and England. While generally accepting the tsar's insistence on the pre-eminence of the army and navy. Senators also wanted old 'ranks', the boyars and so on, to have some recognition, thus paying deference to the aristocracy of blood that Peter wanted to reduce. They also wanted ranks for themselves, too. The War and Admiralty colleges agreed with the Senate and the tsar about the superiority of their charges, although the War college wanted Guards officers to be two ranks up rather than one rank and the Admiralty college wanted more naval ranks to receive recognition. The colleges appeared to agree with the Senate that blood deserved distinction.

Peter recognised that the claims of blood should not be completely ignored; after all, his own position might have been in jeopardy if he did not. But while he acknowledged the existence of an old aristocracy as well as of a new service nobility, he insisted that old as well as new would have to continue to serve in order to retain their position in society and the privileges that went with it. On receipt of the comments of the Senate and the colleges in late 1721, the tsar also agreed with them that remuneration should be adequate at all levels of service, expressing the wish that education abroad because of its high priority should be placed on a par with military service, even when concerning law, foreign trade, state income or economy. (Those educated at home would receive only half the reward of those educated abroad.) But Peter did not want Senators as such to bear rank, believing that the Senate should be considered as a body apart from the main service structure.

After some final discussions, the Table was published in its final version on 14 February 1722 (although bearing the date 24 January in the Complete Collection of the Russian Laws). Its ultimate title was simply 'The Table of Ranks', and it comprised 262 ranks arranged in vertical columns: 126 (48%) from the armed forces; 94 (36%) from the civil service; and 42 (16%) from the court. The armed forces were separated into the land forces, Guards, artillery and navy, with the Guards receiving a two-rank bonus and at least some artillery officers a one-rank bonus. The naval rank of ship's secretary was given singular distinction, being the sole rank at level 11, the result of Peter's decision that the number of levels or classes in the Table would more fittingly be 14 than the original unseemly 13. By the time of the final version, the number of *punkty* had grown, too, from 14 to 19, and there had also been some rearrangement. Added emphasis had been given to dispositions arising in the definitive Table and from earlier discussions concerning the supremacy of service, the seniority of the armed forces and the predominance of the nobility.

Probably no decree of Peter's reign was given such a thorough preparation as the Table of Ranks. As well as the states already mentioned, Austria, Venice, Spain and Poland were also examined from the point of view of their systems of nobility and chains of military, civil and court command. But, without doubt, it was Prussia, Sweden and Denmark which had been of greatest influence and probably in that order. While France may have been preponderant in European politics at the beginning of the eighteenth century, and while several Russians already had some acquaintance with its institutions and a certain admiration for them, the French situation did not appear as comparable to their own as that to be found in central and northern Europe, and, in retrospect, that view seems to have been fully justified. Moreover, while Denmark and even more Sweden may have constituted models for Russian development at the beginning of the eighteenth century, their appropriateness diminished as the century wore on. To take them each in turn, the Denmark of Christian V saw the decline of the old nobility, as was witnessed by the *Apologia nobilitatis Daniae* produced by Olaf Rosenkrans in 1681 and confirmed by the punishment meted out to him for so doing. Christian was able to establish an absolutism maintained by his immediate successors, but the later eighteenth century brought an end of such a form of government. In Sweden, while Charles XII held great power and entertained grand schemes, his death in 1718 and the subsequent recognition of defeat in the Northern War led to the introduction of a Constitution in which the monarch was little more than a 'crowned puppet'. Not only would this be to the distaste of Peter and his successors: the usefulness to Russia of many Swedish institutions was doubted even before Peter's death and almost totally rejected soon afterwards. Meanwhile, in Prussia, Frederick William I was taking much further than Frederick I had been capable or even desirous of taking the process of the consolidation of Prussian absolutism. His General Supreme Finance, War and Domains Directory introduced in 1723 the overall command for which Peter was also striving. Broadly speaking, the junkers were coming to play the same kind of part in Prussia that the nobles were coming to play in Russia, and, if the reign of Frederick William I witnessed the 'complete intermarriage of army and state' that constitutes the 'real meaning of militarism', the same could be said with little less relevance to that of Peter the Great.[23] As the century progressed, so did Prussia and Russia and the formation of what might be called an Eastern European form of absolutism.

All noble *dvoriane* like all junkers had to serve, and the Heralds were to make sure that they did so. To facilitate their service, and to increase their cohesion as a class, the decree of 23 March 1714 was introduced, merging hereditary with service ownership (*votchina* with *pomeste*) and applying to Russia that important hereditary principle that had meant so much to other European nobilities from Castille to Austria, the law of single succession. The traditional Russian practice had been to divide property among all one's children; this was criticised in the preamble to the decree as harmful to peasants, nobles and state alike. The failure of this reform to take root in Russia (the single succession was rescinded at the accession of Anna in 1730 under pressure from her leading subjects) revealed more clearly than anything else the difference between the bureaucratic *dvorianstvo* and most other nobilities of Europe.

Peter's closest henchmen were, of course, top members of the nobility and the Emperor himself behaved like a *primus inter pares*, the empire's first servant. We must be careful then in making statements about the nobility's servile position in the Russian state. While nobles were pressed into service and fined for absenteeism, they were at the same time the elite of the army, navy and government, and as comfortably off as anybody could hope to be in Russia at the beginning of the eighteenth century; as long, that is, as they managed to keep out of the way of the tsar's oak club or other sign of his displeasure.

But occasional noble discontent was categorically different from the dissatisfaction shown by other sections of the community. During the reign of Peter the Great there were several popular revolts. The first large-scale outburst of violence was in Astrakhan in 1705. Standing at the mouth of the Volga, Astrakhan was an important commercial town and fortress. Russian merchants, and others from Bukhara, Armenia and Persia flourished there; fishing, salt and saltpetre industries were carried on. Many peasants, including some runaways, found work there, while *streltsy* and other soldiers formed the garrison. Trouble developed as a harsh *voevoda* named Rzhevsky enforced new taxes and services and persecuted the local Old Believers. Soldiers and *streltsy* grew restless at harsh discipline and pay arrears, inflicted upon them by corrupt officers, several of whom were foreigners. The last straw turned out to be the decree prohibiting the wearing of beards and Russian dress.

The revolt began on 30 July 1705 with an attack on the Astrakhan Kremlin by 300 *streltsy* and soldiers. The *voevoda* Rzhevsky was killed, as were 300 officers and foreigners. The next day the insurgents chose their own administration, including some Old Believers. Emissaries were sent along the Volga, to the mouth of the Iaik, to the northern Caucasus, and to Cherkassk on the Don. All gained support except those sent to Cherkassk, who were arrested by the Cossack leaders and sent off to Moscow. It was a tactical mistake not to have sent them to the upper Don, where there was much more likelihood of their receiving bread, salt and sympathy. Another decision taken at Astrakhan was to send an expedition to Moscow. A rumour had previously spread that Peter had been replaced, and many of the insurgents wanted to find out if this was true. Some believed in the tsar's essential goodness and wished to help him against the boyars and foreigners; others, a smaller group, mainly *streltsy*, wanted to overthrow Peter and restore their former privileges, subscribing to the legend that a foreigner had been substituted for the tsar in his youth. Soldiers and *streltsy* set out from Astrakhan followed by a detachment from Terki in the northern Caucasus. The first band was driven back down the Volga from Tsaritsyn, the second did not even reach Chernyi Iar, while a group of Bashkirs coming to join the revolt did not get to Astrakhan. If the insurgents did not penetrate very far, news of their rising did, and tremors occurred in Moscow. To break disloyal Astrakhan, Peter sent several regiments of regular troops; some Don Cossacks and many Kalmyk tribesmen opposed the revolt, too. Rifts developed among Astrakhan's defenders, and it was retaken on 13 March 1706, other towns having fallen before this. More than 350 people were executed or died after torture.[24]

A year and a half later trouble broke out on the Don. Even though they had remained peaceful at the time of the Astrakhan revolt, the Cossacks were unhappy about being hemmed in from Azov to the south as well as from Voronezh to the north, and also about the attempts of the government to regularise their service. A further cause of their discontent was the attempt of the government to stop the flow of the runaway serfs into the upper Don region, landlords having complained bitterly about the soul drain.

On 9 October 1707 a punitive detachment under guards major Prince Iu. V. Dolgoruky was attacked at a small town to the north-east of Bakhmut by 200 Cossacks under the leadership of the former local hetman, Kondraty Bulavin. The government detachment was destroyed, and many Cossacks answered Bulavin's summons and came to join him. (He had already won at least local fame by burning down the Bakhmut saltworks in 1705.) But not all the Cossacks were in favour of the revolt. The hetman Lukian Maksimov came from Cherkassk with a loyalist band and scattered Bulavin's forces at the end of October.

The second stage of the revolt commenced in March 1708 when Bulavin returned to the Don. Although the Ukrainian hetman Mazepa had commanded the Zaporozhtsian Cossacks who had been concealing Bulavin to give him up, they had refused, and 2,000 of them came with him to the Don. The people everywhere were invited to form Cossack detachments and rise against the princes, boyars and foreigners. Many peasants answered the summons on the Don, the Volga and beyond as Bulavin set up his headquarters on the upper reaches of the River Khoper, and himself planned to mop up local opposition and then to go 'to Rus to kill the boyars'. Loyal Cherkassk to his rear was of great concern, and Bulavin therefore first moved south rather than north. He defeated Lukian Maksimov on the way, many Cossacks coming over to him, and went in triumphal procession to Cherkassk, which gave itself up on 1 May 1708. Maksimov and his henchmen were executed, and Bulavin elected hetman of the whole Don troop. The spoils were shared out; primitive Cossack democracy restored.

As government forces were being sent down to the Don, Bulavin was carrying on negotiations with Kalmyk and Nogai tribesmen, with the Crimean Tatars and with Turkey. He also tried in May 1708 to make his peace with the tsar, ordering his followers not to break out from the Don region. But such an accommodation was impossible. Insurgent detachments of Cossacks, runaway serfs and tribesmen of various kinds roamed a huge swath of the southern countryside from the Dnepr to the Volga. As far north as Kozlov, Tambov and Penza, peasants answered the anti-boyar call of Bulavin and his lieutenants. The second stage of the revolt came to an abrupt end when Bulavin, having returned from an unsuccessful expedition against Azov, was assassinated in Cherkassk on 7 July 1708 by some dissident Cossacks.

Under new leadership the revolt in its third phase took Tsaritsyn and Kamyshin on the Volga, and went on towards Saratov, only to be driven back by the Kalmyks. Bakhmut and Cherkassk were soon lost by the rebels, and Tsaritsyn fell too. Some insurgents went to the Kuban River to join the Turks, others put up a last-ditch resistance, but by January 1709 the revolt was finished.

Many peasants responded to Bulavin's uprising. In 1708 there were disturbances in forty-three districts, including not only the south and the Volga region, but the centre (Tver, Staritsa, Bezhetsk), the north (Unzha, Kostroma), and the west (Smolensk, Dorogobuzh). In 1709–10 the movement spread through sixty districts. But it had an elemental character, the outbreaks were not linked one with another, and so were doomed to failure. A Soviet historian summarises the importance of the revolt in the following manner:

The Cossack movement, like all peasant wars of the 17–18cc., had an anti-feudal character. It is comparable to the revolts under the leadership of Bolotnikov, Razin and Pugachev in such traits as the leading forces of the revolt (above all the peasantry, the Cossack rank and file, the poor townspeople), its anti-serf ideology, its aspiration to a struggle for power, the wide territory seized by the incursions of the insurgents, the existence of a general centre for the movement.[25]

Of course, it also shared with the other peasant wars the traits of 'naive monarchism' among its supporters and of a cruel suppression from its opponents. Small towns on the upper Don were deprived of much of their male population and sometimes destroyed, the whole region was incorporated into Voronezh province, and several former freedoms of the Don Cossacks were abolished.

Besides the revolts in Astrakhan and on the Don, there were others on a smaller scale during the reign of Peter I, such as those in industrial enterprises and among tribesmen. Into the first category fell the rising of workers at the Voronezh shipyards in 1698, of peasants recruited for work in the industrial enterprises at Olonets, 1705–10 and 1715, and of other peasants who besieged Kungur in the Urals in 1703 and had to be suppressed with the help of artillery. At the beginning of the 1720s, in Smolensk, Moscow and Nizhny Novgorod provinces, along the Oka and the Volga rivers, bands of runaway serfs, workers and soldier-recruits were in action, often attacking landlords on their estates. In 1722 there was trouble in the Siberian town of Tara, and, in the same year, the Iaik Cossacks rose against the threat of arduous army service and because of the search among them for runaways. Into the tribal category came the Bashkir rising of 1705–11, again caused by demands for army recruits and, in this case, for horses too. Another outbreak of tribal violence occurred in Kamchatka in 1701–11. From one end of the Empire to the other, then, popular dissatisfaction flared up throughout Peter's reign,[26] His death was widely welcomed, as was well illustrated in a popular woodcut of the time entitled 'The mice bury the cat.'

How many mice had there been for the cat to prey on? Before the reign of Peter the Great there was no census in Russia, and estimates of the population in the seventeenth century are very difficult to make. Even the eighteenth-century censuses are probably unreliable. They were difficult to carry out; there were many reasons why people should want to avoid inclusion in them, or to fiddle the returns. According to the first of them, begun in 1719, there were 7,570,376 'souls', or taxpaying males, in Russia. Most of them came from the central industrial region – 2,278,535; the central agricultural – 1,561,417; the Left Bank Ukraine – 909,651; the middle Volga – 651,405; and the lake region with St Petersburg at the centre – 553, 897. Not included in the census, which was basically an assessment for taxation, of course, would be 218, 551 men in the regular army and fleet. Adding these and other non-taxed groups on, and assuming that there were as many women as men, we arrive at a total population of 15,577, 854.[27] This probably marks a drop from the latter part of the seventeenth century, a phenomenon that would then be common to Russia and other parts of Europe.

Most of these people would be involved in agriculture. Although there are government laws and statistics, confiscation inventories and customs records, instructions to stewards and travellers' accounts for him to use, the historian has great difficulty in building up a composite picture of Russian farming during the reign of Peter the Great. What can be said with confidence is that it was basically the same as it had been for some time past. The old three-field fallow system was still predominant, particularly in the centre. Under this system the arable land of the peasants, and often of the lord, too, was scattered about the fields in strips which could be far apart from each other and from the village. The strips were too narrow to allow cross ploughing, and the boundaries between them and access tracks took up an unnecessarily large amount of land. Everybody had to grow the same crops and work together on the fundamental stages of the farming year. A further disincentive to good husbandry was the periodic redistribution of the strips, and the annual division of meadows. To the north, where there were too few people and too many trees, as well as too harsh a climate for the prosperity of agriculture, arable land was obtained by cutting and burning down a section of the forest, using the ashy soil for a few years, and then repeating the process, allowing the exhausted plot to grow over. Of course the peasants in the northern provinces were basically occupied with hunting and trapping, lumbering and fishing. To the south extensive farming was often resorted to, a piece of land being worked continuously until worn out. The central three-field system encroached on the steppe lands as they became more populated.

The technical level of agriculture was, as before, very low. Manure was sparsely used in the black-earth regions, and insufficiently applied in the less fertile areas. The most common implement everywhere was the ancient and simple plough, with the share only made of iron. It was incapable of producing a deep furrow or tearing out all weed roots, and even more ineffective in the heavy black earth than in other soils. A few improved ploughs were used, and occasionally a better harrow than tree branches lashed together or a wooden contraption with pegs driven into a frame. Sickles were discouraged by government decree, and scythes and rakes encouraged, to little apparent effect. Flails were normally used for threshing, although sometimes the peasants or their horses would tread the grain.

The basic crops were rye, oats and buckwheat, barley and millet, wheat and peas. Specialised farming continued to develop to some extent; as well as flax and hemp being grown for textiles in the south and the north-west, some grain was grown expressly for distillation purposes in several areas. Tobacco flourished in the south Volga region, and silk was prepared near Moscow and Kiev, Astrakhan and the northern Caucasus. Fruit orchards, with some models provided by the government for growers to follow, were to be found near some cities, as was the cultivation of vegetables and medicinal herbs. Broadly mercantilist in outlook, Peter and his advisers were keen to see agriculture flourish, showing particular interest in the cultivation of flax and hemp, tobacco and grapes. The silk industry was fostered by the government, too, experts being persuaded to come for this purpose to Russia from Italy.

Cattle specialisation was to be found in the north and north-west; Russian leather and hides were exported. Sheep were particularly encouraged by Peter's government, a decree of 1724 setting up special highclass flocks. Silesian and Spanish strains were imported, and much advice disseminated on the breeding and care of sheep, which were to be found particularly in the south and the Ukraine. The army needed horses as well as wool, and there were special military studs at Kazan, Kiev and Azov; Bashkirs along the Volga were expert horse breeders. While there had been little or no legislation concerning the apparently inexhaustible timber supplies in the seventeenth century, Peter brought in strict controls over the forests in a series of decrees from 1703 onwards, and since honey and wax were welcome fruits of the forest as well as trees, the all-encompassing shadow of bureaucratic supervision was creeping over apiculture as well as many other branches of rural activity.

Of course Peter and his administrators were not the only directors of peasant life. The noble landlords were interested in their estates, too, if often only from afar. The instructions that some of them sent to their stewards are valuable sources of information on provincial life throughout the eighteenth century; generally speaking they established control over the peasant economy in such a manner that the dues of the landlords and those of the state would be properly paid. The lords had to reckon with the problem of inequalities of property among the peasants; four solutions to it were common. First, the richer peasants could be forced to give some of their land to the poorer so that each would have an equal share. Second, the division of peasant households, which was looked on as the reason for poverty, could be forbidden. Third, stewards might be commanded to make sure that everybody worked hard and to punish parasites and send them into the army. Fourth, peasants could be forbidden to enter into contracts, which through taking them away from their farming were thought to cause their economic ruin. These solutions would vary according to the basis of the peasant economy, which would range between *barshchina* or labour and *obrok*, that is payment in kind or money.

During the first quarter of the eighteenth century agriculture spread into Siberia, along the Volga, deeper in the Ukraine. Of course this expansion involved state, court and other categories of peasant as well as the serfs of the noble landlords. State and court stewards would work in a manner that was similar to the mode of operation of the *dvorianstvo's*. In some areas, however, particularly in the periphery, state peasants might enjoy a somewhat greater degree of independence than the serfs of the nobles. Some of the tribesmen in Siberia and elsewhere came into the state category, too, and would be left to themselves as long as they paid their dues.

With the expansion of agriculture went a growth of small-scale manufacturing. Textiles of various kinds would probably be the most normal products, although there were items worked in iron, silver and gold as well. Lace and ribbons were now made in the capitals, leather-work was carried on in the centre, Kazan and the Ukraine. Footwear and gloves were made in small enterprises, as were soap, lard and various kinds of pottery. Furriers, tailors and carpenters were in business in many towns, and luxury specialists making wigs, chairs, carriages and gowns could be found in Moscow and St Petersburg, which had approximate totals of 2,500 and 7,000 tradesmen respectively. About half of these were peasants although a fair number were foreigners. In other towns the number of indigenous craftsmen was probably higher than in the capitals. In general, small-scale manufacturing can be viewed as supplementary to agriculture. Government policy towards this sector of the economy wavered, although, on the whole, it aimed at regularisation, encouraging guilds and higher standards. For example, the width of certain kinds of cloth was regulated, and the use of tar in shoemaking forbidden. Protected by their landlords, peasants were often able to get round these and other restrictions.

Large scale industry, as is well known, flourished with official support during the reign of Peter the Great. The state extended its own activity as well as supporting that of private entrepreneurs, each type of ownership accounting for half a total of about 180 enterprises, 40 of which were concerned with iron, 15 with other metals, 24 with various kinds of textiles, the others with leather, glass, gunpowder and so on. Most of these enterprises were to be found in the centre, the major exceptions being the metallurgical establishments of the Urals and the Olonets region, and the growing complex in and around St Petersburg. The equal balance between state and private enterprises is somewhat misleading, as the statute of the Manufactures college issued in 1723 made general a policy already clearly apparent in earlier years. the transfer of state-owned factories to private individuals. Although many of the beneficiaries of this policy were from the middle class, nobles did well out of it, too, a group of them headed by Baron Shafirov, Count Tolstoi and Count Apraksin receiving in 1717 the monopolistic rights to silk manufacture. The founder-members of the consortium invested a capital of 81,300 roubles, while assistance from the treasury amounted to 36,700 roubles. The state also helpfully banned the import of silk commodities. State support for industry was still vigorous, then, even after state enterprise was very much reduced.

While considering that the volume of industrial enterprise during the reign of Peter the Great demonstrated that the primitive accumulation of capital was well under way in Russia at this time, Soviet historians also point out the slowing-down influences of contemporary factory labour which was mostly unfree. Some of the workers were taken from the ranks of the nobility's serfs, some were recruited from the lower depths of society, some were included in a special category of 'possessionary' peasants attached to particular enterprises. Many of the establishments set up in the first quarter of the eighteenth century were indeed large-scale. Moscow mills making sailcloth employed more than 1,000 hands; some 25,000 serfs worked in the metalworks at Perm. On the other hand, there was still much cottage industry, in metals as well as textiles.

Trade, like industry, was carried on as a small-scale and large-scale operation; it was also, of course, internal and external. Domestic trade was often local; items of manorial production, both edible and manufactured, were often disposed of at manorial or neighbourhood markets and fairs. On the other hand the all-Russian market was taking on firmer shape around such centres as St Petersburg, Novgorod, Moscow and Nizhny Novgorod. Links with the Ukraine and other peripheral regions were being strengthened.

An impression of Russia's foreign trade can be indicated by data and figures for export and import through the two principal ports, Archangel and St Petersburg, in 1726, the year after Peter's death, when for the most part hides and tallow, flax and hemp, and various kinds of textiles went out, and other textiles, dyestuffs and wines came in. The total value of these exports was 2,688,800 roubles, and of the imports 1,585,500 roubles. The balance was thus over a million roubles in Russia's favour; the picture is much the same if trade through Riga is included, about 4.2 million roubles worth of exports and 2.1 of imports. Great Britain was Russia's major trading partner, although relations fluctuated according to the political situation. Great Britain was becoming particularly interested in Russian naval stores. Russia wanted British tobacco, among other items. In 1698 a contract was agreed with the Marquis of Carmarthen for the monopoly of the tobacco trade, but the British ambassador forced two Englishmen working in a Moscow tobacco factory to leave, brought the factory's operations to a standstill and did considerable damage to Russo-British relations. Holland was another important trading partner; there was a certain amount of commerce from ports other than those mentioned above, and a little over land.

There was trade to the east, too. Although the Black Sea was closed with the loss of Azov in 1711, a company for trade with China and Persia was set up by government decree in the same year. The government showed interest in Central Asia as part of the route to the markets of the middle east and India. This interest was not shared to any great extent by Russian merchants, although a trade treaty was drawn up with Persia in 1715, which gave Russian merchants the right to buy as much silk as they wanted to, and made provision for the institution of a Russian consulate in Persia. Armenian merchants were given a monopoly in the silk trade, and tax relief of various kinds. Trade with the near east was centred on Astrakhan, a cosmopolitan centre where silk would be exchanged for furs, leather and cloth. In 1716 goods to the value of 464,000 roubles were brought to Astrakhan from Bukhara and Persia. As far as the China trade was concerned, the state played an important part, sending a Russian caravan once every two years. In 1708 the value of goods sent to China amounted to 47,000 roubles; by 1710 it had grown to 200,000 roubles. In 1722, however, the caravans were stopped owing to border disputes.

For the achievement and maintenance of an active balance of trade, Peter's government attempted to make foreign contacts for Russian merchants, to develop a Russian fleet, to export manufactures instead of raw materials, and to encourage Russian commerce and industry through a protective tariff, first introduced in 1724. Under the provisions of the tariff, imported goods were subject to a rate of between 25 per cent and 75 per cent *ad valorem*, the rate fluctuating according to the relative volume of the item imported and manufactured domestically. Russian merchants were given preferential treatment by the government, which itself played a vigorous part in Russian commerce, relaxing such activity, it is true, towards the end of the reign. In 1719 the state announced that it would retain potash and pitch only as its province and hand over to private enterprise such items as hemp, flax-seed, lard, caviare and ship timber. Peter took steps to accelerate the growth of St Petersburg and Riga and the decline of Archangel. He also attempted to guarantee the future of the Baltic ports by linking the Volga and the Neva with a series of canals. This arduous project was completed n 1732. Another plan, to bring the Black Sea into the network of waterways as well as the Caspian had to be abandoned with the loss of Azov to Turkey in 1711.[28]

'Money is the artery of war,' wrote Peter to his Senate, and much of his time was devoted to collecting money for this purpose. At the beginning of the Great Northern War over 80 per cent of the budget was spent on it, and even after it was all over, the percentage only just dropped below 65 per cent. The figures of government expenditure are most complete for the last years of Peter's reign after various accounting reforms had been carried out; the following table[29] shows them for 1725.

Debasements of the coinage were much employed as before, and helped the rouble to lose half its value during Peter's reign. Inventive assistants called 'profit-makers' almost literally left no stone unturned in their search for more money, bringing in taxes on such things as hats, boots and beards, water-melons, nuts and cucumbers. Along the Volga and in the Urals, according to one account, those unfortunate enough to have blue or black eyes were asked to pay a special tax. State monopolies,

Item	Millions of roubles	Percentage
Army	5.12	50.4
Navy	1.42	14.1
Total on war needs	6.54	64.5
Central and local administration	2.15	21.2
Court	0.45	4.4
Expenses for tax collection	1.00	9.9
Grand Total	10.14	100.0

although reduced towards the end of the reign, brought in quite a respectable sum, particularly those in drink and salt. Customs duties, still internal as well as external, made a worthwhile contribution, too. But the biggest boost to the income of the armed forces and state in general was the introduction from 1718 to 1723 of the poll tax, which replaced the household tax. Allowing for the debasements in the coinage, the revenues of 1724 were three times as much as those of 1680 and twice those of 1701. The poll-tax revision also helped to keep track of potential recruits as well as taxpayers. Some tribesmen in Siberia and elsewhere paid an alternative tribute known as *iasak*. Because of the great increase of direct taxes, the state was able to claim, not with complete accuracy, it would seem, that the budget was balanced in Peter's last years. Here is his income in 1724:[30]

Item	Millions of roubles	Percentage
Direct taxes (poll and *iasak*)	4.7	55.3
Indirect taxes:		
Levies on trade	1.2	13.5
State trade in drink	0.9	11.4
State trade in salt	0.7	7.2
Total of indirect taxes	2.8	32.1
Other items (including money and post revenues, state *obrok* and leases, sundry duties and levies)	1.0	12.6
Grand total	8.5	100.0

It remains only to be said that if the above picture of finances and other economic subjects during the reign of Peter the Great is clear, it is misleading. The fraud, peculation and theft concealed in the above figures, for example, are indescribable.

We must now turn from matters of finance to those of the mind.

When Peter the Great came to England from Holland in January 1698 he was looking for specialists to serve in Russia, and particularly for teachers to work at his projected school of navigation. In a manner still not certain, Henry Farquharson, tutor in mathematics at Marischal College, Aberdeen, was engaged to go to Moscow as senior teacher in the navigational school in return for free quarters, a food allowance and £50 for each student successfully completing the course under his direction. As assistants to Farquharson two young graduates were enrolled from the Royal Mathematical School at Christ's Hospital, Stephen Gwyn, aged fifteen, and Richard Grice, aged seventeen. An arduous sea voyage brought the three teachers to Moscow in August 1699. Since the tsar was preoccupied with preparations for the Northern War, Farquharson and his companions found themselves unemployed for nearly a year, and then complained to Peter.

Prompted by Farquharson and the others, his interest in the war temporarily diverted, perhaps, by the defeat of Narva, Peter turned to set up his School of Mathematics and Navigation, starting with a decree promulgated on 14 January 1701. This marked the beginning of official secular education in Russia. Farquharson helped Peter work out the organisation of the school, which was largely based on the Royal Mathematical School at Christ's Hospital. An upper limit of 500 students was fixed and the curriculum was to include arithmetic, geometry, trigonometry, navigation, astronomy, fencing, reading and writing. The inaugural years of the school were very difficult, because teachers and pupils could not understand each other, there were no Russian textbooks, and the preparatory education of the students had often been inadequate. Farquharson at first lectured in English, making as he did so notes which were later translated into Russian. Kurbatov, one of the school governors, complained that Farquharson and his assistants enjoyed themselves and overslept too often, and held bright pupils back in favour of backward ones. There was friction between the British teachers and the Russian L. F. Magnitsky, who was brought into the organisation in 1702. Severe punishments, including fines and whippings, were considered necessary to retain the interest of the students. By 1703 the situation was on the mend, with Farquharson, Gwyn and Magnitsky co-operating to produce the first textbooks in Russian and the enrolment totalling 200. By 1706 the school had 400 students, and in 1710 Farquharson could claim fees for fifty graduate navigators sent off to England to complete their training in the Royal Navy.

Peter asked the navigational school to produce not only sailors but artillery-men and engineers, civil servants and teachers, topographers, hydrographers and architects. Farquharson himself surveyed the road from Moscow to St Petersburg in 1712, and supervised the building of a highway connecting the two capitals. He organised regional surveys of the Caspian Sea and published the first detailed map of it. Many graduates of the Moscow school became teachers in the other Petrine schools as they were set up. These included more navigational schools in Novgorod, Narva and Revel.

In 1715 a Naval Academy was opened in St Petersburg: a Baron St Hilaire, who had been associated with French naval schools at Brest and Toulon, receiving the post of director. Farquharson was appointed professor of mathematics there at an increased salary of nearly 1,000 roubles per annum, and Gwyn was to get 400 roubles a year as professor of navigation. (Grice had been killed by robbers in Moscow in January 1709.) St Hilaire quarrelled with Farquharson, exceeded the instructions given him by Peter, and was dismissed in 1717. Farquharson was able to co-operate with the new director, A. A. Matveev, and continued lecturing in the Academy until his death in December 1739. The curriculum of the Academy at first included reading and writing for those who needed it, arithmetic and geometry, artillery and fortification, navigation and geography, drill with muskets, fencing and drawing. There were practical exercises in navigation, too, Peter taking a great interest in these and in all aspects of the Academy's work. He advised the maintenance of strong discipline, saying: 'For the elimination of noise and lawlessness, select good retired soldiers from the Guards, and let one of them be present in each classroom during teaching, with a whip in his hands, and if any pupils start to commit outrages, beat them, from whatever family they come.'[31] This last remark supports an observation made by Weber, the Hanoverian ambassador, that in all Russia there was not one outstanding family which had not sent a son or other relative to the Academy in the first year of its operation. Although many high- and low-born students ran away from the Academy or failed to complete its course for other reasons, it produced good sailors and experts in other fields, too.

Of course many other educational institutions were founded during the reign of Peter the Great. In 1701 a foreign engineer named Gran was put in charge of a Moscow Artillery School He did not last long at the job because he used his pupils as baby-sitters, but the school grew from an initial size of 180 students to 300 in 1704. The number fell to 136 in 1707, partly no doubt because of the inadequacies of the teachers, one of whom was a drunken murderer. Another reason for a continued fall in numbers was the institution in 1712 of an Engineering School in Moscow. Two-thirds of its complement of 100–150 students were to come from the *dvorianstvo*, the juniors concentrating on arithmetic and geometry and the seniors on fortification. Since only twenty-three were enrolled by 1713, seventy-seven more students were to be found at the court, in the lower ranks and at the artillery school. In 1719 an Engineering Company was formed in St Petersburg, to which seventy-four young engineers were transferred from Moscow to help, among other things, with the drawing of maps of the Baltic Coast. Another of the Petrine foundations was the Medical School founded in

Moscow in 1707. Again, difficulties were experienced in the acquisition of students, and some were transferred from the Slavono-Greek-Latin Academy. Medics received a theoretical and practical training, and, as in the other schools, were subject to a strong discipline including bread and water, whipping and irons, and expulsion to the army as ordinary soldiers.

A different kind of school was the Glück Gymnasium, opened in Moscow in 1705 and named after a Lutheran pastor taken prisoner of war who gained state financial support for his project, but did not live to see the other foreign teachers struggle with a broad curriculum including politics, philosophy, literature and rhetoric, oriental languages as well as French, German, Hebrew, Swedish, Latin and Greek, riding, dancing and compliments in the French and German manner. The gymnasium closed ten years after its foundation, having enjoyed no great success but having sent out some 250 graudates with at least a smattering of foreign languages. The Glück Gymnasium, like most of the Petrine schools, had to produce civil servants as well as soldiers and sailors. A special school was ordered for bureaucrats in 1721, but does not appear to have opened, the colleges continuing to train personnel on the spot as the *prikazy* had done before them.

One more special kind of educational institution deserves mention, a School of Mines which was opened in Olonets in 1716, and similar schools which were set up in the Urals in 1721, all under the supervision of the Mines college from 1724 onwards. As well as separate professional schools such as these and the others discussed above, there were three types of general primary institution in existence during the reign of Peter the Great. Most ambitious of these were the cipher or mathematical schools, so called because of the main focus of their curriculum; two of them were supposed to be created in each province, according to a decree of 1714. By 1716 twelve such schools had been opened, and thirty more had started work by 1722. An analysis of the 2,000 or so students who had attended cipher schools by the year 1727 shows that about 45 per cent of them were sons of priests (it should perhaps be hastily reiterated that priests in the lower ranks were able to marry); just under 20 per cent soldiers' children; a slightly lower percentage of civil service origin; less than 5 per cent were young tradespeople; and 2.5 per cent were young nobles. The last two percentages are low because a decree of 1716 excluded *dvoriane* from the schools, and another of 1720 did the same for tradespeople, the first group being assigned to specialist schools and the second taken care of on paper if not in fact by a grandiose scheme for a school in every town being announced in the 1721 decree creating the Chief Magistracy. Cipher schools lasted till 1744, but only eight of them, the three biggest of which were united with garrison schools, These, our second category of general school, were just starting in Peter's reign, and were to expand mostly in the 1730s. The third category, the diocesan schools, were given a boost by the Church Statute of 1721. There were forty-six of them with about 3,000 pupils by 1727, at Novgorod, in the Ukraine, and elsewhere. Their dropout rate was much lower than that of the cipher schools, which produced ninety-three graduates only in the first ten years of operation. Noticing this disparity the Admiralty college, which controlled the cipher schools, persuaded Peter to consider the amalgamation of them with the diocesan schools, but the Synod managed to resist the merger.[32]

For all their disappointments and inadequacies, the professional and primary schools created during the reign of Peter the Great constituted a firm beginning for Russia's educational system, and at least contributed to the spread of literacy and textbooks. Towards the end of his reign the tsar developed an interest, which had been foreshadowed in the Glück Gymnasium, in education in the wider sense. This resulted in the institution of an Academy of Sciences, which was opened soon after its creator's death and gave Russia what France and other enlightened countries possessed: a repository and propagator of higher learning. The Academy is sometimes said to have started its existence with Peter's decree of 13 February 1718 ordering his people to hand over to the authorities freaks, monsters and strange objects with a reward for their finds and a fine for their concealment. The decree explained that it was wrong for such curiosities to be considered the devil's work, because God alone was the Creator of everything, and the devil had no such power. Learned foreigners such as Leibniz and Wolff made their contribution towards the institution of the Academy of Sciences as well as freak-finding, devil-fearing peasants. Undoubtedly there was great incongruity in the situation resulting from the creation of the Academy, including its inauguration by Peter's widow, a former Livonian peasant girl who had never learned to read and write. At the same time, of course, there were probably few French peasants who could have followed the disputations of their Academicians at this time – perhaps even some illiteracy at Versailles.

Many young Russians continued their education or even started it outside the official educational institutions, with various kinds of private tutor. Moreover, war accelerated learning as well as most other aspects of Russia's development during Peter's reign, and soldiers, sailors and officers all received stimulation from the fresh cultural breezes blowing in from the Baltic. Trips abroad were commenced before the end of the seventeenth century, about sixty young *dvoriane* being sent by Peter to Italy and Holland to study navigation before he went west himself. In 1717 there were about seventy Russian navigators in Amsterdam alone. Russians went to study law, medicine and the arts as well as seafaring, a whole group of officials going to Königsberg to study the administrative arrangements there, to give one instance. The emperor encouraged permanent embassies in Russia, and established them abroad in Paris, London, Berlin, Vienna, Dresden, Stockholm, Copenhagen and Hamburg. The Hanoverian ambassador to Russia, Weber, calculated that several thousand young men had gone abroad during Peter's reign for various educational reasons.

Many of the first group to leave the fatherland in 1697 did not care for their mission at all. If they did not think they were going to a pagan land, they were sure they were going to make contact with a questionable faith; they were leaving their families for a long and uncomfortable journey; they would return to be assigned to arduous service. Even one of those in favour of the project. P. A. Tolstoi, spent three days making emotional farewells to his relatives. Arriving in the west, the travellers were struck first of all by the glittering exterior, the whole towns of stone, 'those great round palaces which the Italians call theatres'. A formal garden was described as a lot of grass and exceptional flowers with a considerable number of human likenesses of the male and female sex made of copper. The early Russian visitors were struck by the technical proficiency rather than the aesthetic aspect of works of art. Tolstoi saw pictures of 'marble girls' representing pagan goddesses done true to life. B. I. Kurakin wrote that in a Dutch town square 'stands a lifelike man of copper with a book as a commemoration of the fact that he was an extremely learned man and taught many people'. He was talking about the statue of Erasmus in Rotterdam.

As the visitors grew more accustomed to their new surroundings they began to observe and even enjoy the comparative cleanliness and order of towns, the politeness of some of the inhabitants, the assemblies and meetings in aristocratic houses, the plays and the operas, the coffee-house conversations. They took an interest in real girls as well as those made of marble. Tolstoi was rather surprised that the women in Venice were so well-shaped, tall and thin, and more interested in amusements than handiwork. A. A. Matveev in Paris was impressed by woman's apparent equality with man and the courtesy of the nobility's life. Tolstoi and the others in time became enthusiastic about political as well as social western life. He himself was enthusiastic about the freedom in Venice, the simplicity of the people's relations with the Doge and the correctness of the law courts. Matveev in the France of Louis XIV could see only order and the absence of arbitrary government. He declared that 'The king, although an absolute monarch, cannot exact more than the general taxes'. Property could not be seized by royal decree, and representative assemblies and the law played an important part in government too, pointed out Matveev. In general during the first half of the eighteenth century, French cultural influence was not as great as German.[33] Against the discordant background of such foreign influence and Russian tradition, writers and musicians struggled to produce distinctive contributions in a new formal genre, without as yet much success.[34]

As we turn from a new basis for culture to an old – religion – we may begin by noting that the dominant theme of Peter's policy was subordination of church to state through the elimination of the office of Patriarch and other means. Peter, of course, was a matter-of-fact, not an ideological Erastian. His attitude was mainly formed by his knowledge of the troubles occasioned some of his predecessors by powerful patriarchs, and to a lesser extent by Western European precedents. He was an active churchgoer, taking over direction of the choir when the mood seized him, and spent a lot of money on a monastery for his new capital, the choice of whose name itself appears to imply an elevated place for the tsar in the church hierarchy. But privilege went with onerous duty. As Sumner put it, 'In Peter's eyes man was responsible to his Maker, none more so than the tsar himself: duty to God involved duty to one's neighbour, the active combating of evil and the development of the faculties with which God had endowed his creatures, in particular the gift of reason'.[35]

In 1700 the Patriarch Adrian died, and, busy with his war, Peter did not hurry to appoint a successor. Then he decided to take the opportunity to leave the patriarchate untenanted and to choose instead a 'keeper and administrator of the patriarchal see'. Chosen for the position was Stepan Iavorsky, who had recommended himself to the tsar's attention through a sermon that he had preached at a boyar's funeral. In a by no means unprecedented fashion, Iavorsky soon started to bite the secular hand that had fed him at the promptings of a higher authority or a down-to-earth ambition. But his was not to be the final victory, at least in worldly terms.

The next move in Peter's take-over of the church was the revival in 1701 of the former Monastery *prikaz*, abolished in 1667 but now stronger than ever under the vigorous leadership of Ivan A. Musin-Pushkin, former *voevoda* of Astrakhan. The *prikaz* was necessary, according to the decree of 30 December 1701, because monks had fallen into idleness and luxury and forgotten how 'the ancient monks had supplied food for themselves with the labour of their own hands' and had fed many poor people with their own hands too. A norm of 10 roubles and about 80 bushels (10 *chetverti* or quarters) of grain per annum was established by the decree for each monk, irrespective of rank. The monastic estates were divided into two types, the first assigned for the support of the monasteries, the second paying its income to the state. From this source during the first eleven years of the revival of the *prikaz* came a million roubles.

But this secularisation was not only partial but temporary as well; full secularisation would be completed in the reign of Catherine II. The Monastery *prikaz* died its second death with the introduction of the Synod in 1721. Not that monks were now left alone. A decree of 31 January 1724 said that the large part of them were parasites, and since idleness was the root of all evil so many prejudices, schisms and scandals had arisen. Monks were running away from their tax responsibilities, too, the decree complained. They should learn a useful trade such as spinning. They should not be allowed pen and ink in their cells, but only in the common room under supervision.

The Church Statute was introduced in 1721 with the help of Peter's chief propagandist, Feofan Prokopovich. As he explained, the statute was the result of the fact that the priesthood is a separate social group in the state, and not a separate state. A Church college, soon renamed the Synod, was set up to control the church in general, and so that there would be no reason for fear rebellions and confusion, it was placed under the supervision of a lay chief procurator.[36]

To sum up, more than two hundred and fifty years after his death, the views of his fellow countrymen on Peter and his significance may be represented by those of L. G. Beskrovny and B. B. Kafengauz who tell us that Soviet historians have shown the progressive character of the reform of the army and navy, the construction of factories, the foreign policy of that period and at the same time have underlined the cruel suppression by the government of popular uprisings, the profligate distribution of peasants and land. These policies reflect the circumstance that Peter was 'the representative of the ruling class and expressed its interest, having understood the necessity of reforms as one of the conditions for the successful development of the Russia of the nobles'. Pursuing the realisation of his aims, the tsar showed great energy, willpower and initiative in the use that he made of the example of other countries and of the talents of a wide range of collaborators. And he was not only a practical man:

Peter was one of the greatest ideologues of absolutism. Together with his assistants he gave it a theoretical basis. His views found expression in the 'Military Regulations' and in a series of legislative acts which accompanied sweeping innovations. Peter I considered autocracy to be 'the bastion of justice'. The state was seen by him as a most powerful force, capable of transforming society on the basis of reason. The people must subject itself to laws which were issued in the interests of 'the general good', by which were meant the interests of the ruling class. Together with the theory of the divine origin of power was instilled the secular basis of absolutism – rationalism and the propositions of natural law. These propositions were developed in the works of 'the Learned Guard' the most important representatives of which were F. Prokopovich and V. N. Tatishchev.

The initiatives of Peter were demonstrated particularly clearly in military and naval leadership and organisation of the country's armed forces. He was also a far-sighted and skilful diplomat, and he made a tremendous impression in the sphere of culture. However, Beskrovny and Kafengauz assert that:

these aspects of the activity of Peter must not hide the negative aspects of his character – his neglect of the individual and his cruelty. By means of mass executions Peter dealt with the *streltsy* and generally with political enemies. He himself took part in the executions. Peter confirmed the death sentence for his son and his adherents when he became convinced that Aleksei was at the centre of the forces which threatened the destruction of everything that had been gained in the course of the reforms.[37]

Perhaps Beskrovny and Kafengauz would not disagree with the conclusion of Klyuchevsky that the work of Peter must be accepted in much the same way as 'the impetuous showers of spring, which strip branches from the trees, but none the less refresh the air, and by their downpour bring on the growth of the new seed'. But we should also bear in mind a corrective warning from D. S. Likhachev:

Peter felt himself to be constantly in the public eye, not only of his own people but of the whole of Europe. And he had the gift of imbuing the transformations he effected with a vivid demonstrative character. There was a streak of the actor in him. And so the gigantic figure of Peter really did come to block out the historical perspective.[38]

For a conclusion here, we should perhaps again make our own basic metaphor real and note that, for most of the years from its construction to 1918, St Petersburg replaced Moscow as the Russian capital; except for ceremonial purposes, the Kremlin was no longer the heart of the Russian Empire, which had now been transplanted to the shores of the Baltic. In the beginning the new city grew up in a somewhat temporary and haphazard manner with its buildings mainly of wood, but from about 1714 onwards, when a decree was issued prohibiting construction in stone anywhere else, it began to take on a more planned and permanent shape. Foreign architects, notably at first the Italian Domenico Trezzini and later the Frenchman Jean-Baptiste Leblond, did their best to put the ideas of their impatient Russian employer into practice, even if without complete success. How could they quickly transform a swamp into a 'paradise'?

Peter wanted to catch up with and then surpass the achievement of Louis XIV, a monarch whom he admired for his palaces and also for the glory that he had achieved for himself and his country, even if he did not lead his troops into battle and had not mastered any useful trades. On his visit to Paris in 1717 the tsar particularly admired an equestrian statue of Louis XIV;[39] he would no doubt have been pleased by the famous counterpart of himself that Catherine the Great commissioned for St Petersburg later in the eighteenth century. (Moreover, there may be some significance in the fact that while the mounted effigy of the French king was pulled down at the time of the French Revolution, the Bronze Horseman was to survive for Pushkin to write a famous poem about him in the early nineteenth century and for tourists to admire him rearing up near the banks of the River Neva today. The relation between the French and Russian varieties of absolutism on the one hand and their respective revolutions and aftermaths on the other cannot concern us now, however, although there could be useful discussion of, for example, Stalin as part heir to Peter the Great and Napoleon.) Peter began his reign with the overthrow of Sophie in 1689 at a time when Louis XIV in France and other monarchs elsewhere in Europe, not least William III in England, were facing considerable problems concerning the consolidation of their governments, absolutist and otherwise, even if the general crisis was not as deep as that of the mid-seventeenth-century. Viewed in this wider perspective, Peter's difficulties are not so unique and his resolution of them not so remarkable as they have sometimes been made to appear. We have seen above how such reforms as the Table of Ranks proceeded in rough parallel with the modern organisation of bureaucracies and armed forces elsewhere, especially in Eastern Europe. Eastern Europe, it must be remembered, was the scene on to which Peter's famous Window on the West opened; granted that such influences as the French, Dutch and British were also important, they were not as immediate as the Swedish[40] and the Prussian. The structure of Russian absolutism as erected by Peter is therefore probably as well compared with that of Charles XI and Frederick William I as with that of Louis XIV.

To understand fully the achievement of Peter the Great, which is not to be lightly dismissed even if it has often been exaggerated, it needs to be appreciated not only in its wider European setting but also in relation to the work of his predecessors and successors. For this reason, we have attempted to give a fairly precise estimate of the extent of the growth during his reign of such varied phenomena as trade, industry, finance and secular education, as well as looking at the most significant socio-political measures and developments. While according to Peter the familiar epithet (how widely is he recognised as Peter I?), we need to keep his greatness in proportion, as did Falconet in the celebrated statue, balancing horse and rider against a rough-hewn base.

NOTES

1. Dale Harris, *Guardian Weekly*, 29 July 1979.
2. V. Klyuchevsky, *Peter the Great*, trans. L. Archibald (London and New York, 1958), p. 19.
3. 'The Diary of Patrick Gordon,' located in the Central Military-Historical Archive, Moscow, 7 August 1689.
4. Klyuchevsky, *Peter the Great*, p. 19.
5. *Bishop Burnet's History of his own Time*, vol. 3 (London, 1753), pp. 306–7; Burnet to Reverend Doctor Fall, 19 March 1698, Bodleian MSS, Add. D 23, fol. 10.
6. A. N. Kazakevich, *Vosstanie moskovskikh streltsov: 1698 god (materialy sledstvennogo dela): sbornik dokumentov* (Moscow, 1980), pp. 12–13.
7. Alexander Gordon, *History of Peter the Great, Emperor of Russia*, vol. 2 (Aberdeen, 1755), pp. 315–19.

8. M. S. Anderson, *Peter the Great* (London, 1978), p. 107; James Cracraft, *The Church Reform of Peter the Great* (London and Stamford, 1971), pp. 14, 21. R. Zguta argues that Peter's merry pranks should not be taken too seriously in 'Peter I's Most Drunken Synod of Fools and Jesters,' *Jahrbücher für Geschichte Osteuropas*, Band 21 (1973).

9. M. T. Florinsky, *Russia: A History and an Interpretation*, vol. 1 (New York, 1955), pp. 346, 352. For a somewhat different view, see Anderson, *Peter*, pp. 77–9. Peter's penchant for dynastic alliances was matched by many contemporaries including Frederick William I of Prussia. See also L. A. Nikiforov, *Russko-angliiskie otnosheniia pri Petre I* (Moscow, 1950).

10. Anderson, *Russia*, p. 76. And see W. E. Butler, intro., *P. P. Shafirov, A Discourse concerning the Just Causes of the War between Sweden and Russia, 1700–1721* (Dobbs Ferry, NY, 1973).

11. L. G. Beskrovny, 'Reforma armii i sozdanie voennomorskogo flota' in B. B. Kafengauz *et al.* (eds), *Ocherki istorri SSSR: Period feodalizma: Pervaia chetvert XVIIIv.* (Moscow, 1954), pp. 349–56.

12. Beskrovny, 'Reforma', p. 359; M. D. Rabinovich, 'Sotsialnoe prois-khozhdenie i imushchestvennoe polozhenie ofitserov reguliarnoi russkoi armii v kontse Severnoi voiny' in N. I. Pavlenko (ed.), *Rossiia v period reform Petra I* (Moscow, 1973), pp. 154, 170–71.

13. Beskrovny, 'Reforma', pp. 366–71; Florinsky, *Russia*, vol. 1, p. 357.

14. Previous section taken mostly from N. I. Pavlenko, 'Oformlenie absoliutizma (pervaia chetvert XVIIIv.)' in L. G. Beskrovny *et al.* (eds), *Istoriia SSSR, pervaia seriia*, vol. 3 (Moscow, 1967), pp. 225–42.

15. Quoted in Florinksy, *Russia*, vol. 1, p. 384.

16. L. N. Semenova, *Rabochie Petersburga v pervoi polovine XVIII veka* (Leningrad, 1974), pp. 25–34.

17. Florinsky, *Russia*, vol. 1, p. 424.

18. Ibid., pp. 400–401. See more generally A. P. Vlasto and L. R. Lewitter (trans. and eds.), Ivan Pososhkov, *The Book of Poverty and Wealth* (London, 1987).

19 James Jefferyes to Lord Stanhope, St Petersburg, 13 March 1719; to G. Tilson, 16 March 1719, *Sbornik imperatorskogo russkogo istoricheskogo obshchestva*, vol. 51, pp. 502, 506. See also S. A. Feigina, 'Missiia A. I. Ostermana v Shvetsii v 1719g.' in V. I. Shunkov *et al.*, (eds), *Voprosy vneshnei istorii XVIII i pervaia polovina XIX vekov* (Moscow, 1969).

20. S. M. Troitsky, 'Iz istorii sozdaniia tabeli o rangakh', *Istoriia SSSR*, no. 1 (1974), p. 103. Generally, my analysis of the Table of Ranks draws heavily on this article. And see P. Dukes (trans., ed. and intro.), *Russia under Catherine the Great: Volume One: Select Documents on Government and Society* (Newtonville, 1978), pp. 4–14, for an introduction to the Table and a full translation of the *Punkty*.

21. Nearly all the military and, perhaps to a lesser extent, the naval ranks in the Table were already in use. At least one of them, *kvarter-meister*, was in use in Muscovy as far back as 1630.

22. Troitsky, 'Iz istorii', p. 106

23. E. J. Feuchtwanger, *Prussia: Myth and Reality* (London, 1970), p. 49.

24. V. V. Mavrodin, 'Klassovaia borba v pervoi polovine XVIIIv,' in Beskrovny, *Istoriia SSSR*, vol. 3, pp. 287–90.

25. Ibid., p. 294. For Paul Avrich's verdict, see *Russian Rebels 1600–1800* (London, 1973), pp. 174–7. See also O. Subtelny, *The Mazepists: Ukrainian Separatism in the Early Eighteenth Century* (Boulder, CO, (1981).

26. Mavrodin, 'Klassovaia', p. 295.

27. V. M. Kabuzan, *Izmeneniia v razmeshchenii naseleniia Rossii v XVIII – pervoi polovine XIX v.* (Moscow, 1971), p. 52.

28. Much of the above survey of the economy taken from N. I. Pavlenko, 'Khoziaistvennyi podem' in Beskrovny, *Istoriia SSSR*, vol. 3, pp. 192–224.

29. Adapted from S. M. Troitsky, *Finansovaia politika russkogo absoliutizma v XVIII veke* (Moscow, 1966), p. 243.

30. Adapted from ibid., p. 214. And see E. V. Anisimov, *Podatnaia reforma Petra I: Vvedenie podushnoi podati v Rossii, 1719–1728* (Leningrad, 1982).

31. Quoted by N. A. Baklanova, 'Kultura i byt v pervoi chetverti XVIII v.' in Beskrovny, *Istoriia SSSR*, vol. 3, p. 369.

32. Much of the above section taken from ibid., pp. 368–76; P. N. Miliukov, *Ocherki po istorii russkoi kultury*, vol. 2 (Paris, 1931), pp. 732–46.

33. M. M. Bogoslovsky, *Byt i nravy russkogo dvorianstva v pervoi polovine XVIII veka* (Petrograd, 1918) pp. 10–14; M. Okenfuss, 'Russian Students in Europe in the Age of Peter the Great' in J. G. Garrard (ed.), *The Eighteenth Century in Russia* (Oxford, 1973), pp. 136–45. See also M. Okenfuss, trans. and ed., *The Travel Diary of Peter Tolstoi* (Dekalb, ILL, 1987).

34. See for example A. N. Robinson (ed.), *Russkaia literatura na rubezhe dvukh epokh (XVII–nachalo XVIIIv.)* (Moscow, 1971); G. R. Seaman, *History of Russian Music* (Oxford, 1967), vol. 1, Chapter 3.

35. B. H. Sumner, *Peter the Great and the Emergence of Russia* (London, 1951), p. 139.

36. Cracraft, *The Church Reform*, pp. 267, 306–7; A. V. Muller (trans. and ed.), *The Spiritual Regulation of Peter the Great* (Seattle, 1972); J. Cracraft (ed.), *For God and Peter the Great: The Works of Thomas Consett, 1723–1729* (Boulder, CO, 1982).

37. L. G. Beskrovny and B. B. Kafengauz, 'Petr I' in Beskrovny, *Istoriia SSSR*, vol. 3, pp. 249–50. M. S. Anderson, *Peter the Great*, pp. 160, 174, considers that Peter was not cruel and that he did not have an ideology. Generally, Anderson's appraisal and account nevertheless remain the most satisfactory in English. And see N. V. Riasanovsky, *The Image of Peter the Great in Russian History and Thought* (Oxford, 1985).

38. Klyuchevsky, *Peter the Great*, p. 272; D. S. Likhacherv, 'The Petrine reforms and the development of Russian culture', *Canadian–American Slavic Studies*, vol. 13 (1979), p. 230.

39. N. I. Pavlenko, 'Petr I' in Beskrovnyi, *Istoriia*, p. 53; N. A. Baklanova, 'Otrazhenie ideli absoliutizma v izobrazitelnom iskusstve pervoi chetverti XVIIIv.' in N. M. Druzhinin *et al.* (eds), *Absoliutizm v Rosii (XVII–XVIIIvv.)* (Moscow, 1964)., p. 494. And see J. Cracraft, *The Petrine revolution in architecture* (Chicago and London, 1989).

40. See C. Peterson, *Peter the Great's Administrative and Judicial Reforms: Swedish Antecedents and the Process of Reception* (Stockholm, 1979).

CHAPTER FOUR

Renovation and extension: Anna, Elizabeth and others, 1725–1761

As Russia joined Europe at the beginning of the eighteenth century, the continent itself was in process of reformation. To the West, France was past the peak of its power, and was being increasingly threatened by upstart Britain. The Dutch Republic, Spain and Portugal were all in various stages of decline, if only relatively speaking. The same reservation must be borne in mind as far as Eastern Europe is concerned, for if Sweden, Poland and the Ottoman Empire were no longer the forces they once had been, they remained significant players in the game of international relations down to the end of the eighteenth century, and in the case of the third of them, well into the nineteenth. But Eastern Europe was altered most by the rise of three other powers, Austria, Prussia and Russia, the third of which was establishing its firm foothold on the Baltic Sea. The Baltic provinces, Estonia and Livonia, now replaced the Ukraine as the principal percolator of European culture. Members of the Baltic elite accounted for about a quarter of the Russian army in the 1730s, and about an eighth of the civil bureaucracy between 1710 and 1917. Their German language enabled them to transmit leading ideas of warfare and government, economics and society, education and science, art and literature, and their importance to the Russian Empire was reinforced by the priorities of successive governments in a foreign policy always giving emphasis to the Baltic region.[1]

The development of Russian absolutism in the period 1725–61 has not always been fully appreciated. Just as the seventeenth century has often been looked at as an all-too-imperfect preparation for the reforms of Peter the Great, so there has been the tendency to dismiss the years following them as an era of palace revolutions with an undistinguished series of empresses emerging victorious from them to achieve nothing more than an inactive equilibrium for the ship of state in the doldrums which followed the creative tempests associated with their famous predecessor. Alternatively, in retrospect, these years appear as the somewhat sterile fallow preceding the fecund magnificence linked with another empress as colourful as her predecessors are monochrome:

Catherine the Great. In fact, there may have been some reaction to the work of the tsar reformer in the decades after his death, but there was also some continuation of it, while there was also a perceptible preparation for the enlightened absolutism of his best-known successor. And the involvement with Europe of significance beyond the basic military activity grew to a degree illustrated by the shift from the Great Northern War to the Seven Years War. By 1721 Russia had established itself on the Baltic Sea and opened its window on the West. Forty years later its imperial might had been recognised as a factor of wider significance as its army entered Berlin. To introduce yet another metaphor, if Peter was associated with the entrance of Russia on to the continental stage, his daughter Elizabeth was assessed in a manner which recognised that Russia played one of the principal roles.

Superficial appearances are therefore somewhat deceptive. For this Peter the Great must take some blame, not only because of the illusion created by his towering personality but also through his failure to make the smoothest possible arrangement for the succession. Having killed off the tsarevich Alexis, he himself died without making use of his proclaimed right to appoint an alternative heir. However, doubts were fairly speedily resolved by his widow, now become Catherine I, with the encouragement of several of her late husband's close associates. This was just the first of a series of unpredictable changes of sovereign and of leading establishments, although, as we turn to look at them, we should not entirely forget the all-important relationship in the continuing development of absolutism, that between the ruling group and the ruling class, between crown and nobility.

Born a Livonian peasant girl in 1684 and first baptised Martha according to the Roman Catholic rite, the future Empress became a Lutheran en route to her first marriage to a Swedish officer and then assumed the faith of the Orthodox in 1708 as Ekaterina Alekseevna, some years after having risen through the ranks of the Russian army as mistress first to Count Sheremetev, then to Prince Menshikov and finally to the tsar himself. The union was solemnised in 1712, after Catherine's alleged outstanding performance as saviour of the fatherland at the time of the campaign of the Prut had concealed her lowly origins to an extent sufficient for her to assume her elevated station in life in an official manner. The companion of her husband in his continual journeys and his frequent drinking bouts, his comforter in the hangovers and in the headaches and rages consequent upon his more than occasional fits, Catherine does not appear to have achieved much experience of government beyond the occasional piece of advice or supplication before 1725. On the other hand, by crowning her Empress in 1724, Peter does appear to have indicated that at that time he intended her to follow some Byzantine precedents in becoming the heir to an Emperor, even if he may soon have changed his mind when he suspected Catherine of taking a lover. As the dread day approached in early 1725, one party largely composed of old aristocratic families worked for the succession of Peter Alekseevich, the dying Emperor's eponymous grandson, while another, in which new men, especially Menshikov, predominated, stood out for Catherine, who also at the key moment received the support of the Guards regiments and the oratorical acclaim of Feofan Prokopovich.

During her short reign, which lasted for just over two years, Catherine gave little evidence of talent for or interest in the business of absolutist government, which in fact was increasingly assumed by the ambitious Menshikov, the dominant figure in a newly created advisory body called the Supreme Privy Council, and prospective father-in-law to the young Peter Alekseevich, who became the widely accepted heir to the throne as the health of his step-mother failed. Menshikov was now set to enjoy his finest hour, but, not for the first time in history, a man close to the peak of power was to be suddenly hurled to the depths. Just a week or so after Catherine's death in May 1727, Menshikov was made Generalissimus; before the end of the month his daughter Maria was affianced to the young tsar. But already the Golitsyns and the Dolgorukys along with some of the newer people were scheming towards their rival's downfall, and in early September he was stripped of his many orders and ranks and ordered to go with his family into exile. An ensuing investigation into the misdeeds of the erstwhile favourite was carried out under three main headings, which in descending order of likelihood were criminal, political and treasonable. Certainly Menshikov had misappropriated vast sums of money and huge estates of land; quite possibly in his machinations on behalf of Maria he had worked to the disadvantage of the dynasty; beyond all reasonable doubt he had not sent secret information to Sweden or any other potential enemy. After some delays brought about partly by the court's concentration on the coronation of Peter II, Menshikov's exile to Siberia along with his family was confirmed in the spring of 1728, and he died near Tobolsk a year and a half later. Maria died soon after her father at about the same time as her former fiancé, Peter II.[2]

During his brief reign Peter became the creature of a new establishment headed by the Dolgoruky family, one of whose princesses, Catherine, replaced Maria Menshikov as the tsar's intended bride, and a return to the old ways was reinforced and symbolised by the desertion of St Petersburg for Moscow. The Dolgorukys and other members of a reformed Supreme Privy Council were given precedence over full generals in a decree of 1728, and in late 1729 the engagement was announced between the young tsar and Catherine. Early in 1730, on the day fixed for his wedding, the fourteen-year-old Peter II died of smallpox, and the third question-mark in five years was posed concerning the succession to Peter the Great. This time, in the interpretation of many later analysts, the question concerning the occupant of the throne became inextricably connected with the larger question concerning the very nature of the government.

During the night of 18–19 January 1730 the Supreme Privy Council, led by the Dolgorukys in close association with members of another old family, the Golitsyns, discussed the pressing problem of the succession. One proposal was that the throne should go to Catherine, the Dolgoruky princess, and according to one account a draft testament to this effect made by Peter II was to be supplemented by the posthumous solemnisation of the projected marriage between Catherine and Peter. This macabre suggestion did not get above the ground, and Catherine's candidature was rejected. Peter the Great's first wife, Evdokie Lopukhin, was no more than briefly considered, while the offspring of his second wife, Catherine I, were ruled out on the basis of her illegitimacy as Empress and their illegitimacy as children. The Supreme Privy Councillors now turned attention to another more legal line, that sired by Peter the Great's erstwhile half-brother and co-ruler, Ivan V, and consisting of three daughters. The eldest was turned down because of her unacceptable husband, but the second, Anna, Duchess of Courland, who was a widow, appeared at first sight to be the obliging and humble sort of woman who would know her place, as it were, even on the throne. And so her name was put forward on the morning of 19 January for confirmation by the highest military and civilian officials.

But this was more the beginning of the story than the end, for the Supreme Privy Councillors decided to make their offer to Anna dependent on her acceptance of a series of Conditions. She would not remarry nor designate an heir, and she would retain in existence the Supreme Privy Council of eight members, without whose permission she would not make war or peace, impose taxes, confer civil and military ranks above colonel, grant titles or estates, or make use of state revenues. Moreover, Anna would place the guards and other regiments under the direct control of the Supreme Privy Councillors and not deprive nobles in general of life, honour or property without proper trial. According to a Scotsman on the spot, James Keith, these Conditions were mainly the work of the Dolgorukys, who had formed 'a scheme of government, by which the Empress was to have the name, and themselves the power' in 'a kind of government' which was 'half commonwealth, half Monarchy, and so ill digested, that it was impracticable in any country, but much more in Russia, where the genius of the nation, and the vast extent of the empire, demands a Souverain, and even an absolute one'. Keith is exceptional in his attribution of such a scheme to the Dolgorukys, several other sources making it the work of D. M. Golitsyn, who, it was alleged, wanted to reform the Russian constitution after the model of the Polish or the Swedish. In fact, as far as can now be seen, neither the Dolgorukys nor Golitsyn went explicitly further on paper than the Conditions, although for some historians the accession of Anna was an important opportunity for absolutism to be restricted in the direction of more limited monarchy.[3]

To return to 19 January: the Councillors managed duly to achieve the confirmation of Anna without revealing to their fellow nobles their Conditions. But some of their high-placed rivals somehow got wind of the scheme and sent a delegation to Courland which arrived there soon after the emissaries of the Supreme Privy Council and advised Anna to reject any such limitation on her power. Meanwhile other members of the *dvorianstvo* who had come to Moscow for the wedding of Peter II, stayed for his funeral, and were now anxiously waiting for confirmation of his successor, became seriously alarmed when the announcement was made on 2 February not only of the peremptory Conditions but also of Anna's obliging acceptance of them. In an effort to allay such disquiet, the Supreme Privy Council invited the nobles gathered in Moscow to make speedy written submissions of their own views concerning the advisability and nature of any governmental reforms, some such projects in all probability being already in existence or process of composition. Up to a dozen sets of views were now drawn up, the majority view on the key question being that, although the Empress might well need advice from members of the ruling class, the Conditions as presented by the Supreme Privy Council were too peremptory and could only result in the Russian polity being transformed from an absolutism not to a limited monarchy but to an oligarchical aristocracy. One oft-quoted assessment declared:

God forbid that it turn out that, instead of one autocratic sovereign, we have tens of absolute and powerful families, and thus we the nobility will decline completely and we will be forced more painfully than before to make obeisance and seek favours from everybody – and this will not be easy, because however much they are in agreement now, there will undoubtedly soon be arguments among them.[4]

These and other remarks in circulation in early February 1730 have persuaded some commentators to conclude that the assembled nobles chose the rule of one alone rather than the rule of several. As we shall now see, such an interpretation is as erroneous as that which makes the events of early 1730 into a deep constitutional crisis.

When Anna made her formal entry into Moscow on 15 February, after a brief stay in the suburbs where she had already infringed the Conditions by proclaiming herself officer of the Guards, the Supreme Privy Council found itself pushed towards action as its unpopularity grew. Resolution came on 25 February, when the Councillors attempted in vain to arrest the leaders of the opposition to them and Anna was presented with the clamorous request for the rejection of the Conditions. With a theatrical gesture inspired by such 'popular' demand, the Empress tore up the offending document before the very eyes of her 'true slaves', the nobles disaffected from the previous establishment. However, few of those present expected to be in direct contact with their new sovereign, knowing full well that, while the Dolgorukys and the Golitsyns were now to be ousted from power, a new entourage would soon form around Anna. The Conditions had been the embodiment of a clumsy attempt by the Supreme Privy Councillors to hold on to power after the unexpected death of their puppet Peter II. No doubt his pliability as well as Anna's sex and remoteness had combined with the sudden arrival of the interregnum to make their overtures to her immoderate, even overweening. And their previous confidence, born of their victory over Menshikov, had no doubt caused them to neglect one of the rules of the eighteenth-century patronage game, not only in Russia but elsewhere, and to forget the necessity to maintain the prosperity of a sufficient number of supporters. But this does not add up to a deep crisis, rather to a comparatively superficial change of establishment, illustrated by the ensuing hectic jockeying for position on the part of prospective clients. James Keith, having 'no pretensions to any advancement, being little more than a year in the Empire' saw 'all these favours' being distributed with the detachment of one who was confident that 'being in the service of a generous Princess, I should have my share when time had given me occasions to render any service', and was astonished to be declared Lieutenant Colonel of a Guards regiment. As Keith described the sequel:

All Moscow was as surprised as I was myself; and as the employment is looked on as one of the greatest trust in the Empire, and that the officers of the Guards are regarded as the domestics of the Sovereign, I received hundreds of visits from people I had never seen nor heard of in my life, and who imagined that certainly I must be in great favour at Court, in which they were prodigiously deceived.[5]

If not in great favour at court, Keith was nevertheless an officer in whom the new establishment could put its confidence, and for a time he occupied an important enough position in the new pyramid of power.

While Keith and other new men, many lower, a few higher, were put into place, the Dolgorukys and the Golitsyns, like Menshikov before them, were sent into exile. As Brenda Meehan-Waters has rightly pointed out, there was 'no face-saving way of letting the new "ins" come in without demolishing the "outs"'.[6] Moreover, as the same authority has clearly demonstrated, many of those involved in the eighteenth-century struggle were scions of old noble families prominent in the squabbles of the seventeenth century. But while some of the names of the players remained the same, the rules of the game had been changed by the reforms of Peter the Great. There may still have been no security for individual members of the nobility, but the class as a whole had benefited from the coalescence brought about by the regularisation of service conditions. It was more certain of its inclusion in the imperial structure than it had been confident of its general incorporation in the Muscovite state. The Guards were altogether more co-ordinated than their predecessors, the *streltsy*, and the palace revolutions after 1725 generally as well as in 1730 in particular were far more civilised than those occurring before 1700. And even disgraced individuals must now have derived some comfort from the circumstance that more of them were sent into peaceful if impoverished exile and fewer lost their heads, even if they did lose both face and property. Above all, then, the significance of the dramatic events of 1730 lay not in a bold attempt at constitutional reform nor in a craven acceptance of the system already in existence, but rather in an abrupt change of sovereign without much bloodshed or widespread disturbance.

James Keith was appointed Lieutenant-Colonel of the newly created Izmailovsky Guards Regiment by Count Karl Gustav Löwenwolde, who had been rewarded by the Empress with the Colonelcy of the Regiment 'for the zeal which he had showed for her service', included among which, according to some accounts, were ministrations of a most personal nature. His brother Count Reinhold Gustav, who had been a member of the delegation sent by the rivals of the Supreme Privy Councillors to Courland to dissuade Anna from signing the Conditions at the beginning of the interregnum, was now Grand Marshal of the Court. Other leading members of the new entourage were General Count Burchard Christoph Münnich, commander of the army, Count Andrei Ivanovich Osterman, in charge of foreign affairs, and Count Ernst Johann Bühren (in Russian Biron), who shared with Count Karl Gustav Löwenwolde unofficial responsibilities for certain domestic matters. So great was believed to be the influence of this last favourite over the Empress that her reign has come down in history as the *Bironovshchina*, while conjoined with that of the other top people just listed it has been deemed to have been of such huge and all-pervasive proportions as to have constituted a 'German yoke'. Yet Biron's highest official function was head gentleman-in-waiting at the court, and according to Münnich he avoided learning Russian to avoid being drawn into participation in government, while another contemporary comment on his linguistic predilections was that he addressed men as horses and *vice versa*, a reflection of his priorities in life in general. As for the others, Münnich and Osterman had been in Russia for some years before the accession of Anna without any such all-encompassing comment on the insidiousness of their nationality, and they shared a mutual antipathy with Biron, while other important members of the new establishment were Russian associates of Peter the Great: for example, Prince A. M. Cherkassky, Prince N. Iu. Trubetskoi, V. F. Saltykov and G. I. Golovkin. And so, even though it would be inappropriate to deny a distinctly unsavoury appearance to the reign of Anna, it would be equally inaccurate to paint the 1730s in uniformly foreign dark colours. To emphasise this last point, among the most disagreeable activities were those of the Chancellery for Secret Investigatory Affairs placed at its creation in April 1731 under the supervision of Major-General Andrei Ivanovich Ushakov, who had served his apprenticeship in the Secret Chancellery of Peter the Great.

Among other early moves on the part of the Empress Anna's administration was a return to St Petersburg and the abolition of the Supreme Privy Council; along with some restoration of the power of the Senate, there was the introduction of a new chief co-ordinating body, the Cabinet, supervised by Osterman with the participation of leading Russians, at first Cherkassky and Golovkin, later in turn, after the death of Golovkin, P. I. Iaguzhinsky, already restored to his post of Procurator-General, A. P. Volynsky and then A. P. Bestuzhev-Riumin. These later appointments were all to the dissatisfaction of Osterman, Volynsky falling foul of both this first cabinet minister and the first favourite, Biron, and suffering torture and then execution in the summer of 1740 for his alleged attempt to bring Elizabeth to the throne prematurely. Volynsky was certainly responsible for a 'Project for the Correction of State Affairs' composed about 1739 which echoed some of the suggestions put forward by the nobility in 1730, when Anna's reign was just beginning.[7] Now that it was coming to an end and fresh jockeying for position was about to be inaugurated, the major members of the establishment inside the Cabinet and outside looked around them to make certain that all members of the Dolgoruky-Golitsyn faction had died in exile or prison or by execution, rightly fearful that the demise of their patroness would subject their own lives to comparable extreme perils.

Anna herself was resolved to ensure that the succession passed through the line of Ivan V, her father, rather than that of Peter the Great. This meant that there could be only one candidate for the throne, her older sister Catherine's daughter, Anna Leopoldovna. Biron attempted to marry his son to this young princess, but she chose a petty German prince as a less undesirable alternative, and their union produced a son in August 1740, a couple of months before the Empress Anna died, her last wish having been declared to be that the infant should become Ivan VI with Biron as regent. Unfortunately for Biron, he had failed to take the elementary precaution of winning over a sufficient number of high officials and the Guards, and his negligence allowed his rivals Osterman and Münnich to conspire to remove him along with Anna Leopoldovna, who herself now became regent as he was sent with his family into Siberian exile in commutation of a death sentence. (He was later rehabilitated and died back in Courland in 1769).

The new regency lasted for just over a year. Neither Anna Leopoldovna nor her husband was made of stern enough stuff to maintain their position at the top in the face of the continued machinations of men well practised in such circumstances as had been created. But even old hands like Osterman and Münnich now found themselves outmanoeuvred by a group forming around the daughter of Peter the Great and Catherine I. Elizabeth's politically innocent pursuit of pleasure in the 1730s had acquired for her a sufficient level of popularity among the Guards, while the German origin and Austrian sympathies of the regent's establishment had aroused the antipathies of France and Sweden, which worked for the enthronement of Elizabeth through their ambassadors along with a financial subsidy from the first and a declaration of war from the second. As the regent and her advisers got wind of the schemes for their overthrow, Elizabeth was threatened with the possibility of having to become a nun, a role which according to the English ambassador not one bit of her flesh was qualified to play, and so she threw herself into the lead of a decisive night march on the Winter Palace. In a pre-dawn coup on 25 November, the infant Tsar Ivan VI and his parents were placed under arrest as Elizabeth proclaimed herself Empress. At first the family was sent back towards Germany, but then, through fear of the threat to her own security posed by the baby male Romanov, she recalled them from Riga and sent them off to harsh internal exile and imprisonment (which only a few survived). Meanwhile, Münnich and Osterman were taken into custody along with the rest of the regent's entourage and soon condemned to death, the Field Marshal by quartering, the Minister by breaking on the wheel, while others were to be beheaded. A large crowd gathered for the spectacle in St Petersburg, but were denied their sadistic pleasures by a last-minute commutation of the sentence to Siberian exile.

The events of 1740–41 have been subject to far less academic scrutiny than those of 1730, and yet they possessed their own elements of distinctive significance. While Elizabeth wisely capitalised on her popularity with the Guards and immediately placed herself at their head, the governmental system had become sufficiently bureaucratised for these elite military detachments to have lost something of their earlier freedom of action. In the formulation of John Keep and Brenda Meehan-Waters:

The crisis also weakened the guards regiments' initially close involvement in matters of state security. One might say that from being the agents of surveillance they had become its objects. They would continue to play an important political role at moments of tension, notably in 1762 and in 1801, and until 1825 would remain a significant element in the empire's 'informal constitution'. But henceforth command of the security apparatus would be in other hands. In this domain as in many others a process of institutional specialisation was under way that was essential if Russia were to become a modern state.[8]

Thus it was not surprising that in the informal replacement for the advisory Cabinet one of the few previously prominent officials to retain his position was A. I. Ushakov, the chief of the Secret Chancellery. He and his policemen were kept busy until his retirement in 1744, especially since the new Empress, who it must be remembered had seized the throne through the claims of blood rather than by rule of law, suffered from strong feelings of insecurity. And their justice, if more ordered in its procedures than in earlier times, was still fairly rough in its implementation. For example, in 1743, after an alleged plot to restore Ivan VI to the throne, two fashionable ladies were implicated, had their backs flogged and their tongues branded in public.

Elizabeth's rule was not then necessarily more merciful than its predecessor, nor would it be correct to view it as a Russian replacement for the German yoke, a return to order and probity after a decade of unrestrained lawlessness. The Empress herself was a little less neglectful than Anna of her duties, but not much, while some of her erstwhile playmates could scarcely be said to have donned the mantle of statesmanship after their elevation to high places. Closest to her at first, for example, was probably Alexis Razumovsky, a handsome Cossack who could sing but neither read nor write and was now to become Field-Marshal of the army. On the other hand, it is true that the Shuvalov and Vorontsov brothers, who were also members of her inner circle, did have some taste for government and even a little talent, too. Moreover, in an early decree, Elizabeth attempted to reimpose regularity on the Senate and the rest of the administration, although of course Anna had inaugurated her reign with a similar exercise.

As we turn to consider in close focus these readjustments in the Senate and the other organs of central administration, we must first recall that 'Anna' and 'Elizabeth' have been used just now and on earlier occasions as shorthand terms for their establishments. These ladies themselves did not in fact take any more interest in the business of government than they considered absolutely necessary (such dereliction of duty, however, perhaps being worthy of inclusion among the rights of those deemed to govern absolutely). Like many of her male counterparts including her immediate youthful predecessor, Anna was passionately fond of hunting, and therefore put her personal imprint on the statute book in the shape of decrees reserving the game in certain areas for her own use and others making sure that there would be a plentiful preserve of animals and birds for her to destroy. Among other matters discussed by the Cabinet were the accounts concerning such a delicate matter of the state economy as the purchase on behalf of the Empress of fine lace. The sovereign herself attempted to ensure by law that she would not have to behold such unpleasant sights on the streets as funeral processions or infirm and aged paupers. As far as Elizabeth was concerned, the Saxon ambassador wrote that, not wanting to have her own preferred use of time impeded, and not being able to abide government business, she kept away from it or considered it only with the utmost carelessness, often in annoyance that it inconvenienced her, pronouncing sentences with most cruel severity. As preoccupied with her wardrobe as Anna had been with hunting, Elizabeth ordered foreign and Russian merchants to show her the fine materials that they had imported before putting them on the open market. Showing comparable concern for the appearance of the capital city, she commanded the closure on the principal streets of taverns and the removal from them of 'indecent women and girls', as well as the more certain closure of the graves in cemeteries along the route from St Petersburg to one of her palaces. After an initial flurry of activity marked by seven attendances at the Senate in 1742 and four in each of the following two years, she managed no more than a total of three further appearances in the remaining seventeen years of her reign.[9]

As for the rest of the government apart from the empresses, there was a certain more widely applicable truth in the assertion of Count Nikita Panin that Russia in the reign of Elizabeth was governed not by 'the authority of state institutions' but by 'the power of persons'. We have already made the brief acquaintance of at least some of these persons, and will be meeting at least a few of them again, but neither their appearance nor Panin's observation should blind us to the fact that Peter's reforms had left a lasting legacy of institutional order as well as one of individual wilfulness. Permeating all the organs of state was a pronounced tendency towards bureaucratisation, which was marked in the most straightforward manner by quantitative increase. According to the scholarly calculation of S. M. Troitsky, the number of officials in central and local administration had by the mid 1750s doubled from the end of Peter's reign to between 11,500 and 12,500, and was to grow again by 1763 to about 16,500. About two-thirds of this number were at the lower clerical levels, and although some of them no doubt performed meritorious services for the fatherland, they cannot receive further discussion here. Of the rest, the top third, nearly all were of noble origin, as would be expected. Somewhat more surprisingly, no more than a few started their career at court, a considerable contrast to the seventeenth-century practice and a clear indicator of a bureaucracy separate from the court; the most common previous experience for the highest men in the administration would be in the army and navy, followed by the lower echelons of the civil service. As nobles, these men would tend to be serf-owning landlords, and, naturally enough, the higher the official, the more likely that he would possess a large number of serfs, as well as an advanced education and a title. But more than a few officials had no serfs at all, which made their reception of a salary all the more important and which also presented the possibility of the development of a bureaucratic outlook which would differ from that of the landlords. True, the series of palace revolutions militated against such a development. In the years leading up to the crisis of 1730, for example, as we have seen, the Supreme Privy Councillors entrenched their position by giving themselves precedence over full generals. This and other abuses of the promotion system formed one of the subjects for complaint in the noble projects presented to Anna at her accession, but she continued them with her rewards for those who had given her candidature for the throne their support. And some of these argued that their promotion for special services (*zaslugi*) would produce wider incentives (*ankurazhivanie*) for others. But many bureaucrats were unhappy with elevation for *zaslugi*, preferring the principle of seniority (*vysluga*), so, although elevation for *zaslugi* was by no means forgotten, especially at times of palace revolution, successive governments made concessions to the pressures emanating from their professional servitors in the chancelleries. The consequent movement in the direction of the institutionalisation of *vysluga* led towards a new *mestnichestvo* (placement system), of function and rank rather than of birth, as a consequence of which bureaucrats tended to be ennobled and nobles tended to be bureaucratised, both of which tendencies were not welcome to the governments that had brought them about, since they might alienate their chief supporters. A further response was therefore a series of decrees in the 1750s prohibiting the ownership of serfs by commoner bureaucrats, which would please the nobles, accompanied by the successive exclusion from the poll-tax-paying population of at least some of the lower born bureaucrats, which would appease these commoners.[10]

The greatest increase in the number of civil servants was at the centre; in the provinces, at least in the late 1720s, there was a reduction in their number. This swelling band of pen-pushers and red-tapers worked in an administrative structure that was basically the same as that created by the reforms of Peter the Great, with the Senate and the colleges remaining in existence, although experiencing certain fluctuations of fortune. Soon after the death of the tsar reformer, the creation of the Supreme Privy Council meant some reduction in the power of the Senate, although it must be remembered that even in its early years this state organ had never played as vital a part in the smooth functioning of the body politic as its elevated position might have suggested. The Supreme Privy Council, on the other hand, dominated the government for most of its short life, and during that time three of the colleges – Foreign Affairs, Admiralty and War – were raised in stature over their fellows and made independent of the Senate. At the accession of Anna and abolition of the Supreme Privy Council, the Senate enjoyed a momentary revival, taking care of the enactment of legislation and resuming control over all the colleges. But then Her Majesty's Cabinet was formed, first informally in 1730, then formally but confidentially in 1731, and at last in 1735 publicly as the chief state institution. Yet again after the events of 1740–41 the upstart body was killed off and the Senate resumed its former status, taking responsibility for four-fifths of the decrees issued in the reign of Elizabeth, whose inner circle of advisers were later organised in a regular manner, this time in a Conference. As far as the colleges were concerned, Foreign Affairs, Admiralty and War remained the most important, although never again officially being set apart from the others. As already indicated above, a newly created chancellery of great importance during the period of palace revolutions was that for Secret Investigatory Affairs.

Town government at the time reflected the weakness of urban development, and was largely incorporated into central and provincial government as a whole. True, Peter the Great's magistracies were revived in 1743 after their abolition in 1727, but the burgomasters were subordinate to the governors and *voevodas*, who were empowered, for example, to keep such town officials under arrest until arrears in tax levies were collected. Of course, because of their special position, St Petersburg and Moscow were on a somewhat different footing from their lesser siblings out in the wide reaches of the Russian Empire. Here the limits of the power of absolutism were most clearly revealed, almost as much in the eighteenth century as in the seventeenth; as we shall now see, the grandiose schemes of Peter the Great for the comprehensive revival of the provinces could never come remotely near to completion.

In 1719 Peter had said to one of his henchmen, Admiral Apraksin: 'Although you have always encouraged my actions ..., all the same I read in your heart that if I die before you, you will be one of the first to condemn all that I have done.' While he may not have been one of the first, Apraksin certainly joined his colleagues in government in the years following 1725 to dismantle many of the institutions set up by the reformer. The reaction did not take place immediately after Peter's death, however, even though the situation throughout the empire was recognised at the time as being very serious indeed, and this gloomy appraisal has been corroborated by posterity. According to Klyuchevsky, provincial Russia had not seen such dark times since the early days of Mongol rule:

Bands of pillagers, commanded by deserters, joined together in well-organised and well-armed cavalry groups, and attacked in regular formation, destroying well-populated villages, impeding the collection of taxes, and even penetrating into towns .... The civil servant in the capital, the general on a mission, the noble on his distant estates, all ignored the tsar's terrible ukazes; neither they, nor the brigands in the forests, cared what the semi-autocratic Senate, and ... Swedish-type colleges, with their carefully defined jurisdictions, achieved in the capital. An imposing legislative façade merely concealed the general disorder which prevailed throughout the country.

And at the beginning of the reign of Catherine I the Procurator-General Iaguzhinsky wrote:

Already for several years there have been poor harvests, and the poll tax collections are very burdensome ..., because of which in time of such poor harvests peasants are forced to sell not only horses and cattle, but even their seed corn, and they go hungry, and perhaps the large part are such that they have no hope for future food, and a great number of them already appear to be dying from nothing but hunger ... (one woman threw her daughter into the water and drowned her because of hunger), and many are running away across the Polish border and to join the Bashkirs, and even the military outposts can do nothing about this.[11]

Iaguzhinsky's suggestions for the cure of these and other ills consisted primarily of the completion, continuation and repetition of the reforms. The poll tax was to be retained, but reduced to a level lower than 70 kopecks so that the tax burden would correspond more to the paying power of the people. To bring down government expenditure Iaguzhinsky put forward suggestions for measures comparable to those to which Peter had already resorted. First, there was to be a temporary stoppage of army pay. Second, the serving nobles were to be sent home in rotation, a temporary demobilisation with two beneficial effects: those on leave would not have to be paid; and they would improve the local economy through their personal supervision. Iaguzhinsky went further here than Peter in his proposal that one son in each family should remain permanently on the estate to ensure the collection of state taxes and to carry out the administration of the peasants in general. Local government was to be improved, according to Iaguzhinsky's recommendation, by subjecting it to greater control. In this case, the Procurator-General wanted to put into practice Peter's stratagem of sending inspector senators around the provinces with extraordinary powers. For the government's supervision of tax collection, Iaguzhinsky wanted to revive the State Control (*Revizion*) College. Finally, after making the assertion that the state is based on two foundations, land and commerce, he pointed out the necessity of concentrating on the second. So, generally speaking, Iaguzhinsky aimed at less taxation and less expenditure, more control and more trade.

The Senate discussed the points raised by the Procurator-General in the autumn of 1725. By this time it also had at its disposal several other reports, including some from army officers to the War College and others from provincial bureaucrats to the State Revenue College. On the basis of information and opinions received, the Senate recommended a temporary reduction of the poll tax to 60 kopecks and a correction of the cadastral survey in 1726 so that the rate could be restored to 70 kopecks with the levy being inflicted only on souls who were not dead or absent without leave. Supporting Iaguzhinsky's idea of leave for two-thirds of the landlords, the Senate went further than him in suggesting a reduction in the size of the army which would include the cancellation of the projected call-up of 23,000 recruits. More radically, the Senate proposed the abolition of the arrangements for troop quartering introduced by Peter the Great, which it considered burdensome for the peasantry and harmful to the army and wanted to replace by stationing troops in towns.

The Senate's report was in turn examined by a special commission of generals gathered at the War College. This agreed to the temporary reduction in the rate of the poll tax and to temporary demobilisation for landlords. It opposed the correction of the cadastral survey, however, arguing that it would be very onerous for the landlords and that the first such survey commenced in 1719 was still to be finished. The generals suggested instead an enquiry into the reasons for tax arrears in 1724 and 1725, which they thought could be divided into three categories with three appropriate remedies: popular resistance – corporal punishment; poverty – local inspections, weak officials – fines. The generals opposed the transfer of troops to the towns, because it would leave provincial barracks empty and rural dwellers open to attacks by brigands, and add an unfair burden to the load of duties already borne by the townsfolk. While the generals were against the reduction of army numbers, Field Marshal Münnich was even in favour of their increase, although he was also conscious of the need for commercial development and underlined the necessity for the completion of the Ladoga Canal for this purpose.

After further deliberations, this time by the newly created Supreme Privy Council in 1726, a decree of February 1727 sent two-thirds of the army's officers home on extended leave for the reasons already suggested by Iaguzhinsky, the Senate and the *generalitet*. Other measures proposed by various individuals and groups for the increase of income and reduction of expenditure included the payment in kind of part of the poll tax, the curtailment of unnecessary construction projects, improvements in the coinage, the completion of a new law code, the decentralisation of the Estates College and the systematisation of legal fees and charges for the transfer of property. However, the most significant proposals concerned the provincial reforms of Peter the Great, which were widely thought to be a crippling weight on the backs of the people, especially after the superimposition upon them of the quartering of army units. Listing the many officials in each province, Admiral Apraksin wrote that 'The ordinary *muzhik* does not know who is senior, fears all, and runs from each at sight into the woods.'[12]

And so it came to pass that the provincial edifice, or rather castle in the air, established by Peter the Great was subjected to almost complete demolition. While it was first thought that trouble stemmed from the fact that they had never been completed, the new institutions themselves were soon criticised and their predecessors praised. This process was completed in two years, the speed of the reaction being faster than that of the reform. A series of decrees in 1727 and 1728 transferred the collection of the poll tax from the army to the landlords, abolished many of the innovations brought in by Peter and introduced simple local government by governor and *voevoda* after a pre-Petrine pattern. In the old days the Supreme Privy Councillors considered that 'people were satisfied'. With the restoration of the former system and the growth of interest in provincial affairs on the part of the nobility, wrote an apologist for this class, 'The peasants . . . will be completely satisfied and live in peace and without trouble, and a great advantage will accrue from this to the landlords.' In fact, of course, the popular cup of joy was far from overflowing, and provincial administration continued inefficient and corrupt. The nature and significance of the decrees of 1727–28 were well described by Iu. V. Gote, who wrote:

The counter-reform of 1727 and succeeding years was carried out by the successors of Peter who were seized by the desire to simplify local government and to make it cheaper. In the discussion of measures which were recognised as completely necessary, a reactionary mood broke out, which expressed itself particularly in the idealisation of the old Muscovite institutions and led to the revival of a considerable number of them ... As well as these phenomena recalling the old Muscovite order, we must also mention the hierarchical principle binding all the provincial institutions into one well-constructed chain, with the province (*guberniia*) at the top and the ward (*prigorod*) at the bottom. Simplification on the one hand, idealisation of Muscovite antiquity on the other, led to the complete amalgamation of authority in the hands of the governors and *voevodas*, and this amalgamation, judging by the decree of 24 February 1727, was introduced more completely than in old Moscow. However, the poverty of mind of the governmental men of affairs of the twenties and the thirties was no less clearly expressed in their work. Their reform was not thought out, it was not carried out all at once, but separately ... , in bits and pieces, and it was far from being free of many exceptions, which underlined still more its lack of a creative idea.[13]

In his magnificent study of provincial government from 1725 to 1775, Gote painstakingly builds up a picture of successive attempts to improve its standard during these fifty years. Weighed down by a multiplicity of duties in the field of administration, finance, law and order, the governors and *voevodas* could not begin to cope. In a huge empire with poor communications and a backward society, their task was in any case impossible. Terrified on the one hand by strict directives that could not be implemented and by the threat of fines, dismissal or visits from inspecting officials and commissions, conscious on the other hand of the traditions in their profession of bribery, extortion and corruption of all kinds, the staff of local government from top to bottom made what it could of a bad job. Even for the best of them, this meant following the interests of their class, the nobility, with little realisation of the needs of the community or the state, while the vast majority seized all available opportunities for self-advancement and self-enrichment.

However, the resemblance of this mode of operation to that existing in the seventeenth century should not lead to the conclusion that, after the dismantlement of the complex administrative edifice of Peter the Great, there was wholesale reversion to the provincial government of pre-Petrine times. Although many anomalies and contradictions persisted, and others may well have developed, comparatively speaking, there was after 1727 an harmonious hierarchical system in existence, with an at least perceptible chain of command from the institutions of central government through the governors down to the *voevodas* of county, district and ward. Moreover, there was also after 1727 a certain softening in the conditions of civil as well as military service, for example with the decree of 1736 allowing one member of each family to stay at home to look after the family estates, in a sense a moderate replacement of Peter the Great's 1714 law rescinded in 1730, and provincial life of a settled and peaceful nature was at least beginning to take shape in some regions especially at the centre around Moscow. *Voevodas* were sometimes able to find themselves among a society composed to some extent of members of their own class as the number of landlords in residence on their own estates increased, and probably a growing number of the governors were in a position to exercise an increasing measure of control over the often vast areas under their jurisdiction. Changes in provincial government and society did not occur any more speedily in eighteenth-century Russia than elsewhere, however, whatever the apparent implications of certain decrees such as the so-called emancipation from service of the nobility in 1762, and so we must recognise that the period 1725–61 was a necessary preparation for the continued burgeoning of life outside the capitals in the reign of Catherine the Great. Support for such a contention comes from the rough calculation that of the 50,000 or so landlords in existence in 1762, no more than a quarter would appear to be in state civil or war service, while both the bureaucracy and the armed forces complained of the presence of too few rather than too many nobles in their upper ranks.[14]

In the civil service, as we have seen, by 1762 there were about 5,000 nobles in the upper echelons; at this time, towards the end of the Seven Years War, the number of commissioned nobles in the army and navy probably did not exceed that of their more peacefully occupied classmates by more than a thousand or two. In the immediate aftermath of Peter the Great there were several enquiries into the condition of the army, and some gloomy conclusions, including the most pessimistic observation in 1729 that the Empire's land forces were in complete confusion. Nevertheless in 1731 the army was nearly the same size as it had been in 1720: 4 guards, 55 infantry and 32 dragoon field regiments; and 41 infantry and 6 dragoon garrison regiments. Münnich soon abolished the grenadier regiments and reduced the fire power of the infantry as a whole, while he increased that of the artillery, although making it heavier and less mobile. Too slavishly following foreign fashions, in the view of L. G. Beskrovny, he made the engineers cumbersome as well, spending vast sums of money on fixed lines of defence and the levy of supportive regiments of *landmilitsiia*. True, he did not have everything his own way, and his fellow officers resisted his attempt to reduce the cavalry in size and importance. Moreover, at his fall in 1741, there was a speedy restoration of the military establishment of 1720, and this was maintained in such a manner that by the beginning of the Seven Years War in 1756 the army was in the same physical shape as at the end of the Great Northern War in 1721, although with some administrative changes such as a tightening up of the recruiting system and strengthening of the control of the War College. Meanwhile, contrary to frequent assertion, the navy was not completely neglected, although the dominant strategic view was that Russia was much more a land than a sea power. Towards the end of the reign of Peter the Great, it will be recalled, the navy had consisted of 32 ships of the line, 16 frigates, 85 galleys and 20 or so sundry others, with a total complement of up to 28,000 men. By the early 1740s the numbers had declined to 20 ships of the line, 14 frigates and 40 others of all kinds. The threat of war with Sweden and then with Prussia meant some little increase in naval activity, but the overall size of the navy had not grown much and its quality had probably shrunk by the opening of the Seven Years War. While by 1757 there were 27 ships of the line, 8 frigates, 209 galleys and 11 others, almost a half of them turned out to be incapable of managing more than the lightest of breezes, according to one assessment, while 11 of 27 transport ships sent to Kolberg sank on the way. And the Caspian fleet had become even less usable than that operating on the Baltic. However, the Russian efforts as a whole during the Seven Years War must not be disparaged. Even at sea there was more than a catalogue of pure disaster to report, while on land there were some signal victories, as we shall soon discover. The line tactics of the earlier part of the century received some refinement, partly as a result of the more completely organised forms of officer training, which also allowed the Russian forces to reduce further their dependence on foreigners, the army by far more than the navy. This tendency was clearly illustrated by the later career of James Keith, now achieving distinction as a Prussian officer before being killed at the battle of Hochkirch. By the Seven Years War the Russian army was the largest in Europe, the establishment aimed for at its commencement consisting of 162,430 men in field regiments, 74,548 garrison troops, 27,758 men in the *landmilitsiia*, 12,937 members of the corps of engineering and artillery, and 44,000 irregulars.[15]

The Seven Years War was fought on a world scale, with Russia maintaining a primary interest in central and eastern Europe but also necessarily taking note of developments in other theatres to the west as well as continuing traditional concerns for threats and opportunities on the Asian side. Speaking more generally, in the years following his death, his successors made no major departure from the foreign policy of Peter the Great, even though there were some realignments of allies and enemies. But as with his policies, so with theirs, cool logic or reason of state was sometimes overwhelmed by the loyalties of the rulers towards their German relatives, the baneful influences of gold, intrigue and corruption, the inclinations of the ruling class as a whole and the proclivities of court favourites in particular, and the aims of the 'systems' of their advisers. The two most important individuals were probably Osterman, who was for the most part in charge of foreign affairs from 1725 until his fall in 1741, and Alexis Bestuzhev-Riumin, who took over in 1741 and then fell in his turn in 1758.

The Great Northern War had brought Russia the long-fought-for foothold on the Baltic, which Peter the Great's successors were determined not to let slip. Equally, Sweden was eager to regain what had been lost, gaining important support from France and Great Britain through entry into the Hanoverian alliance in 1727. Therefore, while pouring money into the pockets of influential Swedes likely to support accommodation, the Russian administration also attempted to ensure that at least some Poles would be friendly and others not too hostile, restraining its own desire to bite off at least as much as it could chew of its western neighbour. From the south there was continued pressure from the Crimean Tatars, whose appetites had not been sated by the recapture of Azov and the payment of tribute and who continued their periodic sallies into Russia and the Ukraine from their Black Sea fortress, while their Turkish patrons made little or no apparent effort to restrain them. And although peace with Persia had been formally concluded in 1723, war was in fact being carried fitfully on. Only the Far Eastern frontier was fully stabilised, the Treaty of Kiakhta of 1727 tying up some loose ends left over from Nerchinsk in 1689. With the boundary between the two powers now fixed along the line of part of the River Argun, a tributary of the Amur, China made further gains of territory to Russia's loss, but there was no reason for any immediate conflict and some hopes for expanded trade relations.

As far as Europe was concerned the circumstance that Russia was now a power to be reckoned with to an unprecedented extent was reflected in the recognition gradually given to the imperial title adopted by Peter the Great in 1721. Prussia and Holland made the gesture almost at once in 1722, Sweden in 1723, Denmark in 1724, Saxony in 1733, Turkey in 1741, Austria and Great Britain in 1742, France in 1744 and Spain in 1745, and even Poland in 1764. True, recognition was on occasion withdrawn, by Sweden in 1741 and by France in 1768, but on the other hand the interest in Russia shown by the powers of Europe seeking her neutrality or alliance was frequent and powerful enough to show that the acceptance of this new empire into the family of European nations was almost complete.[16]

Thus, Russia might well have been welcome in the Hanoverian Alliance formed between Great Britain and France in late 1725 had it not been for Catherine I's desire to assist her Holsteinian relatives to re-establish themselves in Schleswig and Menshikov's ambition to become Duke of Courland, as a counter to which a British fleet hovered outside the port of Revel in the spring of 1726. In its turn this action helped the Russian administration make up its mind by the summer of 1726 to join the principal rival of the Hanoverian Alliance, the Austro-Spanish League assembled in Vienna in early 1725. Russia was now obliged to recognise the Pragmatic Sanction of the Austrian Emperor Charles VI, according to which the Habsburg possessions were entailed upon his eldest daughter Maria Theresa, and in return Austria recognised the recent expansion of the Russian empire (if not yet its upstart title) and made secret commitments to assist the restoration of Schleswig to Holstein and to support Russia if war should break out against Turkey. Seeing her two neighbours in central Europe drawing together, Prussia joined them in the autumn of 1726, having been earlier a founder member of the Hanoverian Alliance.

In the early 1730s, after the change of Empress, Russia found itself confronting a changing alignment of European powers. As far as the protagonists of the Hanoverian Alliance were concerned, Great Britain was now drawing close to Russia, while France was drifting further away. Commerce acted as a strong influence upon the British government, which managed to obtain favourable terms for itself in a trade treaty of 1734, including most favoured nation privileges in the overland route to the silk markets of Persia, with whom peace was restored with the return of her lost provinces in treaties of 1732 and 1735. For the French, the 'eastern barrier' of Sweden, Poland and Turkey was of considerable importance and constituted a persistent obstacle to rapprochement with Russia, nothing coming in the end of negotiations for a marriage between Elizabeth Petrovna and Louis XV, who married instead a daughter of Stanislaus Leszczynski. So family as well as state interest persuaded Louis when Augustus II of Poland died in early 1733 to support the candidature of Leszczynski who, having already from 1706 to 1709 sat on the throne of Poland as the client of the Swedish king, was more than happy now to climb on to it again as the client of his son-in-law the French king. Leszczynski was indeed crowned for a second time in September 1733 after French eloquence and money had impeded the advancement of the Russo-Austrian candidate, Frederick Augustus, Elector of Saxony and son of Augustus II. Almost immediately a Russian army under the command of the Irish General Count Peter Lacy assisted by the Scot James Keith invaded Poland, and King Stanislaus left Warsaw for Gdansk. A sufficient number of Polish and Lithuanian nobles could now be found to elect Augustus III in the Polish capital while Lacy laid siege to the Baltic seaport. A French fleet was sent to relieve Gdansk and managed to land a small military force, but this was captured and the fleet was routed. Gdansk fell in midsummer 1734 with Münnich, who had now assumed command of the Russian army, covering himself in glory while Leszczynski made an ignominious getaway disguised as a peasant. He abdicated for the second time at the beginning of 1736, after some Poles had put up at least token resistance to the Russian army which had been joined by another from Saxony. Meanwhile France had declared war on Austria, which had supported Augustus III without actually fighting for him, and enjoyed a number of early successes. But by the time that Russian troops commanded by Lacy came down near Heidelberg to render assistance in the summer of 1735, the French were willing to call the fighting to a halt, no doubt somewhat alarmed at the presence of the Russians on the Rhine. Lacy and his troops were soon recalled from Germany and all Russian and Saxon troops left Poland after an agreement with a confirmed Augustus III in the summer of 1736.

But by the time that the War of Polish Succession had been brought to an official end another conflict had already broken out, this time with Turkey. The struggle between Russia and Turkey for control of the Black Sea had now reached the point where Russians believed that their new-found imperial strength would carry them through to a permanent victory over an empire which was widely agreed to be on the wane. They prepared themselves for this new contest with the aforementioned treaties with Persia, which had promised 'eternal friendship' on the return of many of its Caspian provinces. Immediate reasons for war could easily be found in frontier disputes and the incursions of the Turkish clients, the Crimean Tatars. For their part, the Turks believed that their crescent was still on the wax and that they could consolidate the concessions wrung from Peter the Great at the River Prut. They were also fortified by their possession of powerful friends, the British and especially the French, who through their diplomatic representatives in Constantinople did all they could to stir up the Turks with flattery and cash, although stopping short of full alliance. If the Turks had not already been occupied with war against Persia their annoyance at the threat posed by the successes of the overweening Russians in Poland might well have aroused them sufficiently to strike the first blow. In fact, after frontier clashes with the Tatars in 1735, the Russians made the formal declaration in the spring of 1736, with the main army under Münnich being sent on the offensive towards the Crimea while a detachment under Lacy headed for Azov. In the beginning there was great success, Münnich breaking through the Perekop isthmus into the Crimea and sacking the Tatar capital of Bakhchisarai, while Lacy took Azov. But losses through battle and disease were high, and, apprehensive of Tatar reinforcements returning from the Caspian, both generals made tactical withdrawals before the end of the year. St Petersburg was alarmed, but then as the campaign of 1737 began became heartened by the capture of the Turkish stronghold of Ochakov at the confluence of the Dnepr and the Bug and crossroads of land communications between Turkey and the Crimea. Reassurance was also gained from the long-awaited announcement of Austria's entry into the war and subsequent news of early victories for her armies. Very soon peace negotiations were opened at the Polish border settlement of Nemirov, but the Austrians and the Russians both made exorbitant demands at the same time as each was anxious not to lose Moldavia and Wallachia to their ally, and the congress came to nothing at about the same time as Lacy drew back a Russian force from a second, this time unsuccessful, attempt to break into the Crimea. Lacy was still unable to break open the Perekop bottleneck in 1738, which altogether was a year of disaster for the Russians, who were forced also to give up Ochakov and other Black Sea acquisitions.

The wheel of fortune turned again in 1739, as an army under Münnich crossed the Dnepr to take Khotin and then Jassy, where a group of Moldavian nobles offered their crown to Anna, and the incorporation of the principality into the Russian Empire was soon formally arranged. Meanwhile, however, the Austrians had suffered costly losses and had decided to withdraw from the war even on somewhat humiliating terms. Their allies were now overexposed as well as overextended, and so they too had to talk peace. By the Treaty of Belgrade of September 1739, Russia was almost shut off once more from the Black and Azov Seas, on neither of which were there to be any of her ships, and while Azov was to be retained, the fortress itself was yet again to be taken down. Moldavian gains could not be kept and so in the end, although they held the usual elaborate celebrations, the Russians had little or nothing to show for the loss of 100,000 men and the expenditure of vast sums of money.

The Russian case at Belgrade was probably not helped at all by the mediating power, France, which had been alarmed by the size of potential Russian gains, and was simultaneously encouraging Russia's withdrawal from the Black Sea by doing all it could to build up pressure on the Baltic. With French encouragement a defensive alliance was concluded between Turkey and Sweden, and the negotiations between these two powers provided a reason for moving over to the offensive in the shape of the murder of an emissary from Stockholm to the Porte, Baron Malcolm Sinclair. This dark deed inspired a long and famous doleful Swedish ballad, and was kept fresh in the minds of the Swedish leaders until the right moment for attack appeared to have arrived in the summer of 1741, when Sweden had emerged from political crisis and Russia appeared to be deeply embroiled in it. But a Swedish army was soon routed in Finland, Elizabeth quickly turned out to be more of a patriot than the Swedish and French ambassadors had believed as they worked for her enthronement, and, after the removal of Osterman, his successor Bestuzhev-Riumin continued his rival's policy of antipathy towards France and support for Austria. So Swedish hopes for revenge were coming to nothing when the tsarist family's relations from Holstein made a further appearance on the international stage. The young duke Peter became Grand Duke of Russia in late 1742, a year in which desultory fighting had seen the Cossacks and other detachments continue their advances while diplomatic negotiations moved nowhere. And then, when a peace treaty was finally drawn up in the captured Finnish capital Abo in early 1743, the Russians put forward as one of the conditions for their almost wholesale withdrawal from the occupied territories the Swedish acceptance, as heir to their childless King Frederick, of Adolphus Frederick of Holstein, bishop of Lübeck and *locum tenens* for the infant Peter. But just as the French had been disappointed by Elizabeth, Adolphus Frederick was to dismay the Russians when, soon after arriving in Stockholm with a detachment of the Russian army in attendance, he married in 1744 a clever lady who was to dominate him and was none other than the sister of the recently enthroned Frederick II of Prussia.

Frederick II took quick advantage of the fact that just a few months after his accession in the spring of 1740 the Empress Anna of Russia and the Emperor Charles VI of Austria died within a few days of each other. He invaded Silesia in December, and attempted to carry the advantage home through further encroachments on Habsburg territory and infringements of the Pragmatic Sanction while Maria Theresa looked around in bewilderment for support and he himself received the full encouragement of France and Bavaria. Great Britain and Holland were too remote to take effective action, so Maria Theresa was forced to look principally towards the other new Empress Elizabeth, giving the Russian imperial title her recognition in 1742 and confirming it in 1746 in the hope that Russian leaders might forget the lukewarm support accorded them by their Austrian allies in the war against Turkey. At this time in fact Russian foreign policy contained several contradictions, including a defensive alliance with Prussia in 1743 soon after another with Great Britain promising mutual assistance in case of war and directed essentially against Prussia and its ally France. Although he had previously egged on France to keep Sweden at loggerheads with Russia, Frederick now claimed that he would have given Russia his support against Sweden if only he had not been occupied elsewhere, and hoped that the case for closer ties with him, including recognition of his acquisition of Silesia, would be forcefully put in St Petersburg by his admirers there, who included the Grand Duke Peter, his newly acquired wife and her mother, the younger and elder princesses of Anhalt-Zerbst. But Bestuzhev was more than a match for the Prussian party, whose task was in any case made more difficult in 1745 when after other expeditions elsewhere, Frederick invaded the lands of Russia's ally Saxony, whose elector was also Augustus III of Poland. The elder princess of Anhalt-Zerbst was sent home while her daughter, the future Catherine II, was, with her husband the future Peter III, held under close suspicion by Bestuzhev's agents.

In early 1745 in Warsaw an agreement was signed between Austria, Saxony, Great Britain and Holland, directed against Prussia. The signatories all hoped that, made anxious by the threat posed by Prussia to Courland and Livonia, Russia would soon join them. In 1746 Russia made a partial response by concluding a new treaty with Austria, each party contracting for twenty-five years to assist the other in case of attack by a third party, with some exceptions but especially with regard to Prussia. At about the same time, in a series of conventions, Russia was promising Great Britain in return for annual subsidies a supply of troops to be used against Prussia or its ally France. In January 1748 a Russian force under General Repnin did indeed set out for the Rhine, and, although it took a long time to get there and was never engaged in any actual fighting, it may have had some influence in convincing France that the time for peace had come, Prussia already having made a preliminary settlement with Austria and Saxony at the end of 1745. And so the War of Austrian Succession came to its formal end at Aix-la-Chapelle in October 1748, Prussia's retention of Silesia now being solemnised.

In this somewhat spare account the intractable complexities of mid-eighteenth-century diplomacy have necessarily been subject to much simplification and possibly some distortion. We have omitted such subjects as the feared and hoped-for Russian support for the Jacobite Rising of 1745. Owing to the nature of our primary focus we have so far neglected, moreover, to mention that the wars of the period possessed ramifications stretching not only into Asia but also westwards into the Atlantic world. The largest-scale conflict to which we must now turn, the Seven Years War, cannot be properly understood if we do not recall that as Austria, Prussia and Russia were struggling for mastery in central Europe, France and Great Britain, while by no means ignoring the continental theatre, were simultaneously preoccupied with the fight for dominance in North America and India. This is not to say that sometimes, their attention being given overmuch to the powers of western Europe and their overseas interests, historians have given insufficient attention to the continental theatre. After all, Prussia's consolidation of its Silesian gains was arguably as important for the future of Europe and of the world as Great Britain's victories at Quebec and Madras. Moreover, the prime origins of the war might also be found in the problems of readjustment which followed on from the War of Austrian Succession. According to at least some investigators of the question, the chief initiative for the outbreak of a new conflict came from Russia, which was presenting to its neighbours the problem of an expanding empire.[17]

Another problem was Great Britain's concern for the security of Hanover, in response to which a new alliance was drawn up in 1755 with Russia, renewing the agreements of the 1740s and binding Russia to keep in readiness an army of 55,000 and a navy of 40–50 galleys in return for financial subsidies. Russia's other principal ally Austria was smarting for revenge against Prussia, but Great Britain's major worry was France, a circumstance underlined with dramatic suddenness by the news of the convention signed at Westminster at the beginning of 1756 with none other than Prussia. Their worst suspicions now confirmed, his rivals were able to bring about the downfall of A. P. Bestuzhev-Riumin; even though diplomatic relations with his most favoured nation Great Britain were never completely broken, Russia drew much closer to Austria, and at the end of 1756 joined the defensive alliance agreed earlier on in that year by Austria with the traditional enemy, France. The diplomatic revolution was complete, and the main lines drawn up for a new war in Europe and the wider world.

In August 1756 Frederick II's army had struck the first continental blows, invading Saxony and soon capturing its major cities Dresden and Leipzig. In the summer of 1757, under pressure from a hard-pressed Austria, Russia sent an army into Eastern Prussia, and a great victory was won under S. F. Apraksin and P. A. Rumiantsev at Gross Jägerndorf. Then, perhaps because the Empress Elizabeth was sick almost unto death and might be replaced by the Prussophile Grand Duke Peter, the Commander-in-Chief Apraksin did not press home his advantage, withdrawing his army rather than sending it forward. For this he was arrested and put to trial, the charge of treason being simultaneously levelled at the fallen Bestuzhev-Riumin. Apraksin died before the case against him was completed, while Bestuzhev-Riumin survived to rise again at the accession of Catherine II.

Apraksin's replacement V. V. Fermor, of English descent, was ordered to take Eastern Prussia and duly moved into Königsberg and its hinterland at the beginning of 1758. But after some successes against the Prussian army in 1757 the Austrians had been beaten at Leuthen, Silesia, at the end of that year, just a month after a joint Franco-Saxon force had incurred a defeat at Rossbach, Saxony. Russia's allies were increasingly alarmed at the prospect of her expanding empire, so Austria and France made a secret agreement in May 1758 concerning the territories gained from Prussia. Making some gestures to appease such suspicion, the Russian army pressed on westwards, while the fleet in conjunction with that of Sweden (which had joined the anti-Prussian coalition in 1757) closed the Sound to the British. Frederick II made his stand or rather his swift counterattack at Zorndorf in August. Both sides suffered heavy losses in the bloodiest battle of the whole year, and both claimed victory, the Prussians with perhaps more justification, since the Russians did not press home any advantage that they might have gained and Berlin was at least for the moment saved as Fermor withdrew his army to the Vistula. Meanwhile, the Austrians defeated the Prussians at Hochkirch in Saxony in October, and one of Frederick's most trusted marshals James Keith was killed, but this too led to nothing.

The campaigns of 1759 began too slowly for St Petersburg's liking, and so Fermor was replaced by P. S. Saltykov, whose long service had not been particularly distinguished but who somehow managed to inspire more confidence. After some early successes, Saltykov succeeded in linking up with the Austrian general Laudon, and the joint force routed the Prussians at Kunersdorf near Frankfurt-on-Oder in early August. Once again, however, Berlin was saved, largely because of renewed differences among the anti-Prussian coalition about war aims, the Austrians and the French continuing to see in Russian expansionism a threat if anything even greater than that of the Prussians. And yet in the autumn of 1760 the disaster that had threatened Frederick II for so long, the loss of his capital, at last befell him, with A. B. Buturlin taking the place of the ailing Saltykov. Berlin paid the invading Russian and Austrian forces a large indemnity, but the occupation lasted for no more than a few days and the campaigns of 1760 once again ended indecisively. Voltaire would write to Alexander Shuvalov that the presence of the Russian troops in Berlin made a more agreeable impression than the complete works of Metastasio, but there might be some ambiguity here, and there must be little doubt that beneath the official congratulations of Russia's allies lay a deep unease.

So at the beginning of the year 1761, it was hardly surprising that France should indicate its intention of withdrawing from the war against Prussia and that Austria soon declared its interest in an early arrangement of a peace. Russia was therefore obliged to put a considerable effort into the struggle for Silesia, while also pushing through Pomerania, where the most distinguished Russian officer to emerge from the Seven Years War, P. A. Rumiantsev, managed to take the heavily guarded fortress of Kolberg by the end of the year, with some assistance from a squadron of the Baltic fleet. The way now appeared open again to Berlin, especially since Frederick II had been abandoned by his British ally after the new King George III, less interested in his Hanoverian heritage than George II, had received the resignation of William Pitt at the beginning of October, New Style. But the Prussian king and his cause were saved by the death of the Empress Elizabeth on Christmas Day 1761 according to the Old Style and the arrival on the throne of Peter III, an admirer of Frederick and all things Prussian.[18]

In retrospect, the conclusion of the Seven Years War can be seen to have been brought about by more than such accidents as the resignation of ministers and the death of monarchs. We may now easily enough understand that, having achieved its aims in its war against France after bringing in the New World to redress the balance in the Old, Great Britain had no further need to support its erstwhile ally. Similarly, Russia was beginning to realise that a Prussia defeated would not serve its interests any more than a Prussia triumphant, since a resurgent Poland or an expanded Austria could be at least as troublesome as Prussia still intact but somewhat subdued. As we shall see in the next chapter, a direct consequence of the Seven Years War was a great change in the configuration of states in Central and Eastern Europe, especially the partitions of Poland.

As we shall see now, Russians retained an interest after the death of Peter the Great in the rest of the world as well as Europe. Conscious that they were not active in the ocean that formed the centre of the Western world, the Atlantic, we tend to forget that after their Danish Captain Vitus Bering had given his name to the Strait at the northern end of the Pacific, they developed their interest in the great ocean to the east and completed the European global circle, so to speak, by making landings on the west coast of North America. In the summer of 1728, continuing the work first commissioned by Peter the Great, Bering himself set sail from the river that bears the same name as the peninsula on what has become known as the First Kamchatka Expedition. Back in St Petersburg in 1730, Bering found that the government was not yet convinced that his Strait separated the continents of Eurasia and North America. After others had made further forays down the coast of what was known as the 'Big Land', Bering himself directed the Second Kamchatka Expedition or Great Northern Expedition of 1733–43. This succeeded in charting the coast at the extremities of both sides of the Pacific, and brought the Russians into contact with the human and other animal inhabitants of the adjoining regions. The skins of the otters and seals became a most attractive lure for all kinds of adventurers who roamed further and further in search of such lucrative prizes as the more accessible supplies became exhausted about the middle of the century.[19]

Meanwhile adventurous exploration continued in the by no means completely charted vastness of Siberia, and the grasp of the administration also extended itself further than before. If the entrepreneurs grabbed as many furs as they could, the government officials fleeced the local people as much as possible for tribute. At the same time Russian landward probes were being made into Central Asia, where the Kazakh tribes had been weakened in a bitter struggle with fearsome neighbours and sought a lesser evil in the shape of protection by the tsar. The protectorate was nominal in the beginning, but became more complete as the century wore on. *En route* for Central Asia, Russian expeditions frequently fell foul of the Bashkirs, who were far from happy at the prospect of their incorporation into the Empire, which was signalled in 1735 by the foundation of the fortress of Orenburg at the confluence of the Rivers Or and Iaik (later Ural). Alarmed further by the news of more tribute and greater services, the Bashkirs revolted and were not finally subdued until 1738. The government now set to work to build a new defensive line centred on Orenburg, and then in 1744 created a province with the same name as the capital city. To appraise the extension of the south-eastern frontier in the informed words of Alton S. Donnelly: 'Russians were motivated by much the same complex mixture of economic interest, desire for strategic position, and belief in their own moral and cultural superiority as were the other European imperialistic peoples of the age.'[20] Russian methods were military conquest supplemented by diplomatic manoeuvre of rivalry between Kazakhs, Bashkirs and other peoples and within the ranks of the various tribes themselves.

Immediately behind the frontier regions less pioneering landlords were consolidating their holdings and expanding them. The second census begun in 1744 showed that the population in general had risen by nearly 3 million to a total of 18,250,000 in about twenty-five years, with the steepest percentage increase occurring in peripheral areas such as the Lower Volga and Northern Urals to the east and the Left Bank Ukraine to the west.[21] Most of the population were, of course, peasants belonging to the state or to private owners, of whom members of the imperial family were the greatest, and the highest churchmen not inconsiderable, but the most numerous the nobles. Among these Menshikov was almost in a class by himself, possessing at the zenith of his power in 1727 estates in forty different districts of European Russia with a total register of over 300,000 male and female serfs. He owned about 3,000 villages and hamlets and seven towns, and took a close personal interest in the administration of them, assisted by a large team of stewards and bailiffs. He could hardly be called an improving landlord, however, showing more interest in extracting income than inculcating a higher level of husbandry.[22] In this respect, he resembled his lesser fellows, who also concentrated more on discipline than incentive, and gave detailed instructions to their estate managers for tasks of the farming year to be rigidly executed with appropriate penalties for idleness or insubordination. Generally speaking there were three strata of noble landlords, assessed not so much by acreage as by quantity of serfs. Rather less than a fifth of them each owned over one hundred male serfs and together about 80 per cent of the total; rather more than a fifth each owned between twenty and a hundred souls, about 15 per cent of the total; and the remaining three-fifths each owned less than twenty souls, about 5 per cent of the total. Here was the fundamental underpinning of the socio-political structure of the nobility that influenced the nature of the successive regimes between 1725 and 1762 and the manner of their coming to power.

As far as the economy as a whole is concerned, there has been a persistent assertion that after the death of Peter the Great activity gave way to lassitude with a steep decline in many production figures. In fact, as in many other branches of the national life, the shadow of the larger than life personality of the tsar reformer has led to an inaccurate assessment. In agriculture, the most ubiquitous pursuit yet also the most difficult to assess in any quantitative manner, the overwhelming impression is of peasants following the plough and wielding the sickle in a manner which their grandfathers would have found completely recognisable. But landlords or their officials were increasingly interested in the profitability of their estates, and a continuing tendency towards specialisation may be detected in certain areas, sometimes with the export as well as more often with the domestic market in mind. As for petty manufacturing and heavy industry alike, there appears to have been expansion rather than contraction, especially for the former in and around the old capital and the new, and for the latter in the Urals, where the Demidov family was accompanying the Stroganov towards great riches. As far as trade was concerned, the internal branch was bringing its twigs closer together, so to speak, with the more positive articulation of the all-Russian market around such nodal points as the capitals, Novgorod and Nizhny Novgorod. In Europe, although rarely faring abroad in person, Russian merchants were making their impact through the export of such items as hemp and flax, hides, tallow and naval materials, linen and iron. The balance of trade was in Russia's favour, to the satisfaction of a protectionist government, which was also pleased to see imports consisting partly of useful items such as woollen goods and dyestuffs and partly of luxury comestibles and fabrics for the delectation of its own members and their associates. The most important trading associate to the west was Great Britain, soon to experience the world's first industrial revolution and receiving no small impetus in that direction from its links with Russia, which also extended over to Persia. The Anglo-Russian Trade Treaty of 1734 gave Great Britain special privileges with regard to the Persian silk trade as well as a number of other concessions which aroused the indignation of some Russian merchants engaged in Asia at the time and some Soviet historians swayed by patriotism later.[23]

During the period following the death of Peter the Great the state reversed his policies of control and intervention, lowering the tariff in 1731 if raising it again by 1757, becoming less involved in industry and abolishing internal customs in the 1750s. But, of course, this by no means meant that there was any less interest on the part of state officials in extracting as much income as possible from its subjects, whether by direct or indirect means. Projects continued to abound for making up arrears, achieving set targets and exceeding estimates. At mid century, of a total income of about 11,500,000 roubles, just under half came from the direct poll tax and *iasak* tribute, and somewhat less from indirect taxes and the state trade in alcoholic drinks and salt, the balance being made up by such means as the mint and the post and levies on industry. At about this time over 70 per cent of expenditure went on the army and to a considerably lesser extent the navy, while about 10 per cent each went on administration and tax collection, with most of the rest going on the court.[24] These approximate figures should not be taken to mean that the Russian budget was properly balanced or even anywhere near efficiently organised before the later part of the eighteenth century, even though it was perhaps less rough and ready than during the reign of Peter the Great.

In a somewhat similar manner, the period between his death and the accession of Catherine the Great may be looked on as a period of transition in the cultural sphere. In the stimulating analysis of Paul Miliukov, the Elizabethan generation of educated people embodied a movement from the practical emphasis of the Petrine era to the more philosophical outlook of the Catherinian, with the role of enlightener being taken over by members of the nobility from the hands of the Supreme Power. This socialisation of initiative was assisted by the Supreme Power itself, a decree of early 1748 commanding the Academy of Sciences to attempt 'to translate and print in the Russian language civil books of various kinds in which use and amusement would be united with a pronounced bias towards the secular life'. The St Petersburg newspaper advertised for translators, and publication developed quickly in the 1750s.[25]

The manner in which the subsequent activity affected members of the upper class is well illustrated in the memoirs of an outstanding member of the middle stratum of the nobility, A. T. Bolotov, who was born in 1738 and therefore coming to maturity in the decade in question. 'Everything which is now called the good life was only just coming into existence then,' he wrote of the year 1752, 'as well as a keen popular taste for it all.' Bolotov continued: 'Very tender love, supported by tender and amorous songs in verse, was then just beginning to assert its power over young people, and very few songs were known by heart, but they were all the rage, and whenever one appeared, it was always on the lips of the young girls and ladies.' Many of these came from German or, increasingly, French, but at least some were of Russian composition, including those from the tragedy of *Artistona* by A. P. Sumarokov. Bolotov's consciousness, which was to find ample room for scientific information as well as the words of love songs, was very much developed in service abroad during the Seven Years War.[26]

By this time the first Russian journals publishing articles on an equally wide-ranging number of subjects were making their appearance, the best known of them being the *Monthly Selections* edited by the Academician historian G. F. Müller with a staff including Sumarokov and other young Russians. History and geography were to be found in these journals side by side with more uplifting topics aiming at the victory of reason over the passions and the correction and formation of good morals. Another feature of these journals was their translated presentation of pieces from the *Spectator* and other journals, German as well as English. Translation was difficult enough, but the heavier burden fell upon those like Sumarokov and V. K. Trediakovsky who were trying with mixed success to render European verse forms in Russian. Joining them in this task and engaging in many others was the widely talented M. V. Lomonosov.

It needs to be recalled that the development of Russian literature and thought was carried out by a minute number of people, some of whom like Müller were foreigners. At its peak the journal that he edited, the *Monthly Selections*, had a subscription of no more than 700 readers and the other journals were even less well supported. The majority of educated Russians, learning to read and write in the church, military or civilian schools or under the care of tutors, remained faithful to the ways of their parents, making little attempt to break away from the strict path of service pointed out by Peter the Great. The Academy of Sciences in St Petersburg opened by his widow in 1725 and the University of Moscow inaugurated by his daughter in 1755 were like the journals in that they produced for a select group only, and from this elite there had not yet emerged enough independently minded individuals for discussion to be possible of the formation of a Russian intelligentsia.

On the other hand, even before the arrival on its throne of Elizabeth, the Empire had produced at least a handful of well-educated men capable of setting out their ideas in a coherent manner. It is certainly difficult to agree completely with P. P. Epifanov that 'already in the first decades of the eighteenth century Russia was one of the world centres of the formation of enlightenment and . . . Russian thinkers brought their own original contributions to its progressive movement'.[27] Nevertheless, each of the members of the group known as the 'Learned Guard' to which Epifanov made his principal reference were remarkable enough for his assertion to merit considerably more than summary dismissal. Feofan Prokopovich we have already briefly met as outstanding churchman and apologist for Peter the Great. A. D. Kantemir was an urbane dilettante ambassador, at home in the salons of London and Paris. And V. N. Tatishchev was a man of many parts, historian, geographer, ethnographer and lexicographer as well as diplomat and administrator.

The writings of Tatishchev varied from the first ever study of the mammoth to an early modern rationale for Russian absolutism, which may appropriately be given a closer examination here. Tatishchev's 'Voluntary and Agreed Dissertation of the Assembled Russian Nobility about the State Government' was ostensibly composed at the time of the constitutional crisis accompanying the accession of Anna in 1730, but was in fact probably composed at a somewhat later date. Its essential argument is an unwitting elaboration of the remark concerning Russia made about the crisis by James Keith and quoted above to the effect that 'the genius of the nation, and the vast extent of the empire, demands a Souverain, and even an absolute one'. As Tatishchev put it, 'Great and spacious states with many envious neighbours' could not be ruled by aristocracy or democracy, 'particularly where the people is insufficiently enlightened by education and keeps the law through terror, and not from good conduct, or knowledge of good and evil'. He supported his basic thesis with examples taken from the Europe of his own day and of classical antiquity and was able to make use for his own purposes of the works of such authorities as Pufendorf and Grotius, Hobbes and Locke, Leibniz and Wolff. He was also, in however tentative and restrained a manner, moving forward to a rational acceptance of absolutism which in diluted form would come to be accepted by peers far less learned than he was himself. In such a manner what Peter the Great was attempting to impose from above, the nobility would be coming round positively to welcome from below.[28]

During the reigns of his immediate successors, then, the work of the tsar-reformer was rounded out. If the most significant renovation and extension to the structure of the empire was carried out by their ministers and lesser subjects, the rulers themselves made a distinctive contribution in the patronage that they gave to the architects who were responsible for its actual as opposed to its figurative building. In the comparatively relaxed atmosphere of the mid-eighteenth century, the daughter of Peter the Great could employ Bartolomeo Francesco Rastrelli and his like to refine and enlarge the ideas of her father for the palaces in and around the city of St Petersburg.

NOTES

1. E. C. Thaden, *Russia's Western Borderlands, 1710–1870* (Princeton, 1984), pp. 5–17.
2. R. V. Ovchinnikov (ed.), 'Krushenie poluderzhavnogo vlastelina (dokumenty sledstvennogo dela kniazia A. D. Menshikova', *Voprosy istorii*, no. 9 (1970).
3. James Keith, *A Fragment of a Memoir . . . 1714–1734* (Edinburgh, 1843), p. 84, S. M. Troitsky, 'Istoriografiia "dvortsovykh perevorotov" v Rossii XVIII v.', *Voprosy istorii*, no. 2 (1966); A. Yanov, 'The Drama of the Time of Troubles, 1725–30', *Canadian-American Slavic Studies*, vol. 12 (1978). And see I. de Madariaga, 'Portrait of an Eighteenth-Century Russian Statesman: Prince D. M. Golitsyn,' *Slavonic Review*, vol. 62 (1984).
4. Quoted in A. Romanovich-Slavatinsky, *Dvorianstvo v Rossii s nachala XVIII veka do otmeny krepostnogo prava* (Kiev, 1912), p. 70.
5. Keith, *A Fragment*, pp. 87–90.
6. B. Meehan-Waters, 'Elite Politics and Autocratic Power' in A. G. Cross (ed.), *Great Britain and Russia in the Eighteenth Century: Contacts and Comparisons* (Newtonville, 1979), p. 235; *Autocracy and Aristocracy: The Russian Service Elite of 1730* (New Brunswick, NJ, 1982), p. 142. See also J. P. LeDonne, 'Ruling Families in the Russian Political Order, 1689–1825,' *Cahiers du monde russe et sovietique*, vol. 28 (1989).
7. P. Dukes, *Catherine the Great and the Russian Nobility* (Cambridge, 1967), pp. 36–7.
8. J. L. H. Keep, 'The Secret Chancellery, the Guards and the Dynastic Crisis of 1740–1', *Forschungen für osteuropäishe Geschichte, vol. 25* (Berlin, 1978), p. 193.
9. S. O. Shmidt, 'Vnutrenniaia politika tsarizma vo vtoroi chetverti XVIII v. in L. G. Beskrovny *et al.* (eds) *Istoriia SSSR*, pervaia seriia vol. 3, (Moscow, 1967), pp. 264–73; N. I. Pavlenko, 'Idei absoliutizma v zakonodatelstve XVIII v.' in N. M. Druzhinin et al. (eds), *Absoliutizm v Rossi (XVII–XVIIIvv.)* (Moscow, 1964), pp. 411–12. And generally see E. V. Anisimov, *Rossiia v seredine XVIII veka: Borba za nasledie Petra* (Moscow, 1986).
10. S. M. Troitsky, *Russkii absoliutizm i dvorianstvo XVIIIv: formirovanie biurokraktii,* (Moscow, 1974) pp. 128–32.
11. V. Klyuchevsky, *Peter the Great*, trans. L. Archibald (London and New York, 1958), p. 246; M. M. Bogolovsky, *Oblastnaia reforma Petra Velikogo: provintsiia, 1719–1727* (Moscow, 1902), pp. 463–4.
12. Ibid., pp. 490–91.
13. Ibid., pp. 494, 517; Iu. V. Gote, *Istoriia oblastnogo upravleniia v Rossii ot Petra I do Ekateriny II*, vol. 1 (Moscow, 1913), p. 48.
14. P. Dukes, 'Catherine II's Enlightened Absolutism and the Problem of Serfdom' in W. E. Butler (ed.), *Russian Law: Historical and Political Perspectives* (Leyden, 1977), p. 113.

15. L. G. Beskrovny, *Russkaia armiia i flot v XVIII veke* (Moscow, 1958), pp. 63–9.
16. M. T. Florinsky, *Russia: A History and an Interpretation*, vol. 1, (New York, 1955), p. 353, modified by G. A. Nekrasov, *Rol Rossii v evropeiskoi mezhdunarodnoi politike, 1725–1739gg.* (Moscow, 1976), p. 312.
17. H. H. Kaplan, *Russia and the Outbreak of the Seven Years War* (Cambridge and Berkeley, 1968) develops a suggestion by Herbert Butterfield.
18. This survey of the Seven Years War taken mainly from N. Korobkov, *Semiletniaia voina (deistviia Rossii v 1756–1762gg.)* (Moscow, 1940) including reference to Voltaire on p. 285.
19. D. M. Lebedev and V. I. Grekov, 'Geographical Exploration by the Russians' in H. R. Friis (ed.), *The Pacific Basin: A History of Its Geographical Exploration* (New York, 1967), pp. 175–83.
20. A. S. Donnelly, *The Russian Conquest of Bashkiria, 1522–1740: A Case Study in Imperialism* (New Haven, 1968), p. 273.
21. V. M. Kabuzan, *Izmeneniia v razmeshchenii naseleniia Rossii v XVIII – pervoi polovine XIXv.* (Moscow, 1971), p. 52.
22. S. M. Troitsky, 'Khoziaistvo krupnogo sanovnika Rossii v pervoi chetverti XVIII v. (po arkhivu kniazia A. D. Menshikova)', in N. I. Pavlenko (ed.), *Rossiia v period reform Petra I* (Moscow, 1973).
23. D. K. Reading, *The Anglo-Russian Commercial Treaty of 1734* (London and New Haven, 1938).
24. S. M. Troitsky, *Finansovaia politika russkogo absoliutizma v XVIII veke* (Moscow, 1966), pp. 214, 242–5.
25. P. N. Miliukov, *Ocherki po istorii russkoi kultury*, vol. 3 (Paris, 1937), pp. 267–93.
26. Marc Raeff (intro.), *Zhizn i prikliucheniia Andreia Bolotova*, reprint (Newtonville, 1974) vol. 1, p. 169. And see J. L. Rice, 'The Memoirs of A. T. Bolotov and Russian Literary History', in A. G. Cross ed., *Russian Literature in the Age of Catherine the Great* (Oxford, 1976).
27. P. P. Epifanov, '"Uchenaia druzhina" i prosvetitelstvo XVIII veka', *Voprosy istorii* (1963), no. 3, p. 53.
28. P. Dukes (trans. ed. and intro.), *Russia under Catherine the Great: Volume One: Select Documents on Government and Society* (Newtonville, 1978), pp. 17, 22. On Tatishchev, see various works by A. I. Iukht, including *Gosudarstvennaia deiatelnost V. N. Tatishcheva v 20-kh – nachale 30-kh godov XVIIIv* (Moscow, 1985). See also R. V. Daniels, *V. N. Tatishchev; Guardian of the Petrine Revolution* (Philadelphia, 1973).

CHAPTER FIVE

Enlightened completion: Peter III and Catherine the Great, 1761–1796

The death of Peter the Great's daughter, the Empress Elizabeth, on Christmas Day, 1761, brought to an end the Romanov dynasty as descended through the male line. She was followed by her sister Anna's son, Peter III, also Duke of Holstein, who would rather have been a Prussian, and then by his wife, Catherine II, originally Princess of Anhalt-Zerbst, later widely known as 'the Great', who did her best to assume the nationality of her adoptive homeland. The story of how this couple came from Germany to be part of the Russian court and then in turn its centrepiece forms an important preliminary to a discussion of their respective reigns. Unfortunately, especially for Peter, a much used source for the telling of this story has been the *Memoirs* of Catherine, which not only took the point of view of the narrator but were much amended to her own advantage after their first composition. For example, in an early version Catherine gives her first impression of Peter as really handsome, obliging and well brought up; later he becomes 'a permanent patch upon a very beautiful face'. In the final rewriting she talks more than before about Peter's origin and childhood, possibly to emphasise his foreign origin, and far less than before about her own early days, possibly to disguise her own provenance. Similarly, she gives emphasis to Peter's affection for Lutheranism, while saying very little about her own conversion from it to Orthodoxy. Generally as the *Memoirs* progressed through at least half a dozen versions, not only did Peter appear in a worse light: so did the Empress Elizabeth. Meanwhile Catherine herself took on a more agreeable aura. For example, she stressed the quantity, quality and breadth of her reading. She grew more certain about having learned French at the age of three; the reason for a later serious illness turned out to be her labours into the night to make more rapid progress in learning Russian. Her involvement in intrigue to secure herself the succession received less attention as she became more positive about Elizabeth, making her the heir to the Russian throne in the event of the death of Peter. Altogether, lapses of memory and random changes of mind appear to have been less responsible for successive alterations in the *Memoirs* than a conscious desire to make the best possible impression, and this aim was furthered by the fact that they constitute the most complete and successful of her literary works.[1]

In spite of their bias, a weakness after all shared to some degree or another by any historical source, Catherine the Great's *Memoirs* cannot be ignored when we come to look at the thirty-three years or so of her life that she spent before becoming Empress. On the other hand, we must use them sparingly if at all when we turn first to look at her husband who was about a year older than her, born Charles Peter Ulrich on 10 February 1728 to Anna Petrovna and her estranged husband Charles Frederick of Holstein-Gottorp. Heir not only to his father but also to the King of Sweden, and arguably with a stronger title to the Russian throne than his maternal aunt Elizabeth, the young man was quite a catch for any ambitious woman looking for a good match for a daughter, and into this category certainly came the Princess Joanna Elizabeth of Holstein-Gottorp, an aunt on his father's side, as we shall soon see. For the moment to revert to the aunt who became Empress of Russia, a year or so after she came to power she invited Peter, by now an orphan, to come from Kiel to St Petersburg to consolidate officially his claim to the succession. No doubt she believed that any threat on his part would be less severe if she could keep the young man under her surveillance. Moreover, if he were proclaimed heir presumptive, the claim of the potential Ivan VI, the dying Empress Anna's appointee, would be much reduced. And so, after the customary conversion to Orthodoxy the Grand Duke Peter as he was now to be known was duly announced to the world as next in line to the Empress Elizabeth on 7 November 1742. About three years later, when he was seventeen years old, he took a wife, or rather, as these matters were arranged among royal families at the time, was given one; on 21 August 1745 (at about the time incidentally that Elizabeth herself was receiving proposals made on behalf of Charles Edward Stuart, pretender to the British throne) the Empress of Russia presided over the marriage of the future Peter III to the future Catherine II.

The secrets of the bedchamber and the other rooms in which the young couple attempted to make a life together have been transmitted to us almost exclusively from the point of view of Catherine, as already noted above, so they cannot detain us long. Even she says they were happy enough to play together like children, although she also asserts that Peter was incapable of behaving in the adult manner basic to their marriage. However, if their union was certainly far from perfect, beyond all reasonable doubt it did produce one blessing on 20 September 1754 in the shape of the future Emperor Paul; not only did the young man for better or worse come to resemble his father, but Peter would not have been likely to seek out mistresses for the sole purpose of joining him in his games with toy soldiers. True, his wife's predilection for extramarital dalliance appears to have been stronger and more indulged than his own. Generally speaking, however, neither the sexual proclivities nor indeed the other aspects of the personality of an individual who occupied the throne for a bare six months can be given full investigation here, interesting and controversial though they might be. Just two points should be given brief emphasis, perhaps. The first is that Peter alienated not only his wife but also his aunt; his Prussian sympathies and admiration for Frederick the Great especially made him anathema to her during the Seven Years War. Secondly, both at the time and since there have been commentators on him and his reign prepared to give them a more favourable appraisal than would either Catherine or Elizabeth. R. Nisbet Bain wrote in a biography of Peter III published at the beginning of this century:

Peter was notoriously unfit for ruling an Empire, but he would have made a good average eighteenth-century *junker* or squire. His heart was good if his head was weak; although anything but a hero himself, he was capable of an exalted hero worship; and a Prince who could conduct an orchestra and plan a library should not in fairness be stigmatised as a mere idiot.[2]

Back in the summer of 1762 our man in St Petersburg Robert Keith talked of

this unhappy Prince, who had many excellent qualities, and who never did a violent or cruel action in the course of his short reign, but who from an abhorrence to business, owing to a bad education, and the unhappy choice of favourites who encouraged him in it, let everything run into confusion, and by a mistaken notion he had conceived of having secured the affections of the nation by the great favours he had so nobly bestowed upon them, after his first mounting the throne, fell into indolence and insecurity that proved fatal to him.

In his dispatch of 1 July 1762 to George Grenville in London, Keith went on to give the reasons for the overthrow of Peter III so soon after his accession on Christmas Day 1761. First in Keith's view was his takeover of many church lands and his neglect of the clergy. Next came the severe discipline that the Emperor had attempted to impose upon the army, especially the Guards who had become accustomed to great 'idleness and licence'. Military resentment was intensified by Peter's decision to lead many of his troops into battle against Denmark for the recovery of his ancestral domains in Schleswig and to the further relief of the hard-pressed Frederick the Great of Prussia. Peace would have been welcome to the Russians, Keith believed, but Peter was determined to go further.[3]

In retrospect it is possible to accept the interpretation of Peter's downfall presented by Keith without the attribution to the factors in question of either the same order of precedence or the same lack of rational premeditation. And so, looking around him for models to give him the necessary aura of strength and resolution, Peter III did not make implausible choices in Peter the Great and Frederick the Great, and, in his insecure floundering for survival, his attempt at imposing discipline upon some of the Guards who had already taken 'freedom and liberty' to the point of 'idleness and licence' was perhaps the most characteristic piece of emulation. True, calling the Guards to order would mean running the risk of another palace revolution, but that risk had to be balanced against another, the weariness of those involved in a war which for Russians would not go on for a full seven years, but had certainly lost for many of its participants much of its early glitter. For this reason withdrawal from the war was by no means unpopular, and it is also quite possible that many who had been involved in the hostilities would realise that a Prussia completely defeated would be just as dangerous for stability and security in Central and Eastern Europe as a Prussia carrying all before it. As for the Danish adventure, although the following consideration was in all probability lost on most of those called upon to participate in it, it certainly contained within it more than a distant echo of the policy during the Northern War of the revered Peter the Great, both in its attempt to secure for Russia a greater measure of control over the vital entrance into the Baltic and in its indulgence of a tsar's wish to involve himself in the petty affairs of his German relations. And as for his policy towards the Church, here again Peter III was acting in the tradition of his illustrious predecessor, and at the same time making like him an extraordinary effort to supply the artery of war – money.

Against such a background we must now take a closer look at Peter's most celebrated enactment, the Manifesto on the Freedom of the Nobility of 18 February 1762, about which Richard Pipes has written: 'Altogether, it is difficult to exaggerate the importance of the edict of 1762 for Russia's social and cultural history. With this single act the monarchy created a large, privileged, Westernised leisure class, such as Russia had never known before'.[4] Yet perhaps the most striking aspect of the decree is the relative paucity of its remarks about such a class, even about freedom. Looked at closely, the Manifesto consists of a long preamble and nine clauses. The preamble talks of the compulsion necessarily used by Peter the Great, but then goes on to say that cultural advancement, especially as fostered by the Empress Elizabeth, has rendered that compulsion superfluous:

coarseness in those who neglect good has been eradicated, ignorance has been transformed into healthy reason, useful knowledge and assiduity in service have increased the number of skilful and brave generals in military affairs, have put informed and suitable people in civil and political affairs, to conclude in a word, noble thoughts have implanted in the hearts of all true Russian patriots a boundless loyalty and love for Us, a great enthusiasm and unceasing fervency for service, and therefore We do not find that necessity for compulsion in service, which was in effect up to this time.

And so, freedom and liberty, *volnost i svoboda*, would be bestowed on the whole Russian nobility, but they could then on the basis of the nine clauses not so much live in fruitful retirement as 'continue service both in Our Empire and in other European states allied to Us'.

The nine clauses do indeed discuss continuance in service far more than departure from it. Thus, clause 1 is mostly concerned to point out that officers cannot retire just before or during campaigns, and that permission has to be given by their commanders or, in the case of the top eight ranks, by the Emperor himself. Clause 2 certainly begins by mentioning arrangements for awarding one more rank to those retiring, but then gives instructions about how the transfer may be made from military to civil service. Clause 3 is totally concerned with transfer of service or re-entry into it and contains the insistence that 'those serving should have advantage and preference before those not serving'. Clause 4 begins by stating that an emancipated noble may go abroad, but then insists that he should come back as soon as the necessary order is made 'under pain of sequestration of his estate'. Clause 5 deals with the manner in which nobles returning from service abroad may re-enter the Russian service. Clause 6 is devoted mainly to reviving an order of Peter the Great, that retired nobles should elect annually a fifth of their number to assist the work of the Senate. Clause 7 requires young nobles to undergo an examination at the age of twelve, and specifies the appropriate arrangements to be made for their continued education. The clause concludes:

However, so that nobody should dare to bring up their children without teaching them the subjects fitting for the noble *dvorianstvo* under pain of Our wrath, for this We order all those *dvoriane* who have not more than a thousand peasants to report their children directly to Our Noble Military Academy, where they will be educated with the most enthusiastic care and each will leave with a reward of ranks appropriate to his educational achievement and later enter and continue service according to the above prescription.

As many as 99 per cent of the nobles were obliged to send their twelve-year-old sons to the Military Academy, which would have been bursting at the seams had the obligation been strictly fulfilled, while the other 1 per cent would have to use part of their great wealth to make their own arrangements for the continuation of their children's education. Clause 8 forbade nobles below the rank of commissioned officer to retire unless they had done more than twelve years service. Finally, Clause 9 is clear enough in its encouragement of service and condemnation of its avoidance. Here are its final remarks:

We hope that the whole noble *dvorianstvo*, appreciative of our generosity to them and their descendants, will be inspired by their most dutiful loyalty to Us and their zeal, not to absent or hide themselves from service, but to enter it with pride and enthusiasm, and continue it in an honourable and decent manner to the extent of their ability, and none the less teaching children suitable subjects with diligence and application, because all those who have not been in service anywhere, but spend all their time in sloth and idleness, and do not subject their children to any useful education for the benefit of the fatherland, these as they are negligent of the common good, We command all Our obedient and true sons to despise and scorn, and they will not be allowed to appear at Our Court, or at public meetings and celebrations.[5]

To sum up, in the authoritative view of V. O. Klyuchevsky, the decree did no more than abolish the obligatory *length* of service. The great historian declared: 'The law said: be so good, serve and teach your children, and, nevertheless, he who does neither the one nor the other will be driven from society.' As for the decree's references to freedom, Klyuchevsky argued that these were misunderstood by many contemporaries accustomed to think in a manner less sophisticated than those producing the decree.[6]

We must now turn to look at the Manifesto on the Freedom of the Nobility, as we did at the Table of Ranks, in its international context. The first point to emphasise here is that, if the Northern War brought the Russian Empire firmly on to the European stage, the Seven Years War confirmed it in a leading part. As Marx and Engels said, the war brought face to face with the other powers of the continent 'a united, homogeneous, young, quickly growing Russia, almost invulnerable and inaccessible to conquest'. And if in the early 1720s Russia might have appeared as remote to the advisers of Louis XV as did France to the Senate of Peter the Great, by the early 1760s Louis XV himself was necessarily taking an interest in Russia's policies, and also seeing the sense of his brother monarch Peter III's *volte-face*, observing: 'Europe by no means wanted the destruction of Prussia under the onslaught of two strong powers: on the contrary, she wanted Russia to stand up for Prussia. When peace between the powers was concluded, if Austria had increased her possessions at the expense of Prussia, she would have measured strength with Russia . . .'[7] By this time, too, the reputation of Peter the Great had grown to vast proportions, as had that of the power of the state bequeathed by him to his successors. At the beginning of the Seven Years War, the Abbé Coyer wrote: 'We have seen the Russians not long ago advance towards the Rhine in order to fight us, and in the present crisis they are already preparing their arms.' In order that France could build up its strength, Frenchmen would have to imitate Peter and the Russians, especially the nobility. The Abbé declared:

Gentlemen: Learn to become Nobles. And you, Kings. Contemplate Tsar Peter, to be Great. He was cabin boy in his infant Navy to found the Commerce and the Power of Russia. A leading Magistrate must take all forms to do good; and so everything leads towards order, everything towards his glory; the Arts, the Sciences, Agriculture and Commerce.[8]

The debate between the Abbé Coyer and the Chevalier d'Arcq concerning the part to be played in the French state by the nobility was in many ways running parallel to that being conducted by the Shuvalovs and Vorontsovs in Russia.[9] All the states participating in the Seven Years War were hard pressed for finance and for the best possible method of making use of their human resources including their leading classes.

But the Manifesto of 1762 does not appear to have been as specifically influenced by foreign models as had been the Table of Ranks, to a considerable extent no doubt the result of Russia's burgeoning self-confidence. True, the first recorded mention of the measure by Peter III was at the Senate on 17 January 1762 as follows:

Out of His high mercy towards his loyal subjects, /He/ graciously deigned to order the nobles to continue their service according to their/own/ wish for as long and wherever they want to; and in wartime they would have to present themselves /for duty/; and draft a form /project/ on the same basis as it is done with the nobles from Livland and submit it with all the circumstances for the signature of His Imperial Majesty.

As Marc Raeff says:

The most tantalizing element . . . is the reference to the situation prevailing in Livland, a reference that may also suggest the idea stemmed from the German-Baltic entourage of the emperor. If acted upon, it would have implied introducing into Russia the whole nexus of genuine 'feudal' rights and privileges, most significantly those of local self-government and police, rights and privileges that the Baltic nobles had retained even after the Swedish and Russian conquests. But neither the manifesto itself nor any later legislation pursued these implications.[10]

And so, while there was much talk at this time in Scandinavia, especially in Sweden, of liberty and the parts to be played by the social classes, there appears to have been no more direct connection between it and that being conducted in Russia than in the above-mentioned case of France. Scandinavia, like France, was responding in its own way to the pressures brought about by the Seven Years War. And so was Prussia, where Frederick was finding it necessary to consider again the ideology of his state and the role of the Junkers. But Peter III does not seem to have introduced the Manifesto of 1762 in emulation of his living hero; possibly he was taking a retrospective look of approval at his dead hero and grandfather, Peter the Great, who had certainly contemplated the introduction into Russia of the *landrat* system of the Baltic provinces.

Ultimately the Manifesto on the Freedom of the Nobility is best viewed in a context which establishes both its domestic and its international setting. On the one hand it was an important move forwards in the alleviation of the harsh service conditions that Peter the Great had attempted to impose upon the newly formed *dvorianstvo*, leading onwards from decrees passed in the first years of the reign of Anna towards the Charter of the Nobility to be announced by Catherine the Great in 1785. On the other hand it was a measure partly of demobilisation and partly of readjustment of role to solve a problem confronting nobilities throughout Europe at the end of the Seven Years War. Should the upper class become more of an aloof aristocracy or approach the condition of the Third Estate and become embourgeoisified? Variants of this question were posed from St Petersburg to Lisbon.

However, the significance of the Manifesto should not be too highly evaluated. Several other measures introduced during the short reign of Peter III would call for further examination if they did not share with the Manifesto one fundamental weakness. As noted above by the British ambassador Robert Keith, the secularisation of the church estates and reform of the Guards were of considerable potential importance. So were such other measures as the abolition of the secret police, relaxation of controls over grain exports and limited encouragement of religious toleration. But while his successor could not ignore any of these policies, she would definitely want to give them her own imprimatur, to modify them or even to rescind them as she saw fit. Therefore, fundamentally, the Manifesto on the Freedom of the Nobility as well as Peter III's other enactments must be examined as much from the point of view of their adaptation by Catherine the Great as from that of their initial implementation by her luckless husband Peter III.

Such assessments will be made along with others after we have gone back in time to say something of Catherine's early life and of the manner in which she came to ascend the throne. Of her thirty-three years up to her accession, just under half had been spent in her native land, Germany, from which conglomeration of states also came her two parents. Her father, Christian August of Anhalt-Zerbst, was far from the nonentity that some biographers of his daughter have made of him. True, he was one of the seemingly innumerable minor princes of the Holy Roman Empire that could be found in Northern Germany at the time, but few of them rose as he did in the onerous service of the King of Prussia to become general field-marshal or governor of an important city, which he was when Sophia Augusta Frederika as she was first christened was born on 21 April 1729 in the Baltic port of Stettin. Christian August would probably have preferred a son, although apparently he was pleased enough to sire a daughter in his middle age. He grew quite close to the young girl, and no doubt instilled in her at least some of his ideals of duty and service if not that of punctilious attention to detail. As for the future Catherine the Great's mother, Joanna Elizabeth Princess of Holstein-Gottorp, whom we have already briefly met, she too might have preferred a son as a firstborn but was determined to do the best she could with what she had been given instead, and almost certainly succeeded in transmitting some of her ambitiousness to her eldest child. Like many other people who have made their mark in adult life, Catherine suffered from a serious illness in her youth and had to struggle to overcome this hurdle as well as that of the comparative neglect by her mother when two brothers followed her into the world. Of course, as would be customary with young girls of her rank, the princess had nurses and governesses as well as parents, and these too exerted great influence over her upbringing. To give an example, Elizabeth Cardel, born at Frankfurt-on-Oder into a refugee Huguenot family, not only taught her to read and write at least after a fashion in both German and French and gave her at least a first if somewhat superficial acquaintance with literature, but also afforded a measure of emotional stability in a family which was by no means completely happy as the old soldier bickered with his younger wife. According to Catherine's own later account, the first conscious stirrings of ambition were inculcated in her by her father's official adviser and personal friend, Dr Laurentius Bolhagen, who, observing that a lesser princess, Augusta of Saxe-Gotha, had been married to the Prince of Wales, began to wonder what future awaited Sophia Augusta Frederika herself. The *Memoirs* continue: 'He then proceeded to preach to me wisdom and all the moral and Christian virtues which would make me worthy of a crown, if it were to be my fate to wear one. This idea of a crown began running in my head then like a tune . . .' (According to Klyuchevsky, an old canon from Brunswick had said to Catherine's mother that he could see at least three crowns on her daughter's brow.)[11]

The world outside Germany was fully introduced to the young German princess by a Swedish diplomat, Adolf Henning Count von Gyllenburg, who met her mother and her in the autumn of 1743, and engaged them in cultured conversation, some of which appears to have been a paraphrase of Voltaire. This contact was resumed a few months after Catherine's removal to Russia in 1744, and was continued intermittently for several years onwards. At the first reunion, Gyllenburg accused her of abandoning her philosophical enquiries for the public and behind the scenes activities of court life, but she stoutly defended herself against these charges at the same time as making sure that she was making a full adaptation to her new environment. Her transition was assisted by Simon Theodorsky, an Orthodox priest with pietistic leanings who had studied at both Kiev and Halle and who believed that the theological gap between his own faith and that of the Lutherans was not as great as implied by the respective ceremonials, although the respective rites had to be scrupulously observed by those who shared his ecumenical outlook so that untutored congregations would not perceive any threat to their faith. Catherine was sensitive to the power of such arguments, and was already treading warily with regard to the faith and customs of Russia at the same time as learning as much as she could about life in her new environment. She still liked people, but experience at court soon taught her to be more wary about them than before, especially since she and her husband and their associates were closely watched by a suspicious Elizabeth.

According to her own story, Ekaterina Alekseevna, as she had now become according to Orthodox custom, turned increasingly to her own private world in which a prominent place was occupied by serious literature. She wrote in her *Memoirs*: 'At that time, it could have been said of me that I was never without a book and never without sorrow, but also never without amusement. My disposition, cheerful by nature, did not in the meantime suffer under these circumstances; the hope of a prospect, if not of a heavenly, at least of an earthly crown, kept my spirit and my courage firm.'[12] What did she read? A prominent place on her bookshelf was occupied by Voltaire, with whom she was to enter into a personal correspondence after her accession to power, and from whom before that she gained much of her enlightened outlook. The great man's *Universal History*, for example, would have given her a wider view of human development than she possessed previously, and made her think about the characteristics of peoples as well as the personalities of their rulers. Not that she lacked for heroes among her predecessors as crowned heads of Europe, another of the works that she read with avowed profit being Hardouin de Péréfixe's history of King Henry the Great, that is Henry IV of France. That monarch's version of early enlightened absolutism as represented by Péréfixe and others strongly recommended itself to Catherine as a model for her to follow later. But she also read Machiavelli's *The Prince* and many classics, too, as well as the renowned contemporary of Voltaire, Montesquieu, whose *Spirit of the Laws* was to become her acknowledged 'prayer-book'.

The literary studies of the Grand Duchess did not take up all her time by any means; she still sought human contact, including that of the most intimate kind. In the 1750s she took the first in her celebrated long line of lovers, the Russian Sergei Saltykov and the Pole Stanislaus Poniatowski. And a less amorous if still intense relationship was pursued with one of the British ambassadors, Sir Charles Hanbury-Williams, with whose scarcely moral support and considerable pecuniary assistance Catherine schemed to secure for herself a stronger influence over the succession to the throne. Already perhaps, as the Empress Elizabeth took ill and was obviously nearing the end of her days, Catherine was beginning to think that her own hour was about to come, and that she would be able to manipulate to her own advantage the more immediate right to the crown of her husband and son. She attempted, for example, to ensure the latter's inheritance even if the former's were taken away, and then, if Peter were robbed, she would almost certainly not when the appropriate time came have paid Paul.

An alert woman such as Catherine undoubtedly was could not have been at court for more than fifteen years during late adolescence and early adulthood without assimilating a considerable amount of local history. She learned from some of the participants what had happened at the accession of two other women, the Empresses Anna and Elizabeth, especially after Peter had announced an amnesty for many courtiers banished for alleged misdeeds or support given to failed candidates for the throne. She would therefore have a considerable understanding of what to do and what not to do in gaining the crown that she had promised herself and others had forecast for her. Peter III, as we have seen above, was unpopular, if not so much for his policies as for his methods of carrying them out, and had alienated patriotic Russians in general, and in particular the Guards and sections of the army as well as the Senate and other important administrative bodies in addition to the Church. If the Guards were no longer as powerful as they had been during the reign of Peter the Great, as the process developed of regularisation and modernisation of armed forces and bureaucracy alike, they could still make an Empress or break an Emperor at critical moments such as that arising in the summer of 1762, and Catherine was indeed fortunate that her lover at that time was a popular Guards officer with four conveniently placed brothers and other useful connections. Gregory and the other Orlovs were joined in a party hurriedly gathering around the Grand Duchess by Count N. I. Panin, tutor to the tsarevich Paul, the Princess Dashkova (originally a Vorontsov and also Peter III's god-daughter) and a number of other disgruntled nobles, most hoping for personal advancement, just a few possibly hoping for the dawn of a new age. The actual seizure of power took place in a somewhat confused manner at the time of Peter's proposed march against Denmark, and the Orlovs led the way, relieving Peter of his power and soon afterwards (to Catherine's genuine or feigned dismay) of his life. A manifesto announced to all the people on 28 June 1762 that:

Our Orthodox church is being menaced by the adoption of foreign rites: our military prestige, raised so high by our victorious army, is being degraded by the conclusion of a dishonourable peace. All the respected traditions of our fatherland are being trampled underfoot. So we, being conscious that it is the honest desire of all our loyal subjects, and having God and justice on our side, have ascended the throne as Catherine II, autocrat of all the Russias.

Summarising the reasons for the coup in a more succinct manner in a letter to Poniatowksi, Gregory Orlov's predecessor, Catherine wrote: 'You must know that everything was carried out on the principle of hatred of the foreigner: Peter III himself counted as such.'[13]

Undoubtedly, she now considered herself to be autocrat of all the Russias, whatever the flimsiness of her right to that title, which in the event of her husband's removal should have gone to her son. The new Empress quickly set about the task of consolidating her position on the throne of the Romanovs. One small obstacle was Ivan VI, still alive two decades after his overthrow by the associates of the Empress Elizabeth in 1741 but murdered in 1764 by some of Catherine's supporters among the Guards, and with her encouragement. Peter III, whose death was not so directly her personal responsibility, made an unwelcome posthumous return in the shape of several pretenders claiming to be him, most notably a Don Cossack named Emelian Pugachev whom we shall introduce more fully below. And there were other threats to the new Empress both real and imagined. Throughout the 1760s peasant disturbance was endemic, while William Richardson, a Scottish visitor of the decade, wrote concerning unrest at the higher social level: 'Rumours of conspiracies are secretly propagated; several persons, I have heard, either guilty or suspected of treason, have disappeared: but these things are not noised abroad, they are only mentioned in confidential whispers. The people are prohibited from speaking or writing about politics . . . The spies are busy: the suspected great men are closely watched.'[14]

At least one of the threats has been deemed to have been ideological as well as personal; this was the so-called attempt at oligarchy by Nikita Panin, not only tutor to the Grand Duke Paul but also Catherine's adviser on a number of other matters. Just after her accession there was a considerable amount of discussion about the creation of a top advisory body or imperial council, with the Empress herself issuing a short manifesto on the subject in 1762 and Panin writing a long memorandum about it. Some commentators have seen this as a veiled attempt to create an aristocratic government in the tradition of that sought by the Supreme Privy Councillors in 1730, but Soviet and Western historians now seem for the most part agreed that Panin was aiming at administrative reform as his memorandum said rather than at anything more revolutionary as it could be taken to imply.[15]

Panin began his memorandum by discussing the difficulties of conducting the business of the Senate and other organs of government and of effecting a smooth relationship between them. Confusion compounded natural human idleness, and 'thus a senator, or any other official, arrives at the meetings like the guest to a dinner, who not only does not yet know the food's taste, but not even the dishes which he will be served'. The sovereign could not translate easily into action a concern for improvement in this sorry state of affairs 'except by intelligently apportioning it among a small number of persons specially selected for this purpose'. The reign of Elizabeth had shown how far personal caprice could make worse an already sorry state of affairs, but the new Empress could produce as a result of a long reign, 'the age of Catherine the Great, surpassing in its excellence that of all your predecessors on the Russian throne', especially if she created an imperial council and at the same time divided the Senate into six departments; by such a measure, the legislative branch of government would be separated from the executive.[16]

Upon receipt of Panin's memorandum Catherine moved fairly quickly to reform the Senate, and the six divisions were duly created by a decree of 15 December 1763. The first and most important of the new departments was to concern itself with a wide variety of economic and administrative affairs, and the Procurator-General was to be in charge of it, while the other five were to deal in turn with: petitions and appeals; the Ukraine, Finland and Baltic provinces, higher academic affairs, ports, communications and police; army and navy, young noble academies, the Smolensk nobility, customs posts and New Serbia; state business in Moscow; and appeals against the second department. Here still was a somewhat exotic and over-varied menu for the senators and their associates, but at least there was some improvement on the previous potluck. Moreover, on the same 15 December 1763, there were more decrees announced attempting to put order into provincial government through a rise in the pay of its officials and a regulation of their sphere of duties, as well as an increase in their number. And then in the following year came the biggest revision since the 1720s of the Table of Ranks, which introduced academicians and factory managers and readjusted several of the rungs in the ladder of promotion in both central and local government, one of the more significant upward movements being that of the office of Heraldmaster.

Here was an indication that Catherine and her entourage were interested in putting right the ambiguity in the position of the Empire's chief servants as described in the Manifesto of 1762, although her published papers for the first two and a half years of her reign, down to the end of 1764, reveal no great interest in the emancipation of the nobility, either as a class or as individuals. Most of her statements concerning the *dvorianstvo* or *dvoriane* are concerned with rewards in land or more usually money and with advantages to be gained in service rather than liberation from it. True, she is reported to have written to Nikita Panin at the beginning of 1763 that there was a certain amount of murmuring among the nobility about the non-confirmation of its privileges, although she wrote 'not much' and the editor suggests that she meant 'not a little'.[17] Catherine went on to say that something must be done about the murmuring, of whatever proportion, and she certainly set up at about this time a Commission on the Freedom of the Nobility, to review and tidy up the decree of Peter III. But again, this Commission devoted most of its attention to conditions of duties in the armed forces and bureaucracy and very little of it to emancipation from them, although there was a considerable amount of discussion of their role as landlords.[18] Among the individual cases considered by Catherine was the request by one of the members of that Commission and one of the most prominent men in the government, Michael Vorontsov, for permission to quit his post because of illness and to go abroad for the good of his health. This 'true slave' used the obsequious language customary to all courtiers in the eighteenth century and made no reference to the Manifesto, although he was one of its probable progenitors. Far from granting his abject petition to the full, Catherine met no more than his minimum entreaty, allowing him to leave Russia for two years only, at the end of which period of leave he would have to return to resume his former ranks and functions.[19] If this were the treatment accorded one of the highest men in the land, what could those lower down the Table expect if their wishes did not accord with those of the imperial establishment? While the nobility constituted in most senses the ruling class, its separate members were little more in a position after 1762 than they had been before to make themselves exceptions to the governmental system established by Peter the Great and modified rather than changed by his successors. If many *dvoriane* did indeed request permission to retire from service on the basis of the Manifesto of 1762, there is little evidence that the class as a whole felt that it was starting to play a part in society independent of the state, which it continued to see as the source of its commands but also of its welfare.[20]

True, at a time when there was no great international crisis calling for the full-scale employment of the Russian armed forces and when life in the provinces was becoming more settled, there was the concomitant necessity to contemplate an increased responsibility for members of the nobility in local government. During the first years of her reign Catherine made the attempt to go out from the capitals to see for herself how her administration functioned away from the big cities; she was also the recipient of several suggestions on how it could be improved, from members of the Commission on the Freedom of the Nobility, for example, or from advisers on the preparation of the decrees of 15 December 1763 noted briefly above. Two major schools of thought emerged on the question, both assigning to the *dvorianstvo* a more active involvement in local government, but one giving emphasis to its close integration in the bureaucratic structure, the other wanting to allow it a somewhat more independent elective voice. The gap between these two schools must not be exaggerated, since provincial elections were suggested earlier in the century by Peter the Great to whom any kind of apartness from the state of the ruling class would have been anathema. What was certain was that some kind of wholesale reform of local government was overdue, and that in any new system the functions ascribed to the *dvorianstvo* would be of critical importance.

Meanwhile, as far as central government was concerned, an imperial council, if not as suggested by Panin, took on an informal existence in the shape of the Committee on the Freedom of the Nobility, whose members became the founder members of the Council when it was given formal recognition in 1768. Moreover, her appointment of Prince A. A. Viazemsky as Procurator-General in 1764 showed that Catherine was keen to make this office as important in her administration as it had been in that of Peter the Great. And in her letter of appointment to him, she revealed something of her view of the Empire during the first years of her reign, talking by implication if not by name of the parties attached to the Orlovs and the Panins and the manner in which they must be manipulated to the advantage of the fatherland. She complained of bureaucratic delays, and made an early avowal of her belief as to the only possible cure for them:

The Russian Empire is so large, that apart from the Autocratic Sovereign every other form of government is harmful to it, because all others are slower in their execution and contain a great multitude of various horrors, which lead to the disintegration of power and strength more than that of one Sovereign, who possesses all the means for the eradication of all harm and looks on the general good as his own, and others are all, in the words of the Gospel, hirelings.

From the court itself to the peripheral regions, the Sovereign and her Procurator-General would have to be vigilant in order to ensure uprightness and efficiency. As far as his immediate subordinates were concerned, Viazemsky would do well to recall the observation of the sagacious Richelieu that 'there was less difficulty for him to govern the state and arrange Europe according to his intensions than to rule the King's Antechamber' and he should be encouraged by his possession of an authority not given to the Cardinal – 'to replace all the doubtful and suspicious without mercy'. In his dealings with the Ukraine and the Baltic provinces that possessed their confirmed privileges, Viazemsky must try to ensure that they 'by the easiest of means be brought to the point where they would russify and cease to look like wolves to the forest'. This would be done if reasonable people were chosen as commanders in these provinces. Generally speaking, Catherine declared that the laws of the Empire demanded correction,[21] and for this ostensible purpose she was soon to convene a special Legislative Commission.

But before taking a closer look at this important moment in her domestic policy, we must briefly look at her solutions to the pressing problems of foreign policy that confronted her during the first five years or so of her reign. Immediately on her accession she had to decide what to do about Russia's involvement in the final phase of the Seven Years War, and while she would have been surprised by the observation of Louis XV that she continued in this regard 'to adhere to the system of her predecessor', there is much now to be said for the argument that there was indeed a greater measure of continuity between her aims and those of Peter III than she would have admitted or many analysts have discerned. True, Catherine quickly withdrew her troops from the projected war against Denmark, but although an early manifesto of hers referred to Frederick the Great as Russia's 'worst enemy', she also took her troops out of Prussia and confirmed the peace treaty that Peter III had concluded with Frederick earlier in 1762. Somewhat disappointed at the polite refusal of her offers of mediation in the negotiations bringing to an end the Seven Years War, the Empress had already no desire to be ignored for long by the powers of Europe even though her principal aims in the early years were peace and stability. Moreover, the acknowledged strength of Russian arms would give solid backing to the assertiveness of her personality.

Inevitably she was drawn closer to Frederick, especially after the death of King Augustus III of Poland in late 1763. Earlier in the year Catherine had made Courland a virtual Russian protectorate, and now she wanted to ensure at the very least that its feudal superior, the King of Poland, would not be hostile to her interests. As the customary election drew near, France and Austria both gave their support to continuance of the Saxon line in the shape of the son of Augustus III and former Duke of Courland, Prince Charles. Negotiations in progress between Russia and Prussia now took on an earnest immediacy, and an alliance treaty between the two powers was concluded in St Petersburg at the end of March 1764. Each was to render aid if the other were attacked, and both were to work together for the maintenance of the *status quo* in Sweden and particularly in Poland, where they were also to afford protection against Catholic persecution to the Orthodox and Protestant minorities. For the pursuit of such objectives they agreed that the best candidate for the Polish throne was Catherine's former lover, Stanislaus Poniatowski, who at first appeared pliant enough, and was duly elected in September 1764, without immediate recognition from the Bourbons and Habsburgs but equally without any opposition from them.

In the years immediately following the election of Poniatowski, Russia and Prussia grew closer together in their attitude to the Polish problem and to other questions too. Frederick had recommended as far back as his Political Testament of 1752 that Polish Prussia be 'eaten like an artichoke, leaf by leaf ... now a town, now a district, until the whole has been eaten up'[22] and came to realise that with the acquiescence of Catherine he could fully satisfy his appetite. He made skilful use of her apprehension concerning the Ottoman Empire to bring her over to his point of view. The Empress for her part was coming round fairly quickly to the understanding that vast opportunities had been presented to her through her association with Frederick for the reunification of the historic Western Russian lands with the Eastern. Meanwhile the Poles believed in the maintenance of as much of their independence as possible in the face of this twin threat even if they could not agree among themselves about the best way of realising this desirable aim.

On the wider European stage France, Austria and Turkey would be especially unhappy at any dismemberment of Poland while the suspicions of other powers were somewhat aroused, Great Britain for example holding back from participation in what Catherine's chief adviser on foreign affairs Nikita Panin called his 'Northern System'. A defensive treaty between Russia and Denmark was drawn up in 1765, but Great Britain would not go beyond a commercial treaty in 1766. Panin was soon to discover that a neat theory bringing together like-minded nations and inhibiting precipitate changes in foreign policy could not be fully implemented in the actual messy world.

In a somewhat similar manner his patroness was about to learn that to declare that 'Our laws demand correction' was much easier than to carry out such correction, if that is what she really wanted to do, since motives other than legal reform have been discerned in her convocation in the summer of 1767 of the Commission for the Composition of a Plan of a New Code of Laws.[23] Did she want to achieve a firmer guarantee of her hold on the throne of the Romanovs by calling together in the tradition of the *zemsky sobor* an assembly of the whole land, and to gain more security through her new code just as Alexis had entrenched his position with the *Ulozhenie* of 1649? Was she anxious to impose order on Russian society, especially on the nobility that had harboured ideas above its appointed station ever since the so-called emancipation of 1762, at the same time giving some encouragement to her adopted country's relatively weak Third Estate? Or was this a subtle device for reducing the centrifugal tendencies of the Empire's outlying provinces and subjecting them to gentle russification? Or, now that she was in correspondence with Voltaire and beginning to cut a fine figure in the eyes of enlightened Europe, could the Commission become an effective advertisement of her refined ideas and estimable intentions?

To a certain extent the answer to these questions may be found in the treatise that Catherine composed specially for the Commission, her *Nakaz* or Instruction, although it is also necessary to read between its lines. As the Empress herself said, not everybody would understand the document fully on first reading, yet frequent perusal would give guidance for the deliberations of the deputies to the Commission and to anybody else who cared to make the effort. The variety of interpretation that the *Nakaz* is capable of promoting may readily be gauged in the different evaluations made by the great Klyuchevsky. At first he saw in it 'not an historical stage of our legislative progress, but a purely pathological phase; not a factor in our country's record, but a feature in the biography of the document's composer'. Later he was to argue that it contained the basis for a form of government to be identified as 'personal-constitutional absolutism'.[24] Making acknowledged use of authorities such as Montesquieu, whose *Spirit of the Laws* provided the basis for nearly half of the treatise, and Beccaria, whose *Crime and Punishment* was the source for a further sixth, along with the smaller but still significant borrowings from Bielfeld and Justi of the German 'cameralist' school, from the Encyclopedists and even from Adam Smith, Catherine did manage to put together a fairly coherent argument. Of the various kinds of government identified by political philosophers, absolutism was the most appropriate for Russia because of its size and level of cultural development. Only an autocrat could give life to the necessarily large bureaucracy, whose internal good order coupled with the subordination of all subjects to uniform justice would be a guarantor of the rule of law. Not only the nobility but also the other classes would be expected to perform suitable kinds of service for the fatherland, and while the vast majority enchained in the institution of serfdom could not immediately be manumitted, 'The Law may establish something useful for vesting Property in Slaves.'[25] As a whole the *Nakaz* may be saluted as the most vigorous attempt by a Russian ruler to explain the nature of tsarist power and the necessity for it, even if its practical influence, both short-term and long-term, if far from negligible, was not very profound, partly because its author had to exercise a certain amount of restraint in what she said and did to appease the prejudices of her advisers, high-ranking members of the nobility and usually owners of many serfs.

Such prejudices also severely restricted the fulfilment of the ostensible purpose of the Legislative Commission. Whenever the central problem of serfdom was raised, most deputies from the nobility indicated their strong opposition to any change in the condition of the peasants, and the one or two who (possibly with the encouragement of Catherine herself) supported the suggestion of the *Nakaz* that limited property rights for the 'slaves' might be to the ultimate general benefit, received the most frosty response from their classmates. The serfs themselves were not directly represented at the Commission, which was generally dominated by the nobility with the town representatives playing a secondary part even though they were in numerical majority. As for the meetings, they were unruly for the most part and without much sense of direction of purpose. The *Nakaz*, which was often referred to, might have given inspiration but afforded no direct guidance; the Marshal of the Commission and his associates appear to have been bemused and weighed down by their responsibilities. After mostly regular meetings in Moscow from the end of July to the middle of December 1767, the Commmission adjourned to reconvene in St Petersburg in mid February 1768, which it duly did but with decreasingly frequent sessions; in mid December 1768 it was finally adjourned, never to meet again. The official reason for its dismissal was the outbreak of war with Turkey, and no doubt the attention of the Empress was now concentrated on that and other problems of foreign policy.

However, with the end as well as the beginning of the Legislative Commission, there has been a considerable amount of discussion among historians about Catherine's underlying motives. The level of debate was much too low and open to ridicule for the assembly to lend any support to her campaign to reveal herself to the world as an enlightener. The representatives of the outlying provinces gave little sign of wanting to struggle against their fuller incorporation into the Empire, while those from the Third Estate had found it difficult to hold their own against the more vociferous noblemen. As for Catherine's personal security, this seemed assured as the deputies appeared to be falling over each other in their attempt to achieve the most abject level of obsequiousness, agreeing together to offer her the title of Great and

All-Wise Mother of the Fatherland, which she modestly rejected. As well as all these possible underlying motives and the explicit reason given for the dissolution of the Commission, there is the manifest further consideration that the new law code for the composition of which it was created was no nearer realisation after a year of meetings than it had been before they began. True, some of its committees remained in existence for a number of years, and these did make some small contribution to Russian legal history. More significantly, the *nakazy* or instructions that the deputies elected by the nobility and the Third Estate brought with them to the Commission gave the Empress and her government a vast amount of information about life in the provinces and the worries and wishes of those who lived there. We shall be returning to them as a source for our understanding today of the realities of Russian life over two hundred years ago.[26]

For the moment we must move from internal affairs to consider the foreign problems that confronted Catherine and her advisers at the end of the 1760s and the war that resulted from them. As implied above, the Seven Years War had cleared up some aspects of the international confusion of the mid eighteenth century only to make others more complicated. As far as Eastern and Central Europe were concerned, Prussia and Russia had both firmly established themselves as great powers by the standards of the times, but only at the cost of other former great powers, especially Poland. A strong reaction against the diminution of their country's power set in amongst various Polish groups during the first years of the reign of Stanislaus Poniatowski. The king himself was by no means as pliant as Catherine expected her former lover to be, seeking in the diplomatic field for an improvement in relations with Austria and France as well as leading towards reform in domestic policy. Catherine, who like Frederick II opposed such reform, agreeing with him that 'Poland ought to be kept in lethargy',[27] was also made strongly aware by deputies to her Legislative Commission of fears concerning the drain across the border of runaway serfs and the infiltration in the other direction of ideas tending to undermine Orthodoxy. She therefore used the Russian army in an attempt to oblige the Poles to acquiesce with her preferences for them and their policies, and by 1768 had rendered Poland virtually a vassal state. In February of that year a treaty placed the Polish constitution under eternal Russian protection and gave full rights to non-Catholic religious dissidents. But this in turn led to the formation in early 1768 of an armed Confederation at the Southern Ukrainian town of Bar not far from the Turkish border. Supported by many nobles and aimed at the defence of faith and freedom, the Confederation's activity was accompanied by a widespread revolt among the peasants of the Ukrainian borderlands for similar causes, although differently propounded. With the Russians giving their military aid to royal forces attempting to restore order, a civil war of a somewhat confused nature engulfed large parts of Poland. Further foreign intervention, notably by Austria and France, alarmed Frederick and Catherine and pushed them towards agreement about partition.

In Catherine's case, her worries about the disturbances in Poland were accompanied from the autumn of 1768 by others about the war that broke out then with Turkey. The serenity of the Sublime Porte had already been disturbed for some time by what it considered to be Russian encroachments on its sphere of influence. Like every other power bordering on Poland, it was concerned with the manner in which the decline and impending fall of this once great kingdom was likely to affect its own security, and was especially alarmed when its old enemy Russia appeared to be claiming by far the most generous share in any future dismemberment. Other interested parties, especially France, did all they could to excite the frenzy of the Turks, a task that was made all the easier in the summer of 1768 as the Polish civil war spilled over into Turkish border villages. After Russia had rejected demands for withdrawal not only from the border regions but the rest of Poland as well, Turkey arrested the Russian ambassador and his suite and imprisoned them, and then declared war.

Such an outbreak of hostilities was not completely unwelcome to Catherine's entourage. Even the Empress herself, who had expressed many pacifist sentiments in her earlier life, was already to some extent carried away by the thought of what glory might be achieved by war as well as what she might do to realise the dreams of Peter the Great and other predecessors. She was finding it increasingly difficult to resist the arguments of the brothers Orlov who were pointing out how through the extension of her patronage to the Orthodox victims of Turkish oppression she could help create new independent states around the Black Sea and thus work towards the expulsion of the infidel from Europe. In such a manner the Third Rome would reclaim the inheritance of the Second Rome, Byzantium, for more than three hundred years under Moslem thrall.

Russian strategy for the war almost matched the scale of such grandiose ambitions. Possibly there would be an expedition into the Caucasus; certainly while the army moved on Constantinople by land, the navy would sail from the Baltic to the Mediterranean to break the Turkish fleet and to incite the local Christians to revolt. The revolt did not ensue, but the victories at sea and on land did. True, although they had the ships, the men and the money too, the Russians did not take Constantinople. On the other hand, in the summer of 1770 there were great naval victories at Scio or Chios and Chesme off the coast of Anatolia, where Turkish sea power was reduced nearly to nothing. The fame of this triumph was trumpeted throughout Europe, with Alexis Orlov nominally in charge taking much of the credit for himself, but also being man enough to attribute at least some to the real victors, who included the Russian Admiral G. A. Spiridov and the Scottish Rear-

Admirals John Elphinston and Samuel Greig. Meanwhile, on land, after Russian detachments had taken Azov and Taganrog in early 1769, an army under Count P. A. Rumiantsev later in the year pushed the Turks beyond the Danube. In 1770 and 1771 the Russian army enjoyed mixed fortunes in that region, with some splendid successes but also a few dismal failures; by the end of that period elsewhere the Crimea had been taken while the Polish confederates were suffering some serious reverses.

Negotiations for peace had begun as early as 1770, but the Turks were encouraged to keep going by the French, who saw them, the Poles and the Swedes as the bulwarks of an 'Eastern barrier' against the growing Russian menace. Prussia and Austria were also alarmed at the spread of Russian influence and took what steps they could to counter it without involving themselves in hostilities. These steps included what might be called pre-emptive encroachments on the territory of the other sick man of Europe, Poland, and led in their turn to the First Partition of that by now most unhappy country in 1772. As far as the Russian share was concerned, Soviet historians follow some of the tsarist predecessors in arguing that White Russian and other areas taken over at this time did not include any truly Polish lands and were appropriate for assimilation by their closely related big brother. To be sure, a certain amount of stability, if only temporary, was now brought to Central Europe.[28]

Meanwhile both the war and negotiations to terminate it were continued with Turkey. Because of plague in Moscow and at the front, the threat of war with Sweden and the pressure of other European powers, the Russian government was ever keener for peace. But the ambitions of Orlov, hoping to realise his dreams of empire until he was replaced as official favourite in the summer of 1772, and the more general Russian insistence that the Crimea should be handed over, both proved stumbling blocks. And so, after a pause of several months, the war was renewed early in 1773, and the Empress herself was among the most enthusiastic supporters of the argument that it should now be carried on to complete victory. Although this policy ran the risk of further alienation of the other interested European parties, it proved to be mostly successful as Rumiantsev and Suvorov and other military leaders achieved a series of considerable further victories for Russian arms. The Turks were driven towards acceptance of unfavourable peace terms. By the Treaty of Kuchuk-Kainardzhi of July 1774 the chief bone of contention, the Crimea, was given an independent status, although Kerch and Enikale were retained by Russia, as was a considerable amount of the Black Sea littoral, from the Bug to the Dnepr, around the Kuban and Terek, while possession of Azov was confirmed without restriction and Russia received the right of free navigation in the Black Sea and into the Mediterranean. The Turks paid an indemnity of over 4 million roubles, and although they retained formal jurisdiction over

Moldavia and Wallachia, in fact they lost much of their control over these Danubian principalities. Even the days of an independent Crimea were already numbered, but perhaps the most significant clauses for the future were those containing some rather vague rights of Russian protection over the Orthodox subjects of the Sultan, which could be used as an excuse for an intervention in the future Bulgaria, Greece, Romania and Serbia.

The terms of the treaty might have been even harsher if in the end Catherine had not been pushed towards conclusion of the war by the outbreak of a large-scale internal conflict, the movement led by the Don Cossack Emelian Pugachev. At first dismissed by the government as a rising on the River Iaik with only local importance, by 1774 it had grown to such proportions that it had to be taken very seriously indeed, and regular troops were brought into action in order to suppress it. Not only Cossacks, but also Bashkir and other tribesmen, Ural factory workers and latterly the serfs of the landlords came to be involved, and a great fear penetrated the central provinces to reach as far as Moscow and St Petersburg themselves. More widespread and more profound than its predecessors led by Bolotnikov, Razin and Bulavin, the movement led by E. I. Pugachev deserves most completely the label of 'peasant war', while the man himself was distinguished enough to arouse in Pushkin if not the poet then certainly the writer of fiction and history.

In a historical coincidence stranger than a fictional presentation would dare to suggest, Pugachev was born in the same Don settlement as Razin, the year being 1742 or thereabouts. At the age of seventeen he received the command to enter military service, in which he quickly showed enough acumen to be appointed orderly to a Cossack colonel named Denisov, who by another odd coincidence was to help suppress the rising led by his former underling fifteen years or so later. In the Seven Years War Pugachev was deemed to demonstrate 'outstanding alertness', although he was also soundly whipped for allowing a horse to run away. In 1762 the young Cossack was allowed to return home to his wife and son, but was soon sent off for further service in White Russia and was later involved in the war against Turkey, in which he performed sufficiently well to be promoted to a rank equivalent to cornet. Back home on sick leave he decided not to return to the arduous duties of the military campaign, and this decision made it necessary for him to take flight. At the River Iaik in 1772 he discovered an incendiary situation that inflamed his desertion into open mutiny and promoted him from junior officer to commander-in-chief, from commoner to monarch.

Right from the beginning of her reign by no means all her subjects were happy with their new Empress, and there had been a certain amount of social disturbance in both city and countryside. In 1771, for example, Moscow itself was profoundly shaken by a revolt closely associated with the plague that had struck the old capital after the outbreak of the war with Turkey. Among other groups in the provinces, the Cossacks of the Iaik had already risen up against an unpopular government inspector who had come to investigate their grievances but who appeared to symbolise all the encroachments on their liberties of the central government, and had killed this General Traubenberg and some of their own leaders at the beginning of 1772. By this time widespread discontent had been reflected in the announcement on more than twenty occasions of a return to life of the murdered Peter III, who since his death had been transformed into a symbol of justice and vengeance by the 'naive monarchism' that constituted the basic ideological outlook of the people at large. Pugachev did not find it difficult to include himself in this seditious line of succession, and had already been twice arrested on suspicion of such personating treason before assuming the leadership of the revolt that came to bear his name.

The peasant war under the leadership of E. I. Pugachev was fought in three phases. In his first edict of 17 September 1773, the 'sovereign imperial highness Peter Fedorovich' commanded the Cossacks, Kalmyks and Tatars to serve him in return for rewards consisting of 'the river from the heights to the mouth, and land, and meadows, and money payment, and lead and powder, and grain supplies'. Other decrees soon followed, attempting to bring into the ranks of Pugachev's followers the peoples and factory workers of the Urals and the soldiers, each of which groups was given incentives according to their station, including religious freedom and advancement. In the opening phase of the *Pugachevshchina*, however, top priority was given to the siege of the most important government stronghold on the River Iaik, Orenburg, and other activities near to the original seat of the dissatisfaction of the Cossacks and their allies. Then, at the beginning of 1774, as Orenburg held out, the revolt turned its chief attention to the Ural region, from which it hoped to receive armaments and support from the factory workers and to arouse the hostility towards Catherine and her adherents of the local tribesmen, notably the Bashkirs. Already detachments of these peoples were wreaking havoc and arousing trepidation in places comparatively remote from their homelands and the central insurgent army, and they continued to do so in an elusive manner all the more disturbing to the authorities who did not know where the next blow at them was coming from. The regular army units sent out to squash the impostor and his motley band of followers found it very difficult to locate their enemy, and suffered several defeats when they did, although also inflicting a major reversal on Pugachev and company in March 1774. But the 'vile miscreant' as he was officially designated went into retreat only to plan a more ambitious advance; in the summer of 1774, with an army some 20,000 strong, he advanced to the Volga and took the city of Kazan except for its Kremlin. As the rebel army was preparing for an assault on this citadel, a government detachment engaged it in a bloody battle in which over a third of Pugachev's followers were killed or taken prisoner. Others deserted his cause, especially the Bashkirs, and the leader found himself with a remnant detachment of barely 500 men as he moved down the right bank of the Volga.

Here began the third and most telling phase of the revolt. Pugachev was fleeing, but as Pushkin noted, the flight seemed like an invasion, especially to the landlords, whose serfs were now addressed on 31 July 1774 in one of their sworn enemy's most ferocious edicts. The peasants were offered the rough freedoms of the Cossack life with some echoes of the more sophisticated emancipation bestowed on their masters by the real Peter III in 1762. They were exempted from taxes and given economic advantages as well as religious liberty. In conclusion, the edict declared:

And since now with the authority of God's Right Hand our name flourishes in Russia, therefore we order by this our personal decree: those who were formerly nobles in their estates, these opponents of our authority and disturbers of the empire and destroyers of the peasants catch, execute and hang and treat in the same way as they, not having Christianity, have dealt with you, the peasants. With the eradication of these opponents and villainous nobles, each may feel peace and a quiet life, which will continue forever.

Although the man himself was continuing to make his way down towards the Don, where he hoped to gather sufficient strength for a further assault into the heartland of the Empire, towards Moscow, his very name was now enough to strike terror into the midst of the nobles in the old capital and the surrounding provinces. This was 'Pugachevshchina without Pugachev', which persuaded the government to send some of its best military leaders including the great Suvorov to suppress the movement before it could succeed in producing complete chaos and even a reversal of the natural order of society out of that chaos. But then, if not quite as suddenly as it had flared up, the alarm died away with the reception of the news that, although he was being joined by reinforcements from as far away as the Ukraine, Pugachev had been betrayed by some of his adherents and handed over to the authorities. He was taken to Moscow and executed at the beginning of 1775. His native village was razed to the ground, the Iaik River became the Ural, and the accursed name of Pugachev himself was officially consigned to eternal oblivion.

However cruelly his supporters were punished, the name of Pugachev, like that of Razin and Bulavin before him, in fact lived on in the songs and legends of the peasants, tribesmen and Cossacks. His movement had been more than a disorderly rout; it possessed at least a rudimentary organisation with its own War College and hierarchy of rank, and it had an ideal in the shape of the 'peace and quiet life' that would ensue with the defeat of its opponents. As for them, thrown back on the extreme defensive as they were, Catherine and her supporters necessarily laid bare the fundamental realities of the Russian polity as they perceived them. In one of its own decrees of 23 December 1773, the government declared that human society could not exist without 'intermediate authorities between the Sovereign and the people', while the Empress herself made manifest what could be gathered from her famous *Nakaz* only through to some extent reading between the lines that these 'intermediate authorities' comprised not only the administration but also the nobility. Addressing the beleaguered members of that class in Kazan, she declared herself to be 'proprietress' of that province and avowed that the security and well-being of the *dvorianstvo* were 'indivisible with our own and our empire's security and well-being'. The nobles for their part showed the extent of their agreement with these observations in a speech of thanksgiving composed on their behalf by the poet G. R. Derzhavin who described his and their class as the 'veritable shield' of the country as a whole and 'the supports of the tsarist throne' in particular.[29]

Such a confluence of interest was about to receive a most concrete expression in a reform hastened on by Pugachev's peasant war, but already adumbrated in some of the deliberations of Catherine and her advisers soon after her accession to power in the 1760s. In the introduction to the Institution of the Administration of the Provinces of the Russian Empire of 7 November 1775, the government made clear its intention of completing the work of Peter the Great in an ever expanding vast territory in a manner indicated in the labours of the Legislative Commission. Now that the disruptive war with Turkey had been brought to a successful conclusion, as God had granted 'a glorious peace after six years of uninterrupted land and sea victories with peace and quiet restored together within the wide limits of the Empire', the aim could be resumed 'to furnish the Empire with the institutions necessary and useful for the increase of order of every kind, and for the smooth flow of justice'.[30] Catherine had certainly been made fully aware at the time of the Legislative Commission of the complaints and desires of her ruling class concerning local administration in both criminal and civil spheres. One instruction from the north-west had alleged: 'The *dvoriane* and people of every rank of Pskov country, suffer extreme ravages from brigands, thieves, robbers and other kinds of criminal, which stops very many of the nobility from living on their estates, for the protection of their lives from wicked torment'. Another from Iaroslavl to the north of Moscow had declared: 'The existing extension of cases and the loss resulting from it, forcing the landlords of their stewards, and often the tillers of the soil themselves to live in the town during farming time, and also the multiplication of affairs, often unimportant in themselves, cause both the courts and the nobility great inconveniences.'[31]

From these and other sources, both directly and indirectly, Catherine had built up a reasonably accurate picture of the difficulties in provincial life even in normal times. For a theoretical model, she had supposedly turned from the French *philosophes* and German cameralists to the Englishman Blackstone, whose Justices of the Peace seemed to be the ideal officials for the establishment of order and efficiency in the provinces. But she herself observed that, although she and the commentaries of 'Sir Blackstone' had been inseparable for two years, 'I do not make anything from what there is in the book, but it is my yarn which I unwind in my own way.' In fact, the English JP could no more be transplanted to Russian soil now than could the Swedish *landrat* earlier in the century. More practical advice closer to home came from advisers such as Prince M. N. Volkonsky, Governor of Moscow Province, and especially Jacob Sievers, Governor of Novgorod Province.[32]

In the introduction to the reform of 1775 specific problems were identified: the provinces were too large and insufficiently staffed, business of all kinds being conducted in one chancellery, with the inevitable results of confusion and inefficiency, neglect and delay, corruption and disrespect for the law. Therefore the reform itself recommended for maximum efficiency a province of from 300 to 400 thousand souls, divided into counties where appropriate and certainly into districts. The governor, ruling the province in conjunction with the local military commander and other high personages, would have under him a whole range of officials dealing with the various branches of administration, civil, criminal, financial and social, those appointed by the state being joined by others elected locally. Among those depending on the votes of his neighbours would be the land executive or captain, whose duties would be to preside over a local land court and in this capacity to help preserve law and order, human and animal good health. He would help to apprehend and punish thieves and runaways, and maintain bridges and roads. He would assist the passage through his district of troops, arranging quarters for the men and fodder for their horses. He would do as much as possible to reduce fire hazards, to encourage agriculture and to care for the local poor. This was not a JP, for he was to receive a salary and rank, but he and his fellows were undoubtedly to play an important part in the implementation of the reform. The complaints and desires of the ruling class had been answered, then, but in this response the state bureaucracy had been expanded rather than independent local initiative.

Some of the more ambitious innovations of the decree of 7 November 1775 remained dead letters or never achieved full vitality: a system of courts of equity, for example, and a provision of a doctor and apothecary for each district. The townsfolk and especially the peasants were given less of a voice in provincial government than the nobles. The implementation of the decree was a slow process not brought to

ultimate completion at the time of Catherine's death in 1796. Sometimes it could not be carried out because of circumstance; in Viatka and
Perm, for example, there were not enough members of the nobility to
fill the post of land captain and others, and so army officers had to be
drafted into them. Moreover, the wide and varied range of duties now
given to local government resulted in the atrophy or even demise of
some of the colleges, which process could not ensue smoothly without
a corresponding wholesale reform of central government, which was
discussed but never really planned, far less implemented. Yet the 1775
reform was one of Catherine's greater successes, partly because it was
comparatively well prepared, largely because many of its provisions
corresponded to the preferences of the ruling class and to the stage of
development actually reached by society in many parts of the Russian
Empire.[33]

The mid 1770s constituted something of a watershed in the reign
of Catherine the Great. Not only did they bring the end of a major
war, the outbreak and suppression of a peasant war and the implementation of a significant governmental reform, they also meant for
her a sweeping change in entourage, most notably at the most intimate
centre, where Gregory Orlov was replaced as principal lover by a
man of no smaller ambition and of probably greater talent as well as
the same first name, Gregory Potemkin. To begin with at least, this
was a tender affair of the heart which moved the Empress to some
of the most sentimental passages in her voluminous correspondence,
but the dreams of the newly united couple were not confined for
long to amorous dalliance.[34] Potemkin was quick to appreciate the
expansive nature of his soulmate's territorial ambitions; her appetite
stimulated rather than sated by the gains of her first conflict with
Turkey, she lent a ready ear to his schemes for biting off more of the
Ottoman dominions in a manner which would bring further succour
to the oppressed Christians and revive further some of the glories of
the ancient world. And so they created the 'Greek Project', adopting
for its fulfilment Catherine's grandson born in 1779 and appropriately
named Constantine. Potemkin himself hoped to become King of Dacia,
a state to be created out of Bessarabia, Moldavia and Wallachia (in
unwitting anticipation of the nineteenth-century formation of Romania, and perhaps more conscious pursuit of the lover's refuge from
any future rejection by his mistress or, should her death precede his
own, persecution by her son). In such an emotional atmosphere the
sober schemes of Panin for continuance of his 'Northern System' stood
little or no chance of survival. The man himself fell from office in
1781; already the First Partition of Poland and the estrangement of the
'natural allies', Russia and Great Britain, had struck his grand design a
severe blow which now became mortal.

In 1780 Catherine made her famous Declaration of Armed Neutrality, ostensibly directed at Great Britain's insistence that it needed to

investigate all ships on the high seas under suspicion of rendering aid and succour to its enemies, the revolting American colonies, but also reflecting her progressive alienation from Great Britain's king, whom she dismissed in 1779 as a 'cloth merchant' and was to try to forget in 1783 when writing to Baron Grimm: 'Don't speak to me of brother George, for I never hear his name mentioned without having my blood boil.'[35] Removal from her affections of George III did not mean his replacement by George Washington; in the arguments for American independence she saw little wisdom and much out of place temerity even though these applications of the ideas of the Enlightenment did not offend her nearly as much as those in favour of the French Revolution ten or so years later. And the importance to Russia of commercial relations with Great Britain meant that ties could not be severed with the real cloth merchants or the buyers of naval stores.

A further blow to the 'Northern System' was the undermining of close relations with Prussia. The Russo-Prussian alliance was drawn up originally in 1764 and renewed in 1777 for another ten years came to an unlamented end in 1788. At the end of the 1770s, it is true, Russia came to the aid of both Prussia and Austria as mediator between them in efforts to bring to an end the War of Bavarian Succession, persuading Austria in the Treaty of Teschen of May 1779 to give up nearly all its gains. At the same time Catherine gained for herself protective rights over the constitution of the Holy Roman Empire and the basis for a dream (which she is not in fact known to have entertained) of a personal standard bearing three double-headed eagles, the Byzantine and Habsburg in addition to the Russian. Frederick II was to die in 1786, but a year before then a confederation of fifteen German states led by Prussia was formed to defend the imperial constitution against infringements by Catherine or more directly by Joseph II, who had taken over from Maria Theresa towards the end of 1780. As relations with Frederick grew cooler, those with Joseph warmed up, and a secret Russo-Austrian alliance was arranged already by the spring of 1781, aimed at the maintenance of stability in partitioned Poland and the creation of further instability in Turkey which was deemed ripe for partition. Agreement on joint action remaining elusive after lengthy and detailed negotiations, Russia moved unilaterally in April 1783 to annex the Crimea.

The 'independent' state set up in the Crimea by the Treaty of Kuchuk-Kainardzhi in 1774 stood very little chance of survival between the declining power of Turkey and the rising power of Russia, which made many inroads into the Black Sea peninsula before Potemkin came along to ensure the takeover of what he contemptuously dismissed as 'a pimple on Russia's nose'.[36] While the Crimean Tatars themselves were disconsolate, and most other European powers were unhappy at this latest piece of Catherine's imperial expansion, the Empress herself joined Potemkin and her other adherents in triumphant celebrations which in a sense were capped two years later by her Charter of the Rights, Freedoms and Privileges of the Noble Russian *Dvorianstvo*, issued on 21 April 1785. The preamble to this significant edict contains several passages of congratulation to the class and to individual members of it. The 'bloodless accretion to our sceptre' of the Crimea and adjacent regions was attributed to the 'zealous exploits of our General Field Marshal Prince Gregory Aleksandrovich Potemkin, who answered our commands with judicious enterprise and demonstrated outstanding and unforgettable service to us and the fatherland'. More generally, the nobility as a whole was praised for 800 years of unstinting service culminating in a manner meriting the following panegyrical apostrophe: 'To you deservedly decorated by the victory order we address our words! We praise you, descendants worthy of your forebears! These have been the foundations of Russia's majesty: you have brought to completion the strength and glory of the fatherland with six unbroken years of victory in Europe, Asia and Africa.'[37]

The actual clauses of the Charter are divided into four groups. First and in many ways foremost, there were the personal advantages of the nobility, based on the permanent hereditary retention of this distinguished status except in cases of criminal or dishonourable action, which were to be tried by a court of peers; they consisted primarily of advantages in military or civil service career and in the ownership of property. Second, the assemblies of nobles along with their marshals which had been created originally for the purpose of electing deputies to the Legislative Commission and composing instructions for them and had then been incorporated into the provincial reform of 1775, were to remain in existence on a permanent basis. Third, each province was to keep a genealogical register; and fourth, the necessary proofs of nobility were to be listed.

The Charter provided the context in which have to be assessed charges against the Russian nobles that they failed to take opportunities presented to them to reduce the power over them of the autocrat in observations such as that of Max Beloff:

The nobles of that country seemed in 1785 to want little more than what free men generally possessed in most of the rest of Europe. However one may interpret the policies of Catherine, the nobility, at the end of the eighteenth century was no less a subservient element in the Russian state than it had been under the masterful Peter one hundred years before.

It was rather the case, as Helju Bennett has written, 'that the Russian nobility's charter extended rights that went beyond any to be subsequently guaranteed the European'. The *dvorianstvo* was granted the right to service and to rank, 'a preemptive right to a specific role, a monopoly, as it were, on the valued and honored work that was available in Russia'. The realities of the relationship between the autocrat and the nobility were well caught by V. N. Bochkarev in 1923:

Such were the political and social views of the *dvorianstvo* in the age of Catherine II. The tsar was the autocrat above, the landlords were the autocrats below, and under them, without rights or voice, was the 'common' people, their subjects. Between the all-Russian and the landed autocrats was a strong and close alliance, defensive and offensive, securing the autocracy of the emperor over Russia, and of the *dvoriane* over their subjects, an alliance based on mutual trust. In such a state and social order only the autocrats were free, only they were real people: the all-Russian autocrat was free beyond measure, the freedom of the local small autocrats was limited by the boundaries of their estates and the freedom of the great autocrat, sitting on high.

Yet this alliance was more than the diarchy referred to by some historians, as Bochkarev went on to point out:

However, in this alliance of the political autocracy of the tsar with the social autocracy of the *dvorianstvo*, the actual power of many small autocrats aimed at replacing the power of the great autocrat and restricting the limits of his freedom. The *dvorianstvo*, recognizing itself in words as 'the lowest slaves' of its commander, as a complete nonentity, was at the same time proud of its consciousness that all that was Russia was it, the *dvorianstvo*, and only it . . . its blood and wounds had created Russia, it preserved her, gave her power and glory. Servilely declaring itself a nonentity before the boundless power of the all-Russian autocracy, the *dvorianstvo* was convinced that it alone held on its shoulders both the state and even the very power of the monarch, that only the 'noble' class was able, knew how and was obliged to administer Russia; it had to penetrate into all organs of administration and unremittingly watch over every step of the government. The tsar's protection over the *dvorianstvo*, and the *dvorianstvo*'s over all Russia, that is what, after all, the socio-political convictions of the average Russian *dvorianin* at the moment of the summons of the Legislative Commission of 1767 were leading to.[38]

And after the victories over external enemies such as the Turks and internal enemies such as Pugachev and his supporters, the *dvorianstvo*'s pride and pretensions were even greater in 1785.

And so the Russian polity in the late eighteenth century is best described as a 'noble bureaucratic monarchy'. Not normally recognised as such at the time, when the concept of absolutism was not well developed, still less the concept of an Eastern European variant, the might and majesty of its two principal embodiments were certainly striking enough for David Hume to lament that 'the two most civilised nations, the English and French, should be in decline; and the barbarians, the Goths and Vandals of Germany and Russia, should be rising in power and renown'. The experiences undergone by these 'Goths and Vandals' during the nineteenth and twentieth centuries should not blind us to the realities of their position in the century that went immediately before. As Klyuchevsky put it: 'From Peter, hardly daring to consider themselves people and still not considering themselves proper Europeans, Russians under Catherine felt themselves to be not only people, but almost the first people of Europe.' At that time, the *Scots Magazine* could declare as early as 1776 that: 'Russia enjoys her power, influence, and glory, with a noble and splendid magnificence. All her affairs are conducted upon a great and extensive system and all her acts are in a grand style. She sits supreme between Europe and Asia, and looks as if she intended to dictate to both.'[39]

Nevertheless, in the Russia personified by Catherine, some people, especially the nobility, would enjoy the power, influence and glory more than others. To be sure, a wide-ranging Charter of the Towns was also issued in 1785. It concerned three principal areas: the individual and collective rights of townspeople; regulations for craft guilds; and the organisation of corporate self-government. Certainly, the most comprehensive municipal reform since the time of Peter the Great and before the reign of Alexander II cannot be completely dismissed, and there is some evidence that in certain provinces, for example St Petersburg, it was adapted for local purposes in a fairly successful manner. Nevertheless, any hopes that Catherine might have entertained for a society composed of 'estates' were not fulfilled as far as the towns were concerned. Meanwhile, as far as the peasants were concerned, a draft charter for those attached to the state and envisaging a form of corporate self-government for them, too, was never promulgated.[40]

The theoretical content of the Charters of 1785 was virtually non-existent. Possibly the Empress was already becoming disillusioned with her erstwhile mentors the *philosophes*, giving up her ideas for the development of the Third Estate, for example, or perhaps with the passing of the years she was becoming more russified and therefore more enthusiastic about the distinctive nature of the Russian polity, which she was soon jealously to defend before the ideological onslaught of the French Revolution. But before then she was to become involved again in international conflicts nearer home, as relations with Turkey deteriorated after the annexation of the Crimea in 1783, at which time Russia also encroached towards the Caucasus and established a protectorate over the Transcaucasian state of Georgia. Possibly the power most moved by Russia's consumption of huge stretches of the Black Sea littoral was Austria, which hoped to join in the meal. In 1787 the Empress went on a grand tour of her new possessions, accompanied by an appreciative Joseph II and a large suite, which was entertained by Potemkin in a suitable style which reputedly although not certainly included the setting up of impressive façades of villages to disguise the sordid and mostly empty realities of the broad Southern steppe. But the presence of the new navy in Sevastopol harbour was real enough, and combined with apprehensive deliberations about the purpose of the imperial visit and the promptings of other European powers such as Great Britain and Prussia to provoke Turkey into accusing Russia of violation of the Treaty of Kuchuk-Kainardzhi and resuming hostilities against her in the autumn of 1787. Early in 1788, Austria joined her ally.

The war started badly for Russia. If a Turkish military storm of the fortress of Kinburn was resisted, a metereological storm on the Black Sea could not be beaten back and did great damage to the Russian Black Sea fleet. But it recovered sufficiently to achieve victories in the summer of 1788, and by the end of the year Potemkin had recovered sufficiently from an earlier pessimism to take Ochakov while Rumiantsev had overcome a number of logistical problems to take Jassy beyond the River Prut. Although the Austrians were not doing very well, and although Catherine's dreams of bringing to fruition her 'Greek project' were coming to very little, some progress had been made if at enormous human and material cost. To add to Russian difficulties, Sweden had taken advantage of its old enemy's preoccupation with war on the Black Sea to launch another on the Baltic in the summer of 1788. Great Britain and Prussia were again giving active encouragement, and an old Turko-Swedish treaty could have the dust shaken off it to provide an excuse for an advance on a thinly protected St Petersburg. But the Swedish nobility, unlike its Russian counterpart, was not happy at the lack of consultation extended to it by its monarch, and King Gustavus found it difficult to rouse his armed forces into aggressive action, and so St Petersburg was able to hold out with the Russian army and navy giving as good as it got. True, in 1789, when elsewhere in Europe political events were moving in the opposite direction, Gustavus managed to call his unruly nobles to heel, and in July 1790 his navy inflicted a fairly severe defeat on its adversary. But Great Britain and Prussia did not supply enough continuing aid for this victory to be rammed home, while Russia was too preoccupied with events to the south for her to entertain persistent thoughts of revenge, and so a treaty of no change was agreed in August. A defensive Russo-Swedish alliance drawn up in 1791 did little to inhibit further tension between the two Baltic powers, but there was no immediate resumption of open warfare.

Meanwhile, back on the Black Sea, the year 1789 had been almost as good for Catherine II and Joseph II as it had been bad for Louis XVI in France, Belgrade being among the towns to fall to the Austrians and the future Odessa to the Russians. But the French Revolution soon had repercussions that affected developments at the other end of Europe. Frederick William, apprehensive of renewed isolation for Prussia, entered into alliance with Turkey at the beginning of 1790, promising to fight on until the enemy was driven from the Balkans and the Crimea, and soon afterwards made another military alliance with Poland. Austria was weakened by the death of Joseph II at about this time, as well as by simmering insurgency in Hungary and Galicia, while its provinces in the Netherlands made a declaration of independence as the United States of Belgium. So Austria was forced to make a stalemate armistice with Turkey in the middle of 1790, and a formal peace about a year later.

Russia was now alone, but consoled by the fact that none of the powers of Eastern Europe was likely to attack her, and the Empress still held hopes of realising at least a substantial part of her ambitions if nothing like the whole of the 'Greek project'. Russian victories continued throughout the year 1791, and both Great Britain and Prussia were unable to offer more than threats, which Catherine resisted. And so, feeling ultimately more isolated than its enemy, Turkey was obliged to respond to peace feelers, and at the beginning of 1792, accepted again the terms of Kuchuk-Kainardzhi and recognised the loss of the Crimea, Ochakov and the area between the Rivers Dnestr and Bug. The Peace of Jassy in such a manner marked another triumph for Catherine, although she continued to harbour dreams of a more complete dismemberment of the Ottoman Empire. In the final year of her reign she encouraged the last of her score or more lovers, Platon Zubov, in his youthful 'Oriental project', which aimed at the seizure of the Caucasus as well as Constantinople, opening up the gateway to India and the Far East. Not content with reviving Greece, he wanted to bring back to life the full dimensions of Alexander's Greek empire, and more. Fortunately for everybody else concerned, Catherine died before her young man's scheme had progressed very far towards implementation.

The last years of her reign were fully active in the other direction, an indirect consequence of the French Revolution as well as culmination of a more direct local process being the further partitions of Poland. Under King Stanislaus, Poland had retained what it could of its independence by toeing the line or rather the three lines. Now, towards the end of the 1780s, realising that even continued quiescence might not prolong their country's life, several groups decided that the international situation was ripe for them to drive out the forces of occupation, especially the Russians. And so, while Stanislaus pressed for Polish assistance to Russia in the war against Turkey, a more popular policy was rapprochement with Prussia, duly achieved on the ostensible basis of mutual respect to the level of full military alliance by the early spring of 1790. All seemed to go well at the beginning, Russia withdrawing its troops and Poland drawing up a new constitution. Impressive document though this was, however, its bright aspirations could not be realised in an international atmosphere of gathering gloom, and it soon became no more than one of the scraps of paper with which the history of Poland and other comparatively weak powers of Europe is littered. Brought together in alliance in early 1792 and soon afterwards in war against revolutionary France, Prussia and Austria were sufficiently preoccupied for Russia to send its troops back into Poland. Then, instead of fighting Russia as it should have done, Prussia decided it could do no more than join in what became the second partition in 1793, with

Austria supposedly to receive compensation in Bavaria and the Russian share comprising Vilno, Minsk and the eastern sections of Podolia and Volynia.

Far from taking this new carve-up lying down, the Poles rose up with unprecedented fervour under the leadership of a hero of the American Revolution, Thaddeus Kosciuszko. A national emancipatory movement achieved wide social support, but could not long withstand the full impact of Russian might. Then, although the Prussians and Austrians had done comparatively little to bring the Polish movement down, they were quick to demand their fair share of the spoils. There was a considerable amount of squabbling over policies to be adopted towards revolutionary France as well as insurgent Poland, but in the end the third partition was concluded towards the end of 1795, with Russia adding Courland, Lithuania and the remainder of Podolia and Volynia to the territories already gained in its two predecessors. Their Polish problem was now solved in a manner far more complete than the wildest dreams of the beleaguered Russians could have conceived at the end of the Time of Troubles in 1613. As for the Poles themselves, their last King Stanislaus, living out his last days in St Petersburg for a couple of years or so after the death of his erstwhile mistress who had put him on the throne and then pushed him from it, might well have parodied in anticipation the famous words of the younger Pitt and concluded that the map of Poland should be rolled up for it would not be needed for more than a century.

For centuries before, Poland and Russia had been locked in struggle. Up to the middle of the seventeenth century, Poland had the upper hand, and at times Muscovy had been reduced to the humiliating position of vassal state. The reversal then began with the Muscovite acquisition of a large part of the Ukraine, which also made certain that the question of the Russo-Polish relationship was being posed almost constantly. The fluctuating loyalties of the Cossacks, the uncertainties of the frontier, the clash between Orthodox and Roman Catholic affiliations, the elective nature of the Polish monarchy along with the vagaries of domestic politics in the both countries were just some of the constituent parts of a complex and never completely stable whole. Even the partitions did not settle the question, which was to arise again throughout the nineteenth century, and beyond.

Through the partitions, Russia acquired over 450,000 square kilometres of territory in eastern Belorussia, Lithuania and the Right-Bank Ukraine. About 7.5 million people were incorporated into the imperial body politic, and these included not only Belorussians, Lithuanians and Ukrainians but also Latvians, Poles and Jews. This last group, although probably totalling less than half a million, received a disproportionate amount of attention. Jews had not been numerous at all in Russia before the partitions, and were now, as it were, given a partition of their own in the Pale of Settlement, with a series of attempts, some well-meaning, some not, to accommodate their religion, traditions and customs within the framework of the Empire.[41]

Even before the Polish partitions could have brought about any change in Catherine's title, it clearly demonstrated the manner in which her Empire had been built up:

We Catherine the Second, Empress and Autocrat of all the Russias, of Moscow, of Kiev, of Vladimir, of Novgorod, Tsarina of Kazan and Astrakhan, of Siberia, Tsarina of Kherson-Tavrichesky, Sovereign of Pskov and Grand Duchess of Smolensk, Princess of Estonia, Livonia, Karelia, Tver, Iugorsk, Perm, Viatka, Bolgariia and others; Sovereign and Grand Duchess of Nizhnii Novgorod, Chernigov, Riazan, Polotsk, Rostov, Iaroslavl, Belozersk, Udoriia, Obdoriia, Kondiia, Vitebsk, Mstislavl and of all the Northern Territories; Lady and Sovereign of the Land of Iveriia, the Kar galian and Georgian Tsars and Land of Kabarda, of the Cherkasian and Mountain princes and others the hereditary Sovereign and Proprietrix.

This was in the preamble to the Charter of the Nobility in 1785; twenty years or so before then in her letter to the newly appointed Procurator-General A. A. Viazemsky, it will be recalled, Catherine had recommended that such provinces as Kiev, Smolensk, Livonia and Karelia had now become should 'by the easiest of means be brought to the point where they would russify and cease to look like wolves to the forest'. If her methods of russification became less gentle in these and other provinces as her reign wore on, this would make her policies conform more to the pattern of imperial policies in most places at most times. Certainly during her reign the Russian Empire became consolidated in a typically ruthless fashion from Poland, which we have just dealt with, to Siberia, to which we must now briefly turn. At its eastern extremity explorers like G. I. Shelekhov and G. A. Sarychev, the contemporaries of Captain Cook who himself touched briefly down to Siberian shores, were continuing the work of Bering and others earlier in the century and establishing more clearly the contours of the Northern Pacific. These explorers themselves were often driven by more than a pure love of geography, and made their own contribution to what became the concerted search for profitable enterprise in Russian America. Shelekhov, for example, became a millionaire in the fur trade and helped to found the North-Eastern American Company in 1781. As for Catherine, she was somewhat mistrustful of such distant colonial enterprises, believing that they encouraged monopoly; and having just seen the success of the American Revolution and the failure of the French East India Company, she declared: 'Wide expansion in the Pacific Ocean will bring no lasting gain. It is one thing to trade and another to seize possessions.'[42] This is not to say she was not interested in consolidating Russia's hold on Siberia or probing further into Asia; she promoted several scientific expeditions, such as that of P. S. Pallas in 1768–74, and encouraged missionary as well as commercial contact with the peoples along the Volga and to the east of it who were largely either Moslem or Shamanist. The Kazakhs of Central Asia were among those who fought against the encroachment of the Russian central government in the years following the Pugachev Revolt.[43] At the beginning of her reign especially, under the influence of the populationist theory of the time as well as her growing knowledge of the emptiness of the steppe, Catherine made a great effort to attract German and other foreign colonists to settle in her empire, but for all her efforts achieved only a modest amount of success.[44]

Protection of foreign colonists and suppression of anti-government movements among the many indigenous peoples of the Empire would have of themselves necessitated an army of substantial size even if there had not been great international crises and hostilities to worry about as well. The wars and the expansion of Catherine's reign demanded large armies and a considerable navy as well. Unlike most of the other European armies of the time, the Russian was now largely without mercenaries and dependent on a provincial recruiting system. Some of the officers were still foreign, but the level of domestic military training was now high enough for them to be nowhere near as important as they had been in earlier times. The infantry was the largest component, 63 regiments in 1769 with an establishment of just over 2,000 men each. From about the end of the Seven Years War onwards there was a special attempt to increase the number of chasseur units, and by 1785 there were 7 such corps with 4 battalions each; their mobility was especially appropriate for the column tactics and loose order of the time. By the end of Catherine's reign the infantry consisted of 4 guards regiments, 15 grenadier regiments, 57 ordinary infantry regiments, 2 naval regiments, 10 chasseur corps, 3 separate grenadier battalions, 2 separate modern musketeer battalions (not to be confused with the extinct *streltsy*), 3 separate chasseur battalions and 20 field battalions.

As far as the cavalry was concerned, military thinking at the beginning of Catherine's reign favoured the development of heavy rather than light units, of cuirassiers and carabiniers rather than dragoons and hussars. And so in 1765 the cavalry consisted of 1 guards regiment, 5 cuirassier, 20 carabinier, 7 dragoon and 9 hussar regiments, a total of 42. P. A. Rumiantsev complained that the Russian cavalry was becoming heavier at a time when other cavalries were moving towards lightness, and the experience of the Russo-Turkish War of 1768-74 showed again the importance of mobility, so a trend in the opposite direction set in. By the end of the reign the cavalry comprised: 1 guards regiment, 5 cuirassier, 17 carabinier, 11 dragoon, 2 hussar, 9 light horse, 1 mounted grenadier and 3 mounted chasseur regiments, a total of 49, to which must be added about 27 regiments of Cossacks. Such a force contained all the necessary ingredients for reconnaissance, engagement and pursuit of the enemy.

During Catherine's reign the artillery developed at a relatively slow pace; by the 1790s there were in existence 3 separate artillery battalions, 5 mounted artillery companies and 2 artillery battalions attached to the galley fleet, and in addition about 1,500 cannon in the siege artillery. There was also an engineer regiment and various other engineer detachments. And for internal garrison work there was in 1795 an army of something over 120,000 men, that is about a third as many as in the field army, units of which had to be called in from time to time to help restore or preserve the internal order. For the army as a whole there was a simplification (or deprussification) of its uniform in the early 1780s under the influence of Potemkin, while the weaponry and equipment were both becoming more complicated.

For their administration the army regiments were organised in divisions and brigades in a fairly flexible manner dependent on the needs of whatever kind of war or peace obtained at any given time. In peace the highest administrative body was the War college; in war the field regiments were managed by a Council of War, although the staff situation was not often satisfactory, sometimes receiving interference from civilian outsiders, sometimes in need of the prompting of a Rumiantsev or a Suvorov.[45]

During the reign of Catherine the Great the Russian navy also had its outstanding native commanders, as well as some that were Scots; and having played no small part in Russian successes on the Baltic during the Seven Years War, it was to assume a larger importance on a wider stage during the conflicts of the later part of the century on the Baltic, Black and Mediterranean seas. At the beginning of this period the complement of the basic Baltic fleet was 32 ships of the line, 8 frigates, 4 bombardment or siege ships, 3 prams or flat-bottomed ships and an assortment of others; in a larger version, the complement could be expanded to 40 ships of the line and 10 frigates. At the end of the first Russo-Turkish war a beginning as made towards the construction of the Black Sea fleet, whose complement was established in 1785 as 12 ships of the line, 20 frigates and 23 others. This was not immediately achieved, but by the end of the second Russo-Turkish War the Black Sea fleet consisted of 22 ships of the line, 6 bombardment ships, 12 frigates and many others. By about this time, 1790 or so, its Baltic counterpart comprised 37 ships of the line, 13 frigates and 30 others, plus a galley fleet approximately 200 strong. Overall administration of the navy was under the care of the Admiralty college in time of peace, although obviously in time of war admirals needed even more powers of initiative and control than generals.[46]

To move on to the top civil administration, the salient points of its development on Catherine's reign, the reforms of 1763, 1775 and 1785, have already been noted. On the whole, the principal direction of the bureaucracy at this time was towards increase in numbers and level of professionalisation. In 1763 the establishment consisted of 16,500 officials, by 1775 of 18,000. At the highest level of this pyramid both money and rank could be earned; at the lowest there was a considerable quantity of mean pen-pushers. The condition of the bureaucracy near the beginning of the reign was indicated by the instruction of the Senate to the Legislative Commission, which pointed out that as a result of a regulation that each piece of paper should be kept regardless of its significance, the imperial archives were overflowing; there was 'dangerous prolongation and obscurity' in its business. Some improvement may have been achieved through the Catherinian policies, but after the effective decentralisation of many of the colleges through the provincial reform of 1775, there was a dire need of a reorganisation of the central government, which was discussed but never came.[47]

Such improvement as there was in both civilian and military branches of service could not avoid having an effect on the organisation of Russia's ruling class, the *dvorianstvo*. At the Legislative Commission, the Heraldmaster's office had pointed out that in early 1722 just after the publication of the Table of Ranks it had been ordered to gather together accurate information on the whole class, but, it confessed, 'up to now accurate information on nobles and their children, in service and retired, also deceased and newly born, has still not been received from all regions'. By the end of the reign, especially after the provisions of the Charter of the Nobility of 1785, these deficiencies were probably overcome, and the cohesion of the *dvorianstvo* was certainly greater than that of many of its brother nobilities spread around Europe. And its overall importance in the running of the state was almost in inverse proportion to the insignificance of its numbers, even though the growing importance of the bourgeoisie should not be forgotten.[48]

To consider the population as a whole, there was a great increase in its total from about 23,250,000 in 1762 to just under 28,500,000 in 1782 to getting on for 37,500,000 in 1795. More than half the steep rise was the result of the partitions of Poland, but there was also considerable colonisation of peripheral provinces such as New Russia and the Lower Volga and no small natural increase at the more settled centre.[49] No longer much given to abstract argument anyway, the Empress could not be worried about populationist theory at the end of her reign as she was at the beginning.

But her last years were far from serene. Perturbed at the course being taken by the French Revolution, she did all she could to keep its pernicious influence from crossing the widened frontiers of her Empire, although her greatest fears probably centred around that class of her people least likely to have heard of the events in Paris and beyond, the peasantry.[50] Her most signal failure had been with regard to serfdom and other restrictive institutions, under which laboured to some extent or another more than 90 per cent of her subjects, if subjects they could be called, because in law peasants still had little more standing than inanimate pieces of property, often indeed even less.

True, at the beginning of her reign, she had expended a considerable amount of energy on getting the question at least discussed, up to and including the debates of the Legislative Commission. She sponsored a prize essay competition on one of the central questions connected with serfdom: should the peasants be allowed to possess land or other forms of property, and to what extent? A few entrants suggested at least a limited beginning in the all-important direction, although a more representative view, albeit possibly in caricature, was offered by an essayist with the pen name 'A man who is ungrammatical and has not read any history since birth', who argued that emancipation would lead to interminable lawsuits, and furthermore: 'Their Excellencies the Field Marshals ... who command the glorious Russian army would be compelled to petition the commissars for their brave lads but we in Russia have more brave lads than in foreign parts because the peasants are literate there and in Russia, with God's care, even the priests are not all that literate.' The ungrammatical non-historian went on to put what he obviously believed was the positive point that 'The landlords teach their serfs not only folk-dancing, but also carpentry and part-singing.'[51]

As her reign wore on Catherine's early progressive views were forgotten, and she no longer welcomed even discussion of the serf problem. Such an attitude was considerably at cross-purposes with at least some of the views that she held on economic policy in general, where it would be somewhat anachronistic to call her a free-trader (even if she became familiar with some of the ideas of Adam Smith before they were published by way of a Russian student S. E. Desnitsky who had attended the lectures of the master at Glasgow University),[52] but she did show a pronounced aversion to monopoly and a preference for removal of many restrictions (although she argued in her *Nakaz* that 'Freedom of Trade is not to let the Merchant do as he pleases, this would be rather enslaving Trade; for what confines the Merchant, does not confine Trade'.) And, while she declared herself in the avowal of principle to be in favour of a limited development of industry she gave emphasis to the assertion that the most important element in the Russian economy was agriculture.

In the first years of her reign, according to responses to questionnaires published in the *Works* of Russia's new institution for the dissemination and collection of useful information, the Free Economic Society, surpluses in grains and other produce were rare, and there were not many signs of expansion or improvement of agriculture. However, by the end of her reign, at least partly because of the Society's efforts and government policies, great changes were to take place. In the last two decades of the eighteenth century, according to Soviet calculation, the cultivation of cereals almost doubled, while items connected with the manufacture of cloth, ropes and other shipbuilding materials more than doubled their production. Cattle raising, although also on the increase, lagged somewhat behind other animal developments, including horse and sheep breeding. While the manorial economy remained dominant, peasants and merchants were making considerable inroads into the former exclusiveness of the noble landlords in agriculture.[53]

Statistics, not easily supplied for this most important branch of the economy, can be given for at least some aspects of other increasingly important branches, trade and industry. While the mostly flourishing nature of the internal market cannot be given simply, commercial expansion in general was reflected in a jump in the value of exports from about 12,750,000 roubles in 1762 to just over 43,250,000 in 1793. About 45 per cent of the total exports were in metals and textiles, which, along with hemp and flax, were very important for Russia's chief trading partner, Great Britain, with whom the treaty of 1734 was renewed with minor changes in 1766. In 1774 Mr Foster, the agent of the British Russia Company, argued that without these commodities 'our navy, our commerce, our agriculture, are at end', and more recently economic historians such as the Americans Kahan and Kaplan have suggested that they made a significant contribution to the progress of the British industrial revolution. Meanwhile, imports were rising from something less than 8,250,000 roubles in value in 1762 to over 27,750,000 in 1793; although luxury items for the upper classes such as coffee, wines and fruit comprised a sizeable amount of them, the cotton goods and dyestuffs that also came in were of more directly utilitarian value. The circumstance that even Russia was going through the early stages of industrial revolution was reflected in the maintenance of a protective tariff, albeit with some decrease in 1766 and 1782, followed by some increase in the 1790s.[54]

True, to say that there were by the end of the eighteenth century about 1,200 large-scale enterprises, as opposed to 663 in 1767, might distort the level of the progress although perhaps not so much its rate. Certainly, there was much expansion during the reign of Catherine, but even at its end, many of the bigger enterprises were conducted in a somewhat primitive manner and with the almost exclusive exploitation of serf labour. The most efficient units were probably smaller and involved in light rather than heavy industry, tending to use hired rather than forced labour. Some factory owners were technically serfs and rather more of them were from the merchant class, although noble industrial enterprise remained extremely important at least as far as the early nineteenth century.

All these figures must be taken as the roughest of guides only, especially when they involve money, since the rouble was subject during the reign of Catherine to a considerable amount of inflation. In her letter to Procurator-General Viazemsky of 1764, it will be remembered, she had asserted that there was an insufficient amount of money in circulation, but then the supply of money, like that of people, expanded appreciably, if in this case in a depreciating manner since there was a growing recourse to paper. With such reservations in mind we may note an increase in state income from 24 million roubles in 1769 to 56 million in 1795, the percentage collected from direct taxation increasing from over 40 per cent to more than 46 per cent. Expenditure rose more steeply from less than 23.5 million roubles in 1767 to about 79 million in 1795, the percentage spent on the government going up from less than 25 per cent to more than 36 per cent, while that given to the armed forces declined from nearly 50 per cent to about 37 per cent. In 1795 the budget was out of balance, a gap filled largely by paper.[55]

Catherine's monetary affairs were by no means her sole set of policies running somewhat awry as her years on the throne wore on. Her most famous cultural activities, too, led towards a conclusion that was most unsatisfactory to a certainly no longer and perhaps never liberal Empress. Figuratively speaking, she had wanted to create a new race of men supporting enlightened absolutism and had finished up giving birth to an intelligentsia opposed to it. Such parturition is well exemplified by the career of A. N. Radishchev, one of forty young noblemen chosen soon after the coronation of Catherine II in September 1762 to join the Imperial Corps of Pages, and then selected along with five of his fellows nearly four years later to form half the dozen of young Russians sent by the Empress for their further education to the University of Leipzig. After his return and a quarter-century or so of faithful if undistinguished government service, Radishchev was emboldened by his conscience to write his *Journey from St Petersburg to Moscow*, condemning serfdom as the equal of slavery and warning his erstwhile patroness of the wrath to come if nothing were done about it: 'Everywhere martial hosts will arise, hope will arm all; everyone hastens to wash off his shame in the blood of the crowned tormentor. Everywhere I see the flash of the sharp sword; death, flying about in various forms, hovers over the proud head. Rejoice, fettered peoples! The avenging law of nature brought the king to the block.' Although Radishchev probably had mostly in mind Charles I, the fact that his *Journey* was completed in 1790 soon after the outbreak of the French Revolution obviously had implications for Louis XVI and possibly for Catherine the Great as well. So it was not surprising that, in commutation of an initial death sentence, Radishchev was sent into exile.

Pushkin was perhaps the first among many who in the nineteenth century 'in Radischchev's footsteps . . . praised freedom to the skies', but, as the great writer also pointed out, in the late eighteenth century, 'Radishchev was alone, . . . a minor civil servant, a man without any power, without any support' daring to arm himself 'against the general order, against autocracy, against Catherine!'[56] Allowing for some rhetorical exaggeration, since a handful of other freethinkers along with a somewhat larger group of Freemasons also incurred the deep suspicions of the Empress and her policemen, we do need to realise that the vast majority of the nobility, even those who like Radishchev had been exposed in Russia or abroad to the ideas of the *philosophes*, were broadly conformist. If Catherine had not succeeded in creating a new race of men, her own interests in matters of the mind and sensibility did help to deter most of her like-minded leading subjects from following Radishchev and his ilk down the path of dissidence and opposition towards the creation of an intelligentsia. Outstanding writers like G. R. Derzhavin, Russia's first mature lyric poet, and D. I. Fonvizin, author of some penetrating comedies of manners, were just two of the more noteworthy figures who managed to succumb no more than a little to what must have been strong temptations. And although there has been some interesting Soviet discussion of the formation of a bourgeois 'democratic' and even a 'serf' intelligentsia, such groups could hardly fail to be in no more than an embryonic stage of development until some time after 1801 – especially the latter, one of the estimates of which has been based simply on the number of serfs who had achieved literacy before that date.[57]

Very few of these would have attended such formal institutions of learning as were in existence at this time, nearly 550 with a total roll of something over 60,000 at the death of Catherine according to a widely accepted calculation. Church schools would account for about 20,000 of this number and military schools for about 12,000 more, and some allowance must be made for those attending various special state and private schools. Many of the rest would be enrolled in the major and minor schools set up after Prussian and Austrian models in 1786, with a curriculum and with textbooks aimed at the inculcation of loyalty as well as learning. At the highest level, at the Academy of Sciences, the more newly founded Academy of Arts and similar institutions, Russia was demonstrating that it could produce achievers of domestic growth as well as of foreign importation, even though their names are rarely conjured with today. In the field of activity allegedly closest to the hearts of at least some readers of these lines, M. M. Shcherbatov and I. N. Boltin were in their distinctive ways working on the inheritance of V. N. Tatishchev and handing on to N. M. Karamzin, whose *History of Russia* was to become standard for patriotic Russians throughout much of the nineteenth century.[58]

Especially away from the larger towns the age-old peasant culture was still alive and vigorous, adding songs and legends about Pugachev to those of Razin, even if the year 1768 appears to have brought the last sighting of the descendants of the *skomorokhi*, 120 years after their prohibition, in Western Siberia. Meanwhile, the efforts of N. I. Novikov were bringing at least a veneer of the new urban culture to the provinces in a successful enough manner to provoke the jealousy of Catherine, who liked to be the exclusive source of enlightenment for her people.[59]

The Empress was impressed by the achievements of her folk, and developed to some extent the folk cult, although perhaps as much in imitation of the pastoral romps of the French aristocracy at Versailles as the ceremonial festivities of the Russian peasantry. And, while struck by what could be done to wood by the axe, she was more taken by what Russian and foreign architects could design to be created from stone and brick. The most uncultivated piece of stone that she personally commissioned, although here too art was called in to embellish nature, was the base for the equestrian statue of Peter the Great that she commissioned for the banks of the Neva from the French sculptor Falconet. 'To Peter the First: Catherine the Second: in the year 1782', runs the simple inscription on the Bronze Horseman. With such a direct juxtaposition of the two names, she no doubt hoped to reinforce her claim to the inheritance of Peter in the city founded by him. A similar aspiration for such recognition beyond the Baltic Sea probably occurred to her nearly twenty years before as she presented a great tapestry of the famous victory at Poltava to the retiring British Ambassador, the Earl of Buckinghamshire, while she must have reminded herself of her own ambition whenever she looked at the miniature of her distinguished predecessor on her personal snuffbox. The measure of her success in this endeavour as far as posterity is concerned may be observed in the appraisal presented at the end of the most complete work in English by Isabel de Madariaga, who goes so far as to imply that Catherine was not only a worthy successor to Peter but in some senses his superior.[60]

Turning to other comparisons, Madariaga recommends the avoidance of the 'classical' question of Catherine's enlightened despotism or absolutism, and then goes on herself to assert Catherine's emulation of Louis XIV at the peak of his powers, an anachronistic departure more dangerous than consideration of the Empress in relation to contemporaries such as Frederick the Great of Prussia and Joseph II of Austria, who like her attempted to make use of the ideas of the Enlightenment in their governmental policies. Comparisons of this kind are still being carried on by a number of Western historians,[61] and Soviet colleagues might join them with more enthusiasm if they were not restrained by the negative verdict of Pushkin who wrote of the Empress as a Tartuffe in skirts, and even more by that of Marx and Engels who in over a score of references condemned her ruthless expansionism (Lenin made no more than a couple of passing references to her in his *Collected Works*). At least I. A. Fedosov is prepared to go as far as to say that: 'Without doubt Catherine was one of the outstanding figures on the Russian throne – clever, and educated, and capable, and successful,' while, in the first extended Soviet essay on Catherine, B. A. Kamenskii concludes that she was 'a lively, extraordinary person, leaving a significant mark on the history of the fatherland.'[62]

Undoubtedly she was also lucky to have occupied the throne at a time when Russian absolutism was reaching its apogee, for reasons largely beyond her control (for similar reasons, neither Catherine II nor Peter I would be commonly known as the Great had they come to power around 1900 when Russian absolutism was nearing its collapse). On the other hand, it would be wrong to assert that she had nothing to do with this culmination. As A. A. Kizevetter pointed out in a perspicacious essay, her 'natural egotistic optimism',[63] which was largely formed before her arrival in Russia although it grew afterwards, was well suited to the point of development reached by Russian society, or at least its ruling class. Catherine's concept of a 'personal-constitutional absolutism' that Klyuchevsky detected in the *Nakaz* blended well with the 'noble bureaucratic monarchy' discerned by Bochkarev and others in the outlook of the *dvorianstvo* expressed at the great meeting to which the *Nakaz* was presented, the Legislative Commission.[64] The tacit alliance already formed then was strengthened through the reforms of 1775 and 1785. The earlier fate of her husband (and the later fate of her son) gave ample testimony to the circumstance that this alliance was not automatically dominated by a ruler aloof from the subjects, and Catherine had to tread warily. And so due caution as well as vain hypocrisy explain her reconciliation of little or no ultimate action on the serf problem with a comparatively enlightened policy in other fields. Moreover, if the vast majority of her people were treated by most of the remainder as well as herself as 'unpersons' (especially at the time of social disturbances such as the Pugachev Revolt), such attitudes would conform to a wider eighteenth-century norm.[65] Similarly, although her traits of personality took to an extreme a normal royal desire of the age to be seen as the fount of all wisdom and everything else that was good, her energy as patroness of the arts and her prolificity as a writer helped to impart to Russian culture some of her own unbounded self-confidence.[66] Appropriately, although she travelled widely throughout her ever-expanding dominions and made good use of the cathedrals and palaces of the Kremlin in Moscow, especially for ceremonial occasions, she was most at home in and around St Petersburg, looking out at Europe.

NOTES

1. O. Kornilovich, *Zapiski Imperatritsy Ekateriny II: vneshnii analiz teksta* (Tomsk, 1912), pp. 2–28.
2. R. N. Bain, *Peter III, Emperor of Russia* (London, 1902) p. vii.
3. *Sbornik Imperatorskogo russkogo istoricheskogo obshchestva*, v. 12, pp. 9–10. And see contributions by J. Black and A. G. Cross to *Study Group on Eighteenth-century Russia Newsletter*, no. 13 (1985), pp. 41–2.
4. R. Pipes, *Karamzin's Memoir on Ancient and Modern Russia: A Translation and Analysis* (Cambridge, MA, 1959), p. 15.
5. P. Dukes, *Russia under Catherine the Great: Volume One: Select Documents on Government and Society* (Newtonville, MA, 1978), pp. 28–35.
6. V. O. Klyuchevsky, *Sochineniia*, vol. 8 (Moscow, 1959) p. 277.

7. Quoted in N. Korobkov, *Semiletniaia voina (deistviia Rossii v 1756–1762gg.)* (Moscow, 1940), p. 337.
8. Abbé Coyer, *La noblesse commerçante* (London, 1756), p. 143–4, 210. Compare Voltaire's recommendation of Peter the Great as a model for other monarchs to follow at the conclusion of his *Histoire de l'Empire de Russie sous Pierre le Grand* (Paris, 1759–63). For a further analysis of the debate concerning the role of the nobility see V. Kamendrowsky and D. M. Griffiths, 'The Fate of the Trading Nobility Controversy in Russia', *Jahrbücher für Geschichte Osteuropas*, vol. 26 (1978), and the article by M. Raeff cited in the following note.
9. M. Raeff, 'The Domestic Policies of Peter III and his Overthrow', *American Historical Review*, vol. 75 (1970).
10. Ibid., p. 1292. And see C. Leonard, 'The reputation of Peter III', *Russian Review*, vol. 47 (1988).
11. Catherine the Great, *Memoirs*, M. Budberg, (ed.) D. Maroger (London, 1955), p. 36; Klyuchevsky, *Sochineniia*, vol. 5 (Moscow, 1958), pp. 6–8. See also N. Ia. Eidelman, 'Memuary Ekatering II–odna iz raskrytykh tain samoderzhaviia, *Voprosy istorii*, no. 1 (1968).
12. Catherine the Great, *Memoirs*; K. Anthony (trans. and ed.) (London, 1927), p. 124.
13. Quoted in B. Dmytryshyn (ed.), *Imperial Russia: A Source Book* (New York, 1967), p. 66.
14. W. Richardson, *Anecdotes of the Russian Empire* (London, 1784), pp. 103–4.
15. V. A. Petrova, 'Politicheskaia borba vokrug senatskoi reformy 1763 goda', *Vestnik Leningradskogo Universiteta* (1967) n. 8; D. Ransel, *The Politics of Catherinian Russia: The Panin Party* (New Haven and London, 1975), pp. 73–98.
16. M. Raeff (ed.), *Plans for Political Reform in Imperial Russia, 1730–1795* (Englewood Cliffs, NJ, 1966), pp. 53–68.
17. *Sbornik IRIO*, vol. 7, p. 233.
18. N. Kalachov (ed.), *Materialy dlia istorii russkogo dvorianstva*, 3 vols in 1 (St Petersburg, 1885).
19. SIRIO, vol. 7, pp. 310–13.
20. For an interpretation of the Manifesto of 1762 somewhat different to mine, see R. E. Jones, *The Emancipation of the Russian Nobility, 1762–1785* (Princeton, NJ, 1973).
21. Dukes, *Russia*, vol. 1, pp. 36–9.
22. Quoted in A. Gieysztor et al., *History of Poland* (Warsaw, 1979), p. 267.
23. See also articles by K. Morrison and by R. Givens in *Canadian-American Slavic Studies*, vol. 4 (1970) and vol. 11 (1977).
24. Klyuchevsky, *Sochineniia*, vol. 5, p. 43; Dukes, *Russia*, vol. 2, p. 25.
25. Ibid., p. 77.
26. In English, most use of these materials has been made by Jones, *The Emancipation.*; P. Dukes, *Catherine the Great and the Russian Nobility* (Cambridge, 1967); and W. R. Augustine, 'Notes towards a Portrait of the Eighteenth-Century Nobility', *Canadian-American Slavic Studies*, vol. 4 (1970). See also note 23 above.
27. Quoted in Gieysztor, *Poland*, p. 275.

28. See, for example, L. A. Nikiforov, 'Borba Rossii s Turtsiei i Shvetsiei v 60–90kh godakh' in L. G. Beskrovny *et al.* (eds), *Istoriia SSSR*, pervaia seriia, vol. 3 (Moscow, 1967), p. 527.

29. Documents on the Pugachev Revolt to be found in Dukes, *Russia under Catherine the Great*, vol. 1; Catherine and Derzhavin quoted in J. T. Alexander, *Autocratic Politics in a National Crisis: The Imperial Russian Government and Pugachev's Revolt, 1773–5* (Bloomington and London, 1969), p. 89. On the Moscow revolt of 1771 and much else, see J. T. Alexander, *Bubonic Plague in Early Modern Russia*, (Baltimore, 1980). See also J. T. Alexander (ed.), 'Plague, epidemics and antiplague precautions in early modern Russia,' *Soviet Studies in History*, vol. 25 (1987). See also generally P. Avrich, *Russian Rebels, 1600–1800* (London, 1973).

30. Dukes, *Russia*, vol. 1, pp. 140–43.

31. Quoted in Dukes, *Catherine the Great*, pp. 169–71.

32. Jones, *The Emancipation*, pp. 210–20.

33. Ibid., pp. 244–72; V. V. Grigorev, *Reforma mestnogo upravleniia pri Ekaterine II: Uchrezhdenie o guberniiakh 7 noiabria 1775g.* (St Petersburg, 1910); R. E. Jones, *Provincial Development in Russia: Catherine II and Jacob Sievers* (New Brunswick, NJ, 1984); J. P. Le Donne, *Ruling Russia: Politics and Administration in the Age of Absolutism, 1762–1796* (Princeton, NJ, 1984).

34. G. Soloveytchik, *Potemkin* (New York, 1947) gives a sound enough description of this relationship.

35. D. M. Griffiths, 'Catherine II, George III and the British Opposition' in A. G. Cross (ed.), *Great Britain and Russia in the Eighteenth Century: Contacts and Comparisons* (Newtonville, 1979), pp. 312–13; I. de Madariaga, *Britain, Russia and the Armed Neutrality of 1780* (New Haven and London, 1962); and for Catherine's view of the Declaration of Independence, in which she found too little reason and too much unseemly temerity, see N. N. Bolkhovitinov, *Stanovlenie russkoamerikanskikh otonoshenii, 1773–1815* (Moscow, 1966), p. 97.

36. Quoted in M. T. Florinsky, *Russia: A History and an Interpretation*, vol. 1 (New York, 1955), p. 528. And see A. W. Fisher, *The Russian Annexation of the Crimea, 1772–1783* (Cambridge, 1970).

37. Dukes, *Russia under Catherine the Great*, vol. 1, pp. 162–5.

38. M. Beloff, 'Russia' in A. Goodwin (ed.), *The European Nobilities in the Eighteenth Century* (London, 1953), p. 189; Helju A. Bennett, 'Evolution of the Meanings of *Chin*', *University of California Slavic Studies*, vol. 10 (1977), p. 28; quotations from Bochkarev as in Dukes, *Catherine the Great*, p. 179.

39. Hume, quoted in D. B. Horn, *British Public Opinion and the Partition of Poland* (Edinburgh, 1945), pp. 18–19; Klyuchevsky, *Sochineniia*, vol. 5, p. 370; *Scots Magazine* quoted in M. S. Anderson, *Britain's Discovery of Russia, 1553–1815* (London, 1958), pp. 138–9.

40. See J. M. Hittle, *The Service City: State and Townsmen in Russia, 1600–1800* (Cambridge, MA, and London, 1979) especially Chapter 10; G. Rozman, *Urban Networks in Russia 1750–1800* (Princeton, NJ, 1976); J. Hartley, 'Saint Petersburg Guberniya after the Charter to the Towns of 1785', *Slavonic Review*, vol. 62 (1984).

41. E. C. Thaden, *Russia's Western Borderlands, 1710–1870* (Princeton, 1984)

pp. 32–55.

42. Catherine's title a corrected version of that appearing in Dukes, *Russia under Catherine the Great*, vol. 1, p. 162; her views on the Pacific in Y. Semyonov, *The Conquest of Siberia* (London, 1944), p. 195.

43. See, for example, B. P. Gurevich, *Mezhdunarodnye otnosheniia v Tsentralnoi Azii v XVII – pervoir polovine XIXv.* (Moscow, 1979).

44. See R. P. Bartlett, *Human Capital: The Settlement of Foreigners in Russia, 1762–1804* (Cambridge, 1979).

45. L. G. Beskrovny, 'Armiia i flot' in A. I. Baranovich *et al.* (eds.), *Ocherki istorii SSSR: Rossiia vo vtoroi polovine XVIII v.* (Moscow, 1956), pp. 307–16.

46. Ibid., pp. 307–16.

47. Dukes, *Catherine the Great*, p. 185; N. F. Demidova, 'Biurokratizatsiia gosudarstvennogo apparata absoliutizma v XVII–XVIII vv.' in N. M. Druzhinin, *Absoliutizm v Rossii* (XVII–XVIIIvv.) (Moscow, 1964), pp. 239–40; W. M. Pintner, 'The Evolution of Civil Officialdom, 1755–1855' in W. M. Pintner and D. K. Rowney (eds), *Russian Officialdom: The Bureaucratization of Russian Society from the Seventeenth to the Twentieth Century* (London, 1980), Ch. 8.

48. Dukes, *Catherine the Great*, p. 145; Hittle, *The Service City*.

49. V. M. Kabuzan, *Izmeneniia v razmeshchenii naseleniia Rossii v XVII–pervoi polovine XIXV.* (Moscow, 1971), pp. 53–4.

50. K. E. Dzhedzhula, *Rossiia i velikaia frantsuzskaia burzhuaznaia revoliutsiia kontsa XVIII veka* (Kiev, 1972). Chapter 3 contains some exaggeration but also some convincing argument.

51. Dukes, *Catherine the Great*, p. 95; *Russia under Catherine the Great*, vol. 1, pp. 68–88.

52. A. H. Brown, 'S. E. Desnitsky, Adam Smith, and the *Nakaz* of Catherine II', *Oxford Slavonic Papers*, no. 7 (1974). For emphasis on another source, see Victor Kamendrowsky, 'Catherine II's *Nakaz*, State Finances and the *Encyclopédie*', *Canadian-American Slavic Studies*, vol. 13 (1979).

53. See, for example, N. L. Rubinshtein, *Selskoe khoziaistvo Rossii vo vtoroi polovine XVIIIv.* (Moscow, 1957).

54. *Hansard's Parliamentary History of England* (London, 1913) pp. 1137, 1142; Arcadius Kahan, 'Eighteenth-Century Russian-British Trade: Russia's Contribution to the Industrial Revolution in Great Britain' in Cross, *Great Britain*, pp. 181–90; H. Kaplan, 'Observations on the value of Russia's overseas commerce with Great Britain during the second half of the eighteenth century', *Slavic Review*, vol. 45 (1986). See also A. Kahan, *The Plow, The Hammer and the Knout* (Chicago, 1985), pp. 237–40.

55. S. M. Troitsky, 'Finansovaia politika russkogo absoliutizma vo vtoroi polovine XVII i XVIII vv.' in Druzhinin, *Absoliutizm*, pp. 303, 313, 316.

56. A. McConnell, *A Russian Philosophe: Alexander Radishchev, 1749–1802* (The Hague, 1964), pp. 89, 195–6, 209.

57. M. M. Shtrange, *Demokraticheskaia intelligentsiia Rossii v XVIII veke* (Moscow, 1965); M. D. Kurmacheva, *Krepostnaia intelligentsiia. Rossii (vtoraia polovina XVIII — nachalo XIX veka)* (Moscow, 1983). See also W. J. Gleason, *Moral Idealists, Bureaucracy and Catherine the Great* (New

Brunswick, NU, 1981) and M. Raeff, *Origins of the Russian Intelligentsia, The Eighteenth Century Nobility* (New York, 1966).

58. J. L. Black, *Citizens for the Fatherland: Education, Educators and Pedagogical Ideals in Eighteenth-Century Russia* (Boulder, CO, 1979); M. J. Okenfuss, 'Education and empire: school reform in enlightened Russia', *Jahrubücher für Geschichte Osteuropas*, vol. 27 (1979). Evidence of the continued importance of Orthodoxy may be found in K. A. Papmehl, *Metropolitan Platon of Moscow (Petr Levshin, 1737–1812): The Enlightened Prelate, Scholar and Educator* (Newtonville, MA, 1983).

59. R. Zguta, *Russian Minstrels: A History of the Skomorokhi* (Oxford, 1978), p. 65; and see generally, A. F. Nekrylova, *Russkie narodnye gorodskie prazdniki, uveseleniia i zvelishcha: konets XVIII–nachalo XX veka* (Leningrad, 1984).

60. I. de Madariaga, *Russia in the Age of Catherine the Great* (London, 1981) p. 581. See also K. Rasmussen 'Catherine II and the image of Peter I', *Slavic Review*, v. 37 (1975).

61. See the contributions to M. Raeff (ed.), *Catherine the Great: A Profile* (New York and London, 1972). On Catherine's policies of religious toleration, an important aspect of her enlightened absolutism, see Madariaga, *Russia*, Chapters 7 and 32.

62. I. A. Fedosov, 'Prosveshchennyi absoliutizm v Rossii', *Voprosy istorii*, no. 9 (1970), p. 38; A. B. Kamenskii, 'Ekaterina II', *Voprosy istorii* no. 3 (1989) p. 88.

63. A. A. Kizevetter, 'Portrait of an Enlightened Autocrat' in Raeff, *Catherine the Great*, p. 17. For further interesting analysis of Catherine and her policies, see D. Griffiths, 'Catherine II: The Republican Empress', *Jahrbücher für Geschichte Osteuropas*, Band 21 (1973); B. Meehan-Waters, 'Catherine the Great and the Problem of Female Rule', *Russian Review*, vol. 34 (1975); and J. T. Alexander; *Catherine the Great: Life and Legend* (New York and Oxford, 1989).

64. See notes 11 and 38 above.

65. P. Dukes, 'Catherine II's enlightened absolutism and the problem of serfdom' in W. E. Butler (ed.), *Russian Law: Historical and Political Perspectives* (Leyden, 1977).

66. See note 39 above. There is an abundance of supporting evidence to be found in H. Rogger, *National Consciousness in Eighteenth-Century Russia* (Cambridge, MA. 1960), and K. A. Papmehl, *Freedom of Expression in Eighteenth Century Russia* (The Hague, 1971).

CHAPTER SIX

Improvement or deterioration: Paul (1796–1801) and sons – Conclusion

An epigraph for this final chapter could be an old proverb posed as a question: like father, like son? We shall be examining the brief reign of the Emperor Paul, 1796–1801, and comparing it with those considerably longer of his sons, Alexander I, 1801–25, and Nicholas I, 1825–55. In such a manner, we shall proceed to a concluding discussion of the nature of Russian absolutism, of its making and to a lesser extent of its demise.

To begin with the central character, Paul, beyond all reasonable doubt the son of Peter III and Catherine II, but in his own frequent irrational frame of mind, the offspring of more uncertain parentage. Here we will accept that the boy born on 20 September 1754 was the legitimate child of the grand ducal couple. He certainly appears to have been accepted as such by the Empress Elizabeth, who soon took him away from Peter and Catherine not so much to be a substitute for her own probable lack of issue as to be prepared in an appropriate manner for the onerous responsibilities of the office that he would be called upon to assume, perhaps in preference to his father, certainly in Elizabeth's view before his mother. And later, not only did he wonder who his parents really were, he was often sure enough on this question to worry about another, would he go the same way as the Emperor Peter before he became the Emperor Paul? So strained were the family relationships that the authorities deemed it wise during Catherine's reign to forbid the production in St Petersburg of Shakespeare's *Hamlet*, which in at least one scene might then have become a play within a play within a play. The psychological pressures on the young man made him mad according to some analysts, and there has been some interesting work on his mental make-up by a number of authorities ranging from the psychiatrist V. F. Chizh, who argued in 1907 that he was not mentally sick, to the historian Hugh Ragsdale, who made a bold attempt at psychohistorical analysis in 1988[1].

Not long before her death the Empress Elizabeth appointed as governor to Paul the statesman Nikita I. Panin, who returned from Sweden where he had been ambassador for about eleven years to take up the post in the spring of 1760. Panin drew up an enlightened plan of education for the approval of the Empress, and then started to take the six-year-old boy through a course which included mathematics, most important for purifying reason and training in the bases of truth; history, with 'brief clear essays' especially on the Russian experience; languages, particularly Russian old and new, but with high priority for French and German; and cavalry exercises, dancing and artistic drawing. All this was intended to be done 'according to the child's years and the unfolding of his innate capabilities';[2] care was to be employed in order that he should not be overindulged and yet, possibly because the damage had already been done, his temperament was already far from placid, and his attention was often fitful.

So Paul did not grow up as the model enlightened prince that Panin was hoping for. Nevertheless, he was interested enough to collect a large library and to make use of it, and to welcome the acquaintance of many of the bright young men of the day, for example, the writer D. I. Fonvizin whose play *The Brigadier* was presented to him for its satire of the old-fashioned attitudes of the provincial nobility that the new age was to overcome. At the age of nineteen he married a German princess, who soon became the mistress of one of his best friends and then died in childbirth. Almost immediately, being now twenty-two, he married another German princess, a niece of Frederick the Great, whom he admired as much as his father before him. Maria Fedorovna, to give the lady her adopted Orthodox name, turned out to be a much better wife and a more successful bearer of children, producing four sons, two of them future tsars, and six daughters. For twenty years or more Paul appears to have been an exemplary husband; although forming a mystical, romantic relationship with one of his wife's ladies-in-waiting after about ten years, he did not take a mistress until after his accession to power. Before then his role as a son was much diminished, his contacts with his mother and her court becoming more infrequent after he had attained his majority, an event that caused rumours of a coup on his behalf and a little action as well. After returning from a lengthy grand tour of Europe he retired to Gatchina, an estate near St Petersburg, in 1783, and led a quiet life there as a good landlord if rigorous drillmaster, finding relaxation at the literary salon and theatrical performances sponsored by his wife. Among his entourage there were some reactionary men such as Alexis Arakcheev, who was to gain notoriety during the reigns of his sons, and some enlightened progressives, such as Sergei Pleshcheev, who was to rise to high rank in Paul's reign. Pleshcheev, a naval officer who had been trained in England, encouraged a grand ducal interest in Freemasonry that had first been stirred by Nikita Panin himself.[3]

Kept out of the business of government by Catherine, who in her last years was seriously considering bypassing him for the succession in favour of his son Alexander, Paul nevertheless prepared himself for the position that his birth had appeared to assign him; one of the questions in his mind as he prepared a political testament (his own *Nakaz*) and sketched out policies was the very manner in which the Russian throne was disposed. At an earlier date, at the time of the Pugachev Revolt, he had written: 'The state should be regarded as a body. The ruler is its head, the laws are its soul, morals its heart, wealth and abundance its health, military power its arms and all other parts serving its defence, and religion is the law under which everything is constituted.' Now in 1788, on the eve of his departure for active service in the war against Sweden, he developed this concept of a well-articulated state, taking as a starting-point the basic assertion of his mother's *Nakaz* that for Russia 'there is no better form than autocracy, for it combines the strength of law with the executive dispatch of a single authority'. Paul moved closer to Catherine and away from his mentors in giving emphasis to the part played by the head and playing down the part played by the other limbs and organs of the body politic. Panin and Fonvizin had argued for 'a monarchical government with fundamental, immutable laws'; Paul wanted the autocrat to be bound only by a fundamental, immutable law of succession, an edict issued on the day of his coronation, 5 April 1797, making the house of Romanov the hereditary heir to the throne in a well-defined order.[4]

In the end his own succession in November 1796 was smooth enough, and Paul embarked on the task of implementing his program for reform at the same time as conducting a vigorous foreign policy. He began his reign in what was almost a traditional manner by rewarding his supporters and rather less conventionally by pardoning many of his opponents. He had his father's remains removed to join their predecessors in the Peter and Paul fortress, placing them next to the newly deceased body of his mother who might well have turned over in her grave. Novikov and Radishchev were released along with less notorious convicts, while Kosciuszko was liberated with honour and his fellow Poles.

As far as the administration was concerned Paul's changes at the centre have been seen as a transition from the college system to that of the ministries. True, he at first revived the colleges of Commerce, Manufactures, Mines and State Revenue that had been abolished with the introduction of the new system of provincial government in 1775, but they were all put under the jurisdiction of directors responsible immediately to the tsar, and at least one of them was already known as 'minister'. The State Council and the Senate continued on the whole to function formally as before, although they were subjected to changes in number and procedure, especially as the Emperor made himself increasingly responsible as the active head of state. Similarly his 'prime minister', the Procurator-General, was never as important to Paul as Viazemsky had been to Catherine, and the holder of the office with one possible exception was never retained for long enough to become sufficiently familiar with his various tasks. Paul aimed at the reduction of costs as well as the increase of efficiency, and to these ends simplified somewhat the structure of institutions set up in 1775, reducing the number of courts and court officials, cutting the total of provinces from fifty to forty, and restoring the rights and privileges of the Ukraine, Poland-Lithuania, the Baltic provinces and Finland, at least on paper if not so much in fact.

Nevertheless the restoration of a measure of local autonomy has sometimes been cited as one of Paul's more progressive measures, as have some parts of his social program, notably those dealing with the nobility as a whole. From the end of 1797 they were to pay a tax on their estates, while according to a manifesto of April of that year they were not to oblige their serfs to work on Sundays. A recommendation that the serfs should labour for their masters for three days only and for themselves the other three did not actually receive the full force of law, depending rather on the goodwill of the landlords, even on their determination to break with well-established practice. Because of this supposed limitation on their work, and a favourable attitude with even less foundation stemming from petitions made to Paul as the son of Peter at the time of the Pugachev Revolt, his rating with the peasantry was high. On the other hand the very same measure, as well as other decrees from 1797 to 1800 restricting their rights of election to local governmental offices in addition to an overall approach to them of arbitrary discipline, made the nobles look upon the Emperor as a traitor to the tacit alliance with them. In retrospect, long after the frenetic rumour and energy of the reign have died away, we can see clearly that it did not constitute an exception in its treatment of either the lowest or the highest in the land.[5]

At the time, the anecdotes told of the Emperor's whimsical severity helped create an extreme caricature, and the very reality must have been disagreeable enough for the aristocratic inhabitants of St Petersburg when they were turned out from their comfortable quarters to the parade ground. The crazy atmosphere of the capital during Paul's reign was well caught in the tsar's order that all houses there should be painted in black and white as well as the colourful story of Lieutenant Kije, the non-existent officer born of an imperial misreading of a document that nobody dared to correct as he received successive promotion for meritorious service never carried out. And so a verdict of broad condemnation was arrived at that led to his overthrow and a poor historical reputation. Karamzin was among the first to put this negative appraisal in a literary manner:

Paul came to the throne at that period, propitious for autocracy, when the terrors of the French Revolution had cured Europe of the dreams of civil freedom and equality. But what the Jacobins had done to the republican system, Paul did to the autocratic one: he made people hate its abuses. As a result of a wretched mental delusion and of the many personal unpleasantries which he had experienced, he wished to turn into an Ivan IV.[6]

We will return to more estimates of the Emperor Paul after a look at his foreign policy. For the moment we can at least agree with Karamzin concerning the context of the reign; the French Revolution and its consequences constituted together the most important influence on European development at the turn of the century from one end of the continent to the other. The tsar himself recognised this in an early circular to Russian diplomats announcing his desire for peace and his aversion to the French Revolution and its threat to the terrestrial and divine order. His tendency towards mysticism, encouraged by an association with the Maltese Order of the Knights of St John of Jerusalem, by whom he was to be elected Grand Master in late 1798, encouraged him to think in terms of a crusade against the great monster. However, before building his own dreams, he thought it necessary to dismantle the dreams of others, notably of Catherine's last lover, Platon Zubov, who, it will be recalled, had devised an 'Oriental project' of such dimensions that it surpassed the schemes of Gregory Potemkin and even those of Alexander the Great. So Paul immediately recalled Russian troops from as far as they had reached into Georgia and Persia. Another plan, this time of his mother, for sending more Russian troops over Europe to keep a watch on the Rhine, was also cancelled. For further satisfaction of his initial wish for peace, Paul hoped to revive the idea of his former tutor Nikita Panin – the 'Northern System'. Even when Panin himself was conducting foreign policy, this idea had proved to be very difficult to put into practice, and so it proved to be again now. Withdrawing to the Baltic a squadron of the navy that had been sent beyond it to sail with the British, the tsar attempted to solidify the Russian position in this home sea through closer relations with Sweden, dynastic and then perhaps military too, but negotiations for a marriage between his own daughter and the King of Sweden broke down over the old problem of religion.

No such impediment was allowed to block the marriage of the same princess to Prince Joseph of Hungary, and this led the way towards the revival of the Russian association with Habsburg Austria. Although peace was agreed between Austria and France in late 1797, both sides knew that the cessation of hostilities could not be permanent, especially since after its first striking appearance in Italy, the shadow of Napoleon was now being cast over the rest of Europe. For his part, if Paul were not already sufficiently disposed against Napoleon, he was pushed into that attitude by all kinds of émigrés escaping to his court; a last straw was the occupation by Bonaparte on his way to Egypt in the summer of 1798 of the island headquarters of the knightly order of which he was about to be elected Grand Master. And so Russia joined Austria, Great Britain, Turkey and Naples in the anti-French coalition achieving its formation by 1799.

In consequence of this development a Russian squadron sailed again from the Baltic Sea to join the British fleet along the Dutch coast, while another from the Black Sea moved in concert with its old enemy the Turkish fleet to take islands in the Ionian and Adriatic Seas. On land Suvorov achieved some brilliant military feats in rapid movements through Northern Italy and Switzerland. But the coalition was already subject to powerful strains. In spite of his great talent for leadership, Suvorov could not get on with the Austrians under his command, and victory turned to defeat, alliance to estrangement. The Russo-British operations off the Dutch coast were not a success and led to mutual recriminations; more seriously, after dissuading Admiral Ushakov from making an attack on Malta, the British took it themselves and then stubbornly kept it from the Grand Master.

Having fallen out with Austria and Great Britain, Paul moved closer to Sweden and France. In late 1799 Paul created a new 'Northern System' in a treaty with Gustavus of Sweden, and the two monarchs together revived in 1800 the Armed Neutrality League, much to British annoyance. Now that Bonaparte had taken over in France, and revolutionary zeal appeared to be exhausted in its place of origin, Paul came to believe that he could work with his old enemy for the cause of counter-revolution elsewhere. And at the end of his reign Paul had also developed thoughts similar to his predecessor's for expansion. Between Austria and themselves, Russia and France could carve up a moribund Turkey, and Paul would regain Constantinople. He now grew excited enough to bring to new life the foolish expedition that he had called to a halt at the commencement of his reign. Georgia was formally annexed at the beginning of 1801; a Russian force was sent off in the direction of India. In such a manner, an unpopular foreign adventure was to contribute to the downfall of Paul as it had led to the downfall of his father.[7] Meanwhile, the development of commercial enterprise across Siberia and beyond had been formally marked in 1799 by the creation of the Russian-American Company.

Talk of the removal from the throne of the Emperor Paul can be traced back almost as far as his ascension on it, but the actual conspiracy that achieved the increasingly discussed fell purpose probably took shape towards the end of 1799. The leading figure was the military governor of St Petersburg, Count Peter Pahlen, and most of his collaborators were guardsmen, including Platon Zubov and his two brothers who had not long been recalled from exile by their victim. Another man in the know although not in at the death was the nephew of the Emperor's former tutor bearing his uncle's name, and so a Count Nikita Panin was involved in the elimination of both Peter III and Paul. The latter

Count Panin was responsible for informing the Grand Duke Alexander of the forthcoming event, representing it as the introduction of a regent rather than as a murder of the monarch, but the heir apparent could not have been so innocent of the ways of Russian coups as to have been in ignorance about the probable outcome, whatever his later protestations to the contrary. The dark deed was done on the night of 11 March 1801, and an announcement put out to the people that their ruler had succumbed to a fit of apoplexy.

Guilt concerning this lie and even more concerning the terrible reality behind it definitely had a powerful effect on Alexander I[8] and possibly on Nicholas I as well, but before a concluding brief glance at them and their reigns, let us make a final estimation of their father and his reign, allowing him to compose his own epitaph:

He undertook to create order, but his enthusiastic wish to make it anew hindered him from undertaking this in a reasonable manner. It must be added that there was perhaps carelessness in his character, and therefore he did many things that created a bad impression, which, coupled with intrigues against his person rather than his policies, brought about his ruin and tended to give a bad impression of his deeds. If a reasonable, careful and steadfast spirit had stood in their way, what intrigue could have been conducted?

This passage was actually written by Paul in the 1770s about his father, but might equally be applied to himself, about whom he also wrote at this time: 'I cannot have either party or interest apart from the State ... I prefer to be hated for doing good to being loved for doing ill.' Such an outlook on the part of the Emperor does appear to have been consistent; but his manner of imposing it on his Empire was contradictory to an extreme.[9]

As a consequence there was a large amount of agreement in the nineteenth century with the harsh verdict of Karamzin. By the beginning of the twentieth century, however, the inevitable reappraisal had begun, and E. S. Shumigorsky was among those who saw Paul caught between the influence of the West and the force of tradition, the consequent tension being exacerbated by the French Revolution. Then, just before the fall of tsarism, M. V. Klochkov discerned in his government a coherent system, even if conceding that the hyperactivity of the Emperor himself disguised and even on occasion concealed it. More recently as noted above, Hugh Ragsdale has subjected the man to close psychohistorical scrutiny, while contrasting appraisals of him and his years on the throne have come from Roderick McGrew and John Keep. McGrew writes of Paul as 'one of the first of Europe's modern monarchs to build a program on the principle of preserving the past' while Keep observes that his reign 'represented a crucial stage in the emergence of that modern Moloch, the militaristic-bureaucratic state'.[10]

Karamzin, it will be remembered, made the assertion that Paul wished to become an Ivan IV. Two other models among his predecessors are suggested by his artistic patronage. He commissioned a picture of Michael Romanov at his coronation; he ordered Rastrelli's equestrian statue of Peter I to be moved to the entrance to his new palace in St Petersburg with the inscription 'To Great-Grandfather from Great-Grandson'.[11] Here indeed was a man who wished to place himself firmly in the tsarist tradition, but who also realised that extraordinary measures would have to be taken for such a heritage to be preserved. Hence the curious mixture of knightly mysticism, enlightened rationality and rigid absolutism, and the circumstance that this reign was, to an extent as great as its counterparts discussed above, a reign of transition.

Soviet historians, for their part, also see the last years of the eighteenth century as a period of transition. A. P. Bazhova writes of Paul: 'A monarch, on the throne on the eve of the crisis of the serf system, naturally with full force attempted to strengthen the autocracy, to double the police watch over his subjects, especially the peasants.' She believes that the recommendation in 1797 of a three-day limit on work for the landlords made the condition of the peasants worse rather than better, and points out that in the years 1796–98 there were 184 incidents of peasant insubordination (a pre-revolutionary estimate of 1904 giving the even higher figure of 278 such incidents). While Bazhova characterises Paul as 'unbalanced, weak-willed, neurasthenic, but by no means weak-minded', and a colleague I. A. Fedosov unreservedly dismisses him as a crazy despot who 'threatened to discredit the very idea of absolutism', other Soviet historians appear prepared to move at least some way towards rehabilitation. N. Ia. Eidelman goes so far as to attribute to Paul 'a definite programme, idea, logic' based on a 'conservative utopia' embodying the courtly codes of the medieval past. Hence, the Emperor's emphasis on the duties as well as the privileges of the nobility, his rejection of what he saw as the cynicism and prevarication of Catherine the Great, his admiration for the dedication and inspiration of Peter the Great and his unwitting anticipation of the 'official nationality' to be developed by Nicholas I and his advisers.[12]

To place the Emperor Paul and the transition marked by his reign more fully in their context, we must look back again briefly at his father and mother and the beginnings of this transition when they ruled, and then take a quick glance forward at his sons and the continuation of the transition as they in turn came to the throne. The principal significance of the reign of Peter III lies in its demonstration of the limits placed on Russian absolutism by the nature of its socio-political foundation. A system of government still described by some historians as consisting of a 'state' aloof from society was shown to be dependent on the sufferance of its leading citizens, the members of the nobility, who with virtual unanimity came quickly to decide that Peter had broken many of the unwritten rules of the tacit alliance between the *dvorianstvo* and the tsar. Catherine restored this alliance and then took it to a new peak of development in the Charter of the Nobility in 1785, which, it must be emphasised again, was granted to the class rather than to the members of it. And so Russian absolutism as it had evolved by the accession of Paul took the shape of a collective contract, individual breakers of which, be they rank and file or the supreme commander, invited swift and condign punishment. Nobles such as Radishchev and Novikov were to discover before the end of the reign of Catherine that an over-enthusiastic interpretation of the earlier encouragement by their Empress of free speech and frank criticism could now take them into prison or exile. The autocracy, which under Peter the Great and the younger Catherine the Great had been in the vanguard of progress in many directions, had turned conservative, and Paul discovered that the manner in which that conservatism was practised under the shadow of the French Revolution called for more astuteness than he in his agitated state of mind could furnish.

After his death, his personality was in a sense shared by the sons who succeeded him. Alexander I was the mystic, encouraged by the victory over Napoleon to indulge some of his dreams in the public declarations of the Holy Alliance and others in the private exchanges with a series of like souls. Nicholas I was the martinet, expecting punctilious obedience of his every command by those of high rank as well as low. But beyond the personalities of the tsars, absolutism was being carried by a momentum that they could do little to resist towards decline. Far from marking the apogee of autocracy, as some historians have argued, the reign of Nicholas constituted a descent from a high point that had been reached during the reign of Catherine. Nicholas came to the throne just after, in the footsteps of Radishchev, the Decembrists had revealed that a significant stratum of the ruling class had become alienated from absolutism; he departed from it as the failures of the Crimean War were making clear the inadequacy for survival through the nineteenth century of the whole system. His attempt to maintain a powerful, loyal nobility by reform of the Table of Ranks was in the not-too-distant future to fail as completely as his struggle to maintain its basic underpinning, the institution of serfdom, by readjustment, failed in the shorter run. Meanwhile the opposition movement began to gather strength as it acquired more recruits not only from the nobility but also the third estate.

Students of Russian absolutism, and even more those of the Soviet system of government, have often fallen short of a full understanding of the distinctive nature of the pre-revolutionary polity, by concentrating their attention on the nineteenth century, when it was approaching collapse, and subjecting the late eighteenth century, when it reached its greatest strength, to comparative neglect. To understand in proper historical perspective what came after 1917, the making of Russian absolutism, even though more remote in time than its dissolution, needs to be given its fair measure of analysis.

A certain amount of recapitulation of the period covered by this book now becomes necessary. A standard Soviet view put forward in 1967 of developments between the years 1613 and 1801 would be as follows. Although the first half of the seventeenth century required concentration on recovery from the Time of Troubles, by the middle of the century, 'The vast spaces, the economic advance and the strengthening of external links made Russia a most powerful factor in international life, and the aims put forward in foreign policy had an important influence on the situation of countries to West and East.' The Code of 1649 brought about the juridical confirmation of serfdom, while reinforcing the dominance of the nobility which, along with the nascent bourgeoisie, was to form the main support for the formation of absolutism. The transition to this form of government was accomplished in the second half of the seventeenth century with the curtailment of the national assembly or *zemsky sobor;* the subjection of the church to state power; the growing power of the central institutions known as *prikazy* whose administration was concentrated in the hands of a few influential individuals; and the first attempts at the creation of a regular army. The tendency towards absolutism, especially the entrenchment of serfdom, was resisted by the popular masses in a series of urban revolts and in the peasant war under the leadership of Stenka Razin. The most important aspect of foreign policy was the struggle with Poland for the Ukraine. Wars with Sweden for an outlet to the Baltic Sea and with Turkey for the littoral of the Black Sea failed owing to the economic and military backwardness of Russia. While the acquisition of the Ukraine led to an increase in productive forces, the economic development of Siberia and the Far East could be pursued more easily after the Treaty of Nerchinsk with China in 1689, although it was a blow to the more immediate Russian interests. A new secular culture joined battle with the old, both Christian and pagan, while international cultural connections grew.

The first half of the eighteenth century brought the construction, mainly at state initiative, of large-scale industrial enterprises in metal and cloth. Russian ships were now the equal of the Swedish and the Dutch. But serfdom was intensified, and the economic gains were made through greater exploitation of the people at large. Meanwhile, the administrative apparatus was assembled for what was now 'an empire of the nobility'. The many *prikazy* were now replaced by a smaller number of colleges. The Senate superseded the boyar duma, and the provinces were rearranged. The regular army and navy were important sources of support for the absolutism of the nobility. In foreign policy, the solution of the Baltic problem was most important. The opening of the window on the West was of great significance, not only political and economic, but also cultural. In this latter sphere, the newly created military schools prepared specialists for industry as well as for the army and navy. Secular culture in general was in the ascendancy, at least among the elite, as the Academy of Sciences in St Petersburg became a centre of learning of European reputation.

The second half of the eighteenth century was a period in which the Russia of the nobility flourished and the bourgeoisie also grew. A base for capitalism was formed, while small-scale economic enterprise also prospered. Growing internal demand and increasing export possibilities obliged landlords and peasants to enter wider markets. This process increased social inequalities. The nobility acquired new privileges including freedom from obligatory service, while the lower orders showed their opposition most clearly in the peasant war under Emelian Pugachev. This was followed by the strengthening of the state apparatus and open reaction. In foreign policy two principal tasks were carried out: the achievement of access to the Black Sea and the reinforcement of the position on the Baltic Sea. Lithuanians, Belorussians and Right-Bank Ukrainians were liberated from Polish and Turkish religious and national oppression, while the establishment of a protectorate over Georgia brought to an end threats from Turkey and Persia. In general, the extension of the Empire had a huge influence over the peoples inhabiting it, but the principal beneficiaries were the noble landlords. Through their introduction of serfdom into the southern regions, they weakened social contradiction in the central provinces and slowed down the growth of capitalist relationships. On the other hand, the struggle for national independence and the struggle of the popular masses against serfdom facilitated the formation of the Russian and other nations inhabiting the Empire. Meanwhile, elite Russian culture also moved ahead, preparing the way for the flowering which occurred in the first half of the nineteenth century. At the same time, ties were strengthened between Russian and foreign thought in the international movement known as the Enlightenment.[13]

Most Western historians would agree to reject several aspects of this standard Soviet view. First, they would not be happy with a periodisation based on vulgar fractions. Second, the identification of 'tasks' in foreign policy injects too much retroactive wisdom into the minds of those statesmen who made the 'correct' choices. Third, the argument is suspect that Russian imperial expansion brought about the strengthening of ties between the lower orders of the various nationalities at the same time as a convergence of interest between their leaders and the Russian nobility. Fourth, and more generally, many foreign readers are not prepared to accept the flag-waving patriotism of the standard Soviet account. Granted that Russia became a great power in the eighteenth century, we no longer need to celebrate the victory over Sweden or even the reduction of the Turkish threat to Europe: in the partitions of Poland, Russia was hardly pursuing a less acquisitive policy than Austria and Prussia. Moreover, in the cultural sphere, was the reputation of the Academy of Sciences in St Petersburg so firmly established in Europe in the first half of the eighteenth century? In the second half of the century, was Russian thought in reality such an integral part of the international movement known as the Enlightenment? Fifthly, and most comprehensively of all, the majority of Western historians would want to reject the overall Marxist approach of their Soviet colleagues, their insistence on the significance of classes, and of the struggle between them.

The response that might be made to these objections must in part be given on the basis of conversations rather than the written record, for although there has been much reconsideration among Soviet historians, especially since 1985, by no means all the new thinking has made its appearance in print. On the first point, of periodisation, they might say that to insist on divisions by reigns rather than chronological slices is to exaggerate the importance of certain rulers. Conceding, indeed often asserting, that individuals such as Peter the Great made an enormous impact on Russian development, they would also argue that there were others who made little mark on history. If, however, allowance is made for the fact that a change of monarch usually meant a new entourage, a fresh establishment, then the case for personal rather than arithmetical delineation becomes somewhat stronger. As for 'tasks' in foreign policy, the second point, it could be maintained that some direction needs to be given to discussion of any theme in the story of a state, or there will be no possibility of comprehensive grasp. Soviet historians might suggest here, as elsewhere, that all practitioners of their craft cannot avoid at least a little of the spirit of patriotism when dealing with their own country. More of this below. Similarly, when dealing with any nation or empire, somehow or another a rationalisation of the present situation needs to be, or at least often is, given. From empire to commonwealth, the overseas extension of the *patrie*, the proclamation of 'manifest destiny' or whatever, Britain, France, the USA and others advance a justification not always accepted by outsiders. Granted that the formula of the 'friendship of peoples', like its predecessors, can be severely criticised, the USSR, like all contemporary political units, has needed the cohesion that an appropriate account of the past provides, and Soviet historians in their own way perform the service rendered by their colleagues all over the world. Thus, there may be at least some flag-waving in the historiography of the USSR, but where will it not be found, it could be asked? Do not all nations tend to exaggerate the importance and the unique contribution of their own culture? Finally, as far as an overall approach is concerned, the Soviet reaction might be at once defensive and aggressive. In other words, while defending their own version of Marxism as a serviceable framework for their research and publication, they would also ask, what is your alternative?

Needless to say, since 1985 not all Soviet historians would assert their Marxism as much as before, and at least some of them would deny it. In such a manner, they would approach the diverse nature of the approaches of their Western colleagues, who would normally cite such diversity as the reason for the absence of any agreed over-arching key to explanation in their own work. Here, however, at least some of them make too much of a virtue out of heterogeneity, especially when finding minor exceptions to major observations, even detecting 'Marxist' influence in any attempt to apply sociological findings to their own discipline. At the very least, concepts provide a basis for discussion, generalisations counter random prejudice and structures develop a sense of proportion. These advances were realised during the Enlightenment, from which Marx took much of his argument. In 1852, he wrote:

Long before me bourgeois historians had described the historical development of this class struggle and bourgeois economists the economic anatomy of the classes. What I did that was new was to prove: (1) that the *existence of classes* is only bound up with *particular, historical phases in the development of production;* (2) that the class struggle necessarily leads to the *dictatorship of the proletariat;* (3) that this dictatorship itself only constitutes the transition to the *abolition of all classes* and to a *classless society.*

Allowing Marx proprietorial rights over (2) and (3), at least some challenge can be made on (1) from the vantage point of the Scottish Enlightenment in particular, from, for example, that of Adam Ferguson, John Millar and Adam Smith.[14]

Such an argument is unlikely to hold much sway with those who hold that use of the term 'class' is both Marxist and anachronistic. There will be many who will want to reject nearly all attempts at sociological explanation, whether Marxist or not, arguing that they cannot be applied to the complex process of history. On the other hand, there may be more widespread agreement about the employment of at least some terms not current in the seventeenth and eighteenth centuries while also to be found in sociological, even Marxist analysis: for example, 'absolutism' and 'autocracy'.[15] The mode of explanation applied here to the process of the making of Russian absolutism has adopted a middle course, an approach chosen not so much for balance as through conviction. Beyond all reasonable doubt, the evidence bequeathed to us from the period of history under discussion demonstrates that 'the existence of classes is only bound up with particular, historic phases in the development of production'. Those fully familiar with the Scottish and other areas of the Enlightenment should have no difficulty in accepting that basic circumstance, even if it does have Marxist overtones. Meanwhile, points (2) and (3) from Marx's letter of 1852 can be left on one side since, especially for the making of absolutism, they are predictive rather than descriptive. Moreover, it remains difficult, even impossible, to accept fully some of the structuralist and other sociological modes of explanation to a developmental process. In other words, moving towards a conclusion, we may be well advised to give some emphasis to a summary which can indicate the evolutionary nature of the subject under discussion, and recall again in particular the manner in which Russian absolutism took shape as part of an international, even world-wide, process.

This book began with a description of the 'discovery' of Russia. Of course, Russia was not previously unknown to Europeans, but 1553 marked the first occasion on which it had been involved in the seaborne voyages of discovery and exploration that gave a new dynamic impetus to the history of the continent as a whole from the sixteenth century onwards. In particular, the opening up of the New World across the Atlantic Ocean helped to create a world system dominated by European capitalism. Among the many important consequences of this sea-change was an increased pace in the movement towards the creation of modern, centralised states including those controlled by the form of government known as absolutism. Another significant development was the shift in the European 'core' first from Italy to Spain and Portugal and then on to Holland and England. To a considerable extent, then, Central and Eastern Europe, for the most part land-locked, became 'semi-periphery' or 'periphery' to the core.[16] Another feature of central and especially the eastern areas was a relatively sparse population situated in a vast plain without the kind of natural geographical divisions – mountains as well as water – to be found in much of the West. On the Russian frontier of the continent, therefore, there was a marked tendency towards absolutist control before its 'discovery' by an expedition seeking a new route to the riches of the Orient in the middle of the sixteenth century. The reign of Ivan the Terrible, even more from this time onwards than before, involved the attempt to construct a stronger system of government that could simultaneously maintain law and order throughout Muscovite Russia while expanding its boundaries towards the Baltic, Black and Caspian Seas and into Siberia. The Time of Troubles ensuing soon after Ivan's death underlined his failure, but then, under the new Romanov dynasty, Russia moved more surely if slowly and painfully towards the making of its own form of absolutism.

We have followed that process through five phases, which we will now attempt to summarise, concentrating on nine distinctive features of absolutism in general and the Russian variety in particular, while placing them in their broad European setting. For the sake of simplicity and ease of comprehension, let us begin with a list of the nine features before following them through the five phases which, it will be recalled, have been demarcated by the reigns of the Romanovs:

1) An all-powerful figurehead, normally a monarch;
2) An ideology, basically divine right, but with a growing secular component – the 'general good' and so on;
3) Accommodation with the church, sometimes the assumption of superiority over it;
4) A tendency towards unified law and permanent bureaucracy;

5) The coalescence of nation and/or empire from older provinces and newer acquisitions;
6) A standing army, often a fleet in being;
7) Nobility as the ruling class, although sometimes counterbalanced by a middle class or bourgeoisie, and always accompanied by a huge peasantry;
8) An integrated taxation network and market, tendency towards a national or imperial economy;
9) Development of a secular education system and culture in general, coexisting with, and often establishing superiority over, the earlier church-based counterparts.

The 'broad European setting' of Russian history included the international relations of the states comprising the continent, especially the wars in which they became involved. These conflicts accelerated the establishment of a leading presence for some while, bringing about the decline or even the downfall of others. For many analysts, the first all-European conflict was the Thirty Years War of 1618–48.

The years 1613–45 marked the reign of Michael against the background of most of the Thirty Years War. Except for the Smolensk War of 1632–34, Russia played no direct part in the greater conflict, although the expulsion of the Poles and Swedes at the end of the Time of Troubles was among its precipitators. However, if mostly on the sidelines, Muscovy was on constant alert not only on its western frontier but also to the south, from which the Crimean Tatars might attack at any moment. Meanwhile, exploratory probes into Siberia continued. Under Michael, political and social emphasis was on restoration, with the tsar himself at the apex of the system. An all-powerful figurehead, gathering unto himself the full majesty that had accrued to his predecessors, he does not appear to have exercised his authority to the full, especially during the lifetime of his father Filaret, who played Richelieu to his son's Louis XIII. Even though both monarchs were less than fully self-assertive, however, both France and Russia witnessed during this period the decline of representative assemblies, the *Estates-General* and the *zemsky sobor,* and the increased bureaucratisation of government.[17] Everywhere, nascent absolutism took on the traditional ideology of monarchy, divine right, without as yet much secular component, or attempt to assert control over the church. Indeed, at this stage of development, the distinction between state and church was not yet apparent. Modernisation was in fact most apparent in the army, which needed to come to terms as fully as possible with the 'military revolution' taking place throughout Europe, either through the employment of mercenaries or the re-training of indigenous forces.[18] Michael's government followed the former path for the most part, yet this and other policies could not unfold without an impact on society, from top to bottom.

In the Russian case, the three estates were far from fully fledged as elsewhere, especially the clergy, which had rarely considered itself separate from the secular authority, partly because there was no Orthodox Pope, partly because any kind of centrifugal force had been discouraged in Muscovy from the very beginning. Thus, the nobility, too, possessed very few characteristics of an independent aristocracy, local loyalties and more general exclusiveness having been eradicated in the reigns of Ivan III and IV, the Great and the Terrible. But this did not mean that the nobility was in every way subservient. Indeed, as has been pointed out on several occasions above, Russian absolutism was a socio-political structure closely involving the tsar with the *dvorianstvo*: the individual and the class stood together. Meanwhile, the role of the Third Estate was more passive, since it had little or no independence from, and shared little interdependence with, the absolutist establishment. Even more than the nobles of such principalities as Tver and Vladimir, the burghers of Pskov, Novgorod and other towns had been reduced to obedience. To be sure, leading merchants, the 'guests' in the seventeenth century and their successors in the eighteenth, made extremely important contributions to the prosperity of the state, but they were not often involved in its inner counsels. Of course, these observations apply much more to the vast mass of the population, the Russian peasants and comparable groups within the nationalities. Of these masses, it might be said that their world overlapped with the world of absolutism but was not fully part of it: for them, the world was the village rather than the wider community. Paying dues and taxes, toiling in the fields and workshops, maintaining lines of communication or defence, building churches or palaces, serving in the army or as domestics, they made an enormous contribution to the success of an enterprise from which they benefited little and felt themselves almost completely alienated. Such circumstances and sentiments intensified in all probability as the system of serfdom was intensified during Michael's reign.

Feeling the winds of change blowing in from the west, the government had to protect and extend the prosperity of the national economy, resorting not only to a more energetic attempt to extract as much labour and, increasingly, money from the peasants and their like, but also to the wider, if not more coherent, adoption of policies that might broadly be called mercantilist. These included the reservation unto itself by the tsarist state of special privileges in the fur trade, for example, and the careful restriction of the activities of foreign trading partners.[19]

Old Russian culture, old Slavic folkways with a superimposition of Christianity whose powers of penetration into nature worship and pagan magic have been much debated, was as yet little threatened by the newer secular humanism. On the other hand, although the classical 'humanism' of the Renaissance, the revived interest in the culture of Greece and Rome, and the Protestant Reformation, the breakaway by Luther, Calvin and others from Roman Catholicism, had not made any great impact on Russia, which was remote from the mainstream, there were Muscovite eddies detectable in a range of activities from architecture and icon-painting through to abstract thought. The determination of Michael's father and co-ruler, the Patriarch Filaret, to restore and maintain the cloistered culture of Orthodoxy against all threats from outside, of both older and newer origin, was an indicator of their strength.

The middle of the seventeenth century produced a signal moment in the history of Europe in the shape of a political crisis varying in size and characteristics from one part of the continent to another. While the most severe shock was felt in England, Scotland and Ireland with the execution of Charles I, almost no country was untouched, and Russia was certainly among those affected. We have noted above and described in fuller detail elsewhere how Tsar Alexis, son of Michael, was confronted by a serious revolt in Moscow and elsewhere soon after his accession. However, just as Louis XIV recovered from the threat posed to his throne in the series of disturbances known as the Frondes, sufficiently indeed for his kingdom to threaten dominance in Europe and beyond, so was Alexis able to survive and then to place his absolutism on a firmer foundation. To be sure, Alexis remained the supreme autocrat, and his ideology, – almost exclusively divine right – or, at least, this was still the imposing façade. But interpretation of divine right became more exclusively the domain of the tsar as the accommodation with the church reached the point of assumption of superiority over it: the Patriarch Nikon carried out a comprehensive reform causing a split with the Old Believers, and then succumbed in a confrontation with his former patron, Alexis himself. Before then, in 1649, a *zemsky sobor* had given its imprimatur (or rather its 'rubber stamp') to a new law code, or *Ulozhenie*, which gave official confirmation to the evolving social structure. Throughout the reign of Alexis and his immediate successors, there were at least some signs of bureaucratic rationalisation.

The Code of 1649 was to a considerable extent of Lithuanian origin, and, generally speaking, in this phase cultural influences in the broadest sense came largely from the immediate west, from Poland-Lithuania, with the Ukraine as one of the percolators. The acquisition of the Ukraine was altogether of great and wide importance, although attempts to establish a presence on the Baltic and Black Seas resulted in comparative failure, and movements into Siberia and towards Central Asia and the Far East were mostly of a consolidatory nature. Meanwhile, the army, still substantially trained by mercenaries, was becoming more regular, with a corresponding demotion for the old levies and not so old musketeers (*streltsy*). Some ships were built on the River Don for participation in the struggle against the Crimean Tatars and their patrons, the Ottoman Turks. And so, as in many other directions, the way was prepared for Peter the Great by his father.

Military developments affected the structure of the ruling class, which was also becoming more regularised. The abolition of the Muscovite system of precedence (*mestnichestvo*) in 1682 did not mean so much, as has sometimes been suggested, that old blood was being ousted by new, as that attitudes towards service, involving both traditional members of the tsarist establishment and upstarts, were becoming modernised, in line with developments elsewhere in Europe. It is also significant that the abolition took place half-a-dozen years or so after the death of Tsar Alexis, during a period when the figurehead of absolutism was less obtrusive, even if to be sure, the Regent Sophie was a much more remarkable person than her elder brother Theodore or Fedor (1682 was the year of his death and her 'accession'). The gap between the death of Alexis and the overthrow of Sophie by the future Peter the Great in 1689 bore witness to the fact that the tsarist system could survive and prosper without a charismatic and energetic autocrat on the throne, and that, therefore, it was a socio-political amalgam centrally involving the nobility as a ruling class rather than the dependency of a single individual. In the seventeenth century, certainly, the latter was the majority view, but it was more fervently held by the peasants than by their landlords, even when they were rising up in vast numbers to support the revolt of Stenka Razin from 1670 to 1671. For the most part and most of the time, however, the peasants accepted in patient resignation their unhappy lot, while waiting perhaps for a 'true tsar' who would lead them to a promised land, often giving their adherence to Old Belief, or in some cases running away to the frontier to join the Cossacks.[20] Meanwhile, the merchants and other upper members of the Third Estate were continuing to make their adjustments to changes in the international markets while making as much use as possible of internal opportunities, which now include the Ukraine as well as Siberia and Central Asia and the traditional heartland of Muscovy.

Absolutism could not develop without full economic support, and the government was therefore concerned that merchants and peasants alike should flourish, although it was at least as interested in extracting income from them. In other words, while the Russian policy, like that of other states in Europe at the time, could be called mercantilist, it was neither integrated nor comprehensive. The finalisation of the process of enserfment by 1649 was both a response to the general crisis of the mid-seventeenth century and an attempt to compensate for remoteness from the European 'core' but in by no means a coherent manner.[21] The economic consequences of the acquisition of the Ukraine are important enough to be mentioned again, as were the cultural, too. For not only the winds of religious reformation blew in by way of Kiev, but also some breezes of secular change. Their force must not be exaggerated, and we must remember that throughout Europe as a whole, new ways of thinking were only just beginning to make their way. After all, the world-views of the outstanding figures of the period such as the Englishmen Newton and Locke were, each after its own fashion, centred on religion. If such Protestants, and others who were Roman Catholic, were still in such a manner traditional in outlook, one could hardly expect the Orthodox to be iconoclastic.

An important individual example may be taken in the person of the future Peter the Great, whose early education certainly included instruction in the faith of his fathers, but also possessed a considerable amount of exposure to other ideas at the hands of inhabitants of the Foreign Settlement from Germany, Scotland and elsewhere. Following in the footsteps of Alexis, he had a confrontation of considerable seriousness with the Patriarch, and then went further in deciding that there should be no successor at the death of the head of the Russian church in 1700. But Peter himself was staunchly Orthodox, a believer in divine right and an upholder of the concept of the brotherhood of the Christian monarchs of Europe, which he hoped to strengthen through the promotion of a latter-day crusade against the infidel Ottoman Turks, whose expansionist ambitions had taken them as far as the gates of Vienna in 1683. However, at about the turn of the century, the secular concept of Europe was taking hold[22], and Russia shared in this, too: the Northern War mainly against Sweden from 1700 to 1721 had little religious element in it and was mostly for control of the Baltic.

Many of the reforms accompanying the war reflected the spirit of early eighteenth-century Europe as well as constituting the completion of the structure of absolutism on the foundations laid during the preceding period. Thus, at the same time as reducing the Orthodox church to a department of state, Peter added a secular rationale to his continued divine right, particularly through his adoption of the tenets of German cameralism, a variation of the still dominant mercantilist outlook. Although connected with Protestant Pietism, cameralism also possessed ideas of welfare and service in a well-regulated state. Calling himself that state's first servant, Peter attempted to blend theory imported from the German states, Scandinavia and elsewhere with the traditional Russian views of community.[23] His administrative reforms, both central and local, were similarly intended to make optimum use of modernised practices from Sweden through Prussia over to Western Europe. Of particular importance here was the acquisition of the Baltic provinces, which played a similar kind of role now to that assumed by the Ukraine from about the middle of the seventeenth century, as per-colator of cultural influences in the broadest sense. Peter did not forget the Black Sea or the Caspian, and continued, even extended, the interest of his predecessors in Siberia and Asia. According to some accounts, like Louis XIV before him, Peter aimed at domination of Europe, even of the world, but neither allegation is easy to substantiate.[24] Certainly, the wars of the early eighteenth century cut France down to size while advancing the claims of Russia (as well as those of Britain) to be a great power.

Such an assertion could not be made without an appropriate performance by the armed forces, and Peter made a great effort to make sure that it was given. In no other area did he make so much reality of his role as first servant, starting service in the ranks and awarding himself promotion only when he considered that he deserved it. Nevertheless, here as elsewhere, it has been all too easy to exaggerate the individual and to minimise the mass, to give too much emphasis to the innovation and not enough to the continuity. If military and even naval developments are considered in their European context and against their Russian background, they are not so far out of step or on the wrong tack. This is also the case with society. Here, an all too persistent image is of Peter coming back from his Great Embassy to Western Europe in 1698 to cut off the beards of the nobles, to force them to change their kaftans for uniforms, and to galvanise them from idleness into action, while promoting a comprehensive transfusion of new blood into the old blue. In fact, the vast majority of leading members of high society were members of families and patronage networks established before the end of the seventeenth century, already accustomed to service and to the demands imposed as well as the opportunities presented by it, if more rarely aware of European fashions in facial hair and clothing.[25] Similar observations could be made about commoners, too, merchants and peasants alike: with the middle and lower class as with the upper, already existing trends were reinforced rather than fresh departures taken. Moreover, even much of the opposition to Peter's reforms was conducted along lines already apparent before 1698, firmly rooted in Old Belief. On the other hand, of course, if historical development consisted of nothing but the reinforcement of already existing trends, there would never be any change at all. And so, if we look at the Table of Ranks and the nobility, the Chief Magistracy and the middle class, the poll tax and the peasantry, we cannot but see a measure of originality.

Similarly, in economic development, invention does occur and so do other breakthroughs. It was also possible for a government to force the pace: as in the Soviet Union in the 1930s, so in tsarist Russia in the first years of the eighteenth century. But the degree of success enjoyed by both bouts of artificial acceleration has been questioned. On the other hand, there are experts today who argue that the revolution associated with the name of Stalin was vital for the USSR's survival and victory in the Second World War, while Prince Shcherbatov calculated late in the eighteenth century that Russia would have needed two hundred years to catch up with the progress achieved under Peter the Great had the reformer not existed. Certainly, as in most other fields, much work remains to be done in this. On the whole, however, the balance of available evidence would appear to indicate that the leap forward that took place during Peter's reign resulted from the demands of war and other international pressures combined with an accumulation of internal trends begun before the reign started. In other words, Russia was a participant in rather than a spectator of the quickening of the pace associated with the European continental colonial rivalry and the early stages of industrial revolution at the same time as responding still to the pressures for the formation of a national market and taxation network.

We can see again a similar dual process as we attempt to detect the broad outlines of the picture of cultural change during the reign of Peter the Great. Let us recall the widespread image of Peter as secular reformer, but then also think of its context. To repeat the most important circumstance, Russia was becoming secularised at roughly the same time as much of the rest of Europe: the idea of Europe itself as a lay rather than religious concept was taking shape at about the turn of the century as the tsar was embarking upon the Northern War after his return from the Great Embassy to the West. The revolutionary interpretation of the cosmos advanced by Sir Isaac Newton was brought to Russia soon after 1700 at a time when it had still to meet with full acceptance back in Britain. Scientific and educational developments in general were in rough parallel with those elsewhere in the continent, as was the persistence of an older outlook among the majority of the people as a whole. However, recalling that even emphasis on generalities should not be made without some qualification, we should note again that Europe could be divided from many points of view into at least two major sections, East and West, and perhaps more. Bearing this in mind, and looking for bases of comparison, we should turn again to Scandinavia or the German states, especially Prussia, which provides us also with a personal counterpart to Peter the Great: Frederick William I, the 'Sergeant-King'.[26]

Frederick William was King of Prussia from 1713 to 1740 and therefore outlasted Peter by some fifteen years, during ten of which Russia was said to be suffering under the 'German yoke'. To be sure, neither Prussia nor its king was blamed for this imposition, which was charged rather against immigrants from other, smaller German states. But in fact, the 'German yoke' was a caricature of what actually transpired during the reign of the Empress Anna, when Russians as well as foreigners were to be found in the establishment. If the dominant foreign influence was still German, this was not just the personal choice of Anna, any more than it was exclusively the decision of her successor Elizabeth that the most important foreign influence during her reign became French. Generally speaking, indeed, the reigns between those of Peter the Great and Catherine the Great – that is, between the years 1725 and 1762 – demonstrated again that it was possible for the Russian absolutist system to function smoothly enough without a charismatic or forceful individual at the top. Some might even argue that a breathing space after the frenetic pace set by the great reformer was everywhere welcome. Certainly, although neither empress has yet been subject to full academic scrutiny, Anna and Elizabeth appear to have shared an aversion to government and to have left such business to their advisers. During their reigns, the bureaucracy increased in size and importance, and exerted a greater, and probably more efficient, control over the affairs of the Russian Empire, which consequently became a more cohesive polity. This was partly because no further major expansion occurred between the reigns of Peter and Catherine the Great.

However, the armed forces remained active throughout the interim, involvement in a series of international conflicts culminating in a major role during the Seven Years War from 1756 onwards. There is a still persistent misunderstanding that the army, and even more the navy, entered into a steep decline after the death of Peter the Great. To be sure, there was some diminution of activity at sea, but, for all Peter's efforts, the early record of the Russian navy had been far from glorious, and so there was no high standard to maintain. On land, there were some failures, again not without precedent, but also many successes, with impressive performances by the rank and file, and distinguished leadership from Rumiantsev, Suvorov and others.

Dominating the civil service, and providing virtually all the officers for the armed forces, the nobility also threatened to take on a larger part in the conduct of government at the highest level. At least, so runs a still extant interpretation of the events of 1730 at the accession of the Empress Anna. However, those events serve rather to underline the basic emphasis of this book, that Russian absolutism was a socio-political amalgam rather than the rule of one. Coincidentally and significantly enough, it was not long after this time that Montesquieu made a celebrated similar assertion in *The Spirit of the Laws*: 'no monarch – no nobility: no nobility – no monarch'. This axiom must be borne in mind when Montesquieu's further observation is considered, to the effect that the events of 1730 demonstrated clearly that Russia could not become an aristocracy. While Montesquieu did not fully spell out his view on the relationship between the autocrat and the *dvorianstvo,* he strongly implied that it should be one of interdependence, and that this interdependence would act as a restraint on the tendency of Russian absolutism towards despotism. More recent and more complete research has revealed that Russia was in fact further down the road that Montesquieu would have liked it to travel than he himself could appreciate.[27]

As in France, so in Russia, there were those who would have liked the nobility to take on some of the characteristics of leading members of the Third Estate, but there was a widespread reluctance on the part of the landlords to countenance any departure from economic activities rooted firmly in the soil of their estates. Equally, the leading members of Russia's traditional 'Third Estate' were restricted in their activities by the circumstance that they could normally encroach on the land and serf monopoly of the landlords only by becoming members of the nobility. But it would be wrong to draw from such limitations the conclusion that merchants were unable to enjoy a full measure of prosperity in commercial and manufacturing enterprises. As for the peasantry, weighed down though it was by serfdom or comparable encumbrances, to which it showed its continued opposition in persistence of flight and occasional revolt, the process of stratification showed clearly that at least some members of the lowest class could react to market opportunities. In other words, along with an official social hierarchy of a rigidly stratified nature, there were unofficial developments of a freer variety.

Opportunities for enterprise were to be found more frequently during the years 1725 to 1762 than is often thought. The old idea that a kind of depression set in after the death of Peter the Great has been shown to be false: it was rather the case that some of the attempts made by him artificially to increase the pace of economic change were revealed as failures. State enterprises set up during his reign were now often sold off to private entrepreneurs or allowed to languish. On the other hand, the state in general continued to play an important part in the management and direction of the economy through its tariff and taxation policies, for example.

Similarly, in the cultural field, even without the constant compulsion of the tsar reformer, progress continued in the formation of a secular outlook. If the cipher schools and some of the other institutions set up by him fell into decline, education of a formal, and even more of an informal, nature brought into its embrace an even greater number of members of the nobility, in all probability. Most assuredly, at least some of the individuals benefiting from it, first under predominantly German, later increasingly of French, influence, began to produce written literary and artistic testimony to the fact that genres for the most part originating abroad could be adapted and developed in the domestic environment. By this period, the dominant church-centred culture of less than a hundred years before was giving way more completely to the lay upstart. Recall just for a moment the halting, guarded manner in which such new modes were introduced into the Muscovy of Tsar Alexis. Now that shy infant was about to enter a confident adolescence under the patronage of a French-speaking German – the Empress Catherine the Great.

For the first time, an autocrat was about to compose a justification for absolutism – the celebrated *Nakaz* or Instruction to the Legislative Commission of 1767. Although this document was drawn mostly from Montesquieu, Beccaria and other writers of the Enlightenment, it begins, we should recall, with the observation: 'To do all the Good we possibly can to each other, is the great Rule of Christianity.'[28] In such a manner, the Empress may be said to be completing the process of incorporating the old idea of divine right in a secular framework. At the same time, she was astute enough to realise the powerful hold that Orthodoxy still possessed over the majority of her adopted people, a consideration that had helped her to power five years earlier. As she put it in the Manifesto at her accession in June 1762 alleging a tendency towards Protestantism of Peter III: 'Our Greek Church has been... subject to the ultimate danger by the change of the ancient Orthodoxy in Russia and the adoption of an infidel law.' On the other hand, as the Empire expanded into Poland-Lithuania, Catherine showed a degree of toleration towards Roman Catholics and Jews: when it moved south and east into Moslem lands, again, there was no persecution and a degree of recognition. To a considerable degree, then, while recognising the special position of Orthodoxy, the Empress made a considerable effort to act as the protectress of all her peoples.

Along with imperial expansion, there was consolidation and rationalisation of the administrative framework. We will not examine again here the detail of the provincial reform of 1775, the Charters of 1785 and other measures, but simply recall the manner in which they brought near to completion the socio-political basis of Russian absolutism: as put most succinctly by V. N. Bochkarev, 'the tsar's protection over the dvorianstvo, and the dvorianstvo's – over all Russia'. Reinforced by the traumatic experience for autocrat and nobility alike of the Pugachev Revolt, the 'monarque–noblesse' interdependence as identified in general terms by Montesquieu reached the culmination of its peculiar Russian formation. As we have seen, the preamble to the Charter of the Nobility was a celebration of centuries of military and civil service, a panegyric especially to those who had brought 'six unbroken years of victory in Europe, Asia and Africa'. Meanwhile 'the subordinates are stimulated by the example of their leaders to deeds which attract praise, honour and glory'. This, we can be fairly certain, was not the view from the towns and villages, of merchants and peasants, even though the former would be less discontented than the latter. Moreover, although envious outsiders would seek to undermine the old order at the first available opportunity, it would be premature to find in the ranks of Russia's Third Estate a bourgeoisie in the Marxist sense, even if prosperous peasants are included along with 'official' masters of commerce and manufacture.[29] As for the vast mass of the people, their outlook appeared to fluctuate between long periods of resigned obedience and short bouts of frenzied opposition.

However, having reached its culminating point in or around 1785, the old order began to crumble, from both inside and outside. In the first place, the more complex the government became, the more the bureaucracy developed as an order wedged between the upper echelons of the establishment and the ruling class as a whole. This was not just a question of obstructionist red tape, although it certainly was that, too. Mostly, it was the formation of the corporate discernment of a state interest which differed from that of high society.

The difference in outlook will become clearer when we turn to examine socio-economic rather than socio-political aspects of the

Russian situation towards the end of the eighteenth century. How were government and society to respond to the ever-increasing pace of change? At least in the early years of her reign, Catherine sought to respond constructively to new opportunities, to begin to dismantle the serf system and to encourage the growth of free trade. The nobility opposed such innovations, reacting to the international demand for grain and other products of the manorial economy by holding on firmly to what they possessed, at the same time as seeking to extend their possessions. A further difference of interest could be detected in the sphere of finance. In a burgeoning economy involving a steep rise in prices, the income of the state could not keep up with inflation, especially since the landlords increased the pressure on their own peasants while resisting any attempt by the government to put up the rate of the poll tax and other such dues. The early stages of industrial revolution, then, involving Russia along with the other states of Europe, were beginning to undermine absolutism as it reached its mature formation, even before the more dramatic threat posed by the French Revolution.[30]

Again, even before 1789, a cultural gap was beginning to open up between the autocracy and at least some members of the ruling class. The manner in which some young nobles found themselves at a crossroads between old and new outlooks was well caught by Miliukov:

One can imagine that spiritual confusion, that panic which possessed the serious and conscientious youth, when he had to make that decisive choice and when in making this choice he felt himself completely left to himself. Something similar must have been felt by those medieval medical students who went to the cemetery at the middle of the night in order to study the secrets of life on corpses.

Soviet historians have gone further than Miliukov in stressing the emergence of the intelligentsia in the last years of the eighteenth century, arguing that the process involved members of the middle class and even of the peasantry. Western historians in general would reject much of this assertion, as indeed would at least some of their Soviet colleagues.[31] But nearly all would agree that with Radishchev, if not before him, some kind of a break was made between the autocracy turning conservative and an emerging opposition. The French Revolution, as well as the final partition of Poland, served to make the break wider and more certain, during the reign of Paul, and after.

Historical perspective is not only a matter of time, but of place, too. The nation state, just like any other phenomenon, cannot be understood in isolation from its fellows; the history of one country alone is impossible. Russia, to which had been attributed an extraordinary degree of exclusive apartness, may be viewed in several ways, the most objective of which must be based on a global foundation. The broadest geographical division would be either East–West, which has been dominant in human enquiry for more than a century, or North–South, which has recently been receiving vigorous advocacy. Russia does not fit in neatly to these divisions, since it occupies something of a borderline position. And yet, if it does not seem to be quite part of the West or the North when examined from the remainder of the inside of these groupings, the view from the East or the South would probably be more positive. Especially in the centuries before 1917 and for some decades afterwards, Russians, white in colour, European in language and Christian in religion or Marxist in ideology controlled in turn the Empire and then the Soviet Union. Now, if yellows or browns with a native Asiatic tongue and Moslem religion or adaptation of Marxism are coming to play an increasingly important part in the affairs of at least some of the Socialist Republics and even in those of the Soviet Union as a whole, they, like all the other citizens of the USSR, are among the Northern haves, even if they do not have very much, rather than among the Southern have-nots, who often have nothing and only a fleeting grasp on life itself.

As part of the West, Russia may be appropriately placed in a category along with other absolutist states, particularly those of Eastern Europe, whose distinctive features, size and so on, have been given emphasis by investigations from Tatishchev and Montesquieu onwards. Among several analysts who have devoted searching attention to this type of government, Perry Anderson has talked of

one basic characteristic which divided the Absolute monarchies of Europe from all the myriad other types of despotic, arbitrary or tyrannical rule, incarnated or controlled by a personal sovereign, which prevailed elsewhere in the world. The increase in the political sway of the royal state was accompanied, not by a decrease in the economic security of noble landownership, but by a corresponding increase in the general rights of private property.[32]

The special position of Russia with regard to the second of the above observations, to which Anderson gives emphasis, has been indicated in the foregoing chapters. 'Rights of private property' were certainly consolidated by the nobility during the process of the making of Russian absolutism, and secured by some members of the third estate during the same period. However, even for the nobility, property rights were attached more to the class and less to the individuals and families comprising it. Primogeniture and entail, the guarantor of the estates of leading citizens in other parts of Europe, never took firm root in early modern Russia, partly because of Slavonic tradition concerning the obligations of parents to their children, partly because the nature of the service state on the European frontier militated against the development of an independent society. Peter the Great's introduction of the single succession or *maiorat* in 1714 undoubtedly constituted an attempt to adapt the Western system of succession to Russian conditions, but it proved difficult to administer and was opposed bitterly by the nobles themselves, being withdrawn soon after the accession of Anna in 1730.

In Catherine the Great's Charter of the Nobility of 1785, property was prominently listed among their personal advantages that could not be taken away without due process of law, but service to the state was still implicitly featured as an accompaniment to the enjoyment of these advantages. In spite of differences in social organisation and local affiliation between the position of the *dvoriane* and the Junkers, the Russian nobility is probably best compared with the Prussian, and, with similar allowance for variation under the general heading of European absolutism, Russian expansion in the eighteenth and nineteenth centuries in general is perhaps most appropriately compared with that of Prussia and Germany. The almost simultaneous collapse of the Romanovs and the Hohenzollerns at the end of the First World War, and then the struggle of their successor regimes for dominance in Europe, take the comparison well into the twentieth century.[33]

However, the failure of Nazi Germany to grasp world power and the success of Soviet Russia in the acquisition of at least a vast share of it combine with the earlier disappearance of absolutism to render this comparison inappropriate from the Second World War and to make another historical comparison, that with the United States of America, much more suitable than when first introduced towards the end of the eighteenth century as one of Catherine the Great's correspondents, the Baron Melchior von Grimm, observed:

Two empires will then share all the advantages of civilisation, of the power of genius, of letters, of arts, of arms and industry: Russia on the eastern side and America . . . on the western side, and we other peoples of the nucleus will be too degraded, too debased, to know otherwise than by a vague and stupid tradition what we have been.

Comparison of the USSR and the USA and their antecedents becomes increasingly significant as they rise to world power with the all-too-complete fulfilment of the Baron's prophecy, viewed in either East–West or North–South direction. While the nature of Russian absolutism now loses its central importance, it remains an important determinant of the Soviet variation of super-power.[34]

To revert finally to the basic metaphor of this book, and to note the popular identification of the Soviet government with that walled complex of buildings that the Romanovs inherited as the centre for their recuperating state of Muscovy soon after the beginning of the seventeenth century. The Kremlin has experienced many vicissitudes of fate since the end of the Time of Troubles and the coronation of Michael; as the task of the making of Russian absolutism necessitated a largely new state structure, it was mostly deserted for the new capital, St Petersburg. For two centuries or more, while absolutism reached its peak, then moved into decline and finally collapsed, the cathedrals and the palaces grouped at the heart of Moscow were often unoccupied. In the early spring of 1918, however, after the fall not only of tsarism but also of its first republican successor, under the threat of attack from the Baltic, Lenin took the capital of the nascent state back to Moscow and soon set himself up in a modest apartment in the Kremlin. What was first a necessity became transformed into a virtue; new adornments such as ever shining red stars and ever waving red banners embellished the Kremlin which is now proclaimed as the formal, almost sacred centre of the Soviet Union. Some historians have taken the contemporary Muscovite period as an indication that the USSR may be virtually equated with the empire of the tsars, as distorting an exaggeration as the argument that 1917 marked the dawning of an era with no historical provenance. Obviously, the making of the Soviet Union owes something to the making of Russian absolutism; as Lenin pointed out to over-optimistic supporters, the new order would have to be constructed from the bricks of the old. The estimation of the extent of the rebuilding, and of its dismantlement, remains an important task for historians and social scientists alike.[35]

NOTES

1. H. Ragsdale (ed.), *Paul I: A Reassessment of his Life and Reign* (Pittsburgh, 1979); H. Ragsdale, *Tsar Paul and the Question of Madness: An Essay on History and Psychology* (London, 1988).
2. D. Ransel, *The Politics of Catherinian Russia: The Panin Party* (New Haven, CT, and London, 1975), pp. 209–10.
3. Ibid., pp. 255–61.
4. Ibid., pp. 225–6, 283–5.
5. This section takes mainly from M. V. Klochkov, *Ocherki pravitelstvennoi deiatelnosti vremeni Pavla I* (Petrograd, 1916).
6. R. Pipes, *Karamzin's Memoir on Ancient and Modern Russia: A Translation and Analysis* (Cambridge, MA, 1959), p. 135. On Karamzin himself in this context, see A. G. Cross, 'The Russian literary scene in the reign of Paul I', *Canadian-American Slavic Studies*, vol. 7, no. 1 (1973).
7. See, for example, N. E. Saul, *Russia and the Mediterranean, 1799–1807* (Chicago and London, 1970); H. Ragsdale, *Detente in the Napoleonic Era: Bonaparte and the Russians* (Lawrence, KA, 1980).
8. A. McConnell, 'Alexander I's Hundred Days: The Politics of a Paternalist Reformer', *Slavic Review*, vol. 28 (1969) pp. 375–6.
9. D. Kobeko, *Tsesarevich Pavel Petrovich, 1754–1796* (St Petersburg, 1883) introductory epigraph and p. 173.
10. E. S. Shumigorsky, *Imperator Pavel I: zhizn i tsartvovanie* (St Petersburg, 1907), pp. 5–6; Klochkov, *Ocherki*, pp. ii–iii, 142; R. E. McGrew, 'The Politics of Absolutism: Paul I and the Bank of Assistance for the Nobility', *Canadian-American Slavic Studies*, vol. 7 (1973), p. 38; J. L. H. Keep, 'Paul I and the Militarization of Government', ibid., p. 14.
11. V. D. Kuzmina *et al.*, 'Russkoe iskusstvo' in A. I. Baranovich *et al.* (eds),

Ocherki istorii SSSR: Rossiia vo vtoroi polovine XVIIIv. (Moscow, 1956), p. 562; David Ransel, *The Politics of Catherinian Russia: The Panin Party* (New Haven, CT, and London, 1975), p. 283.

12. A. P. Bazhova, 'Vnutrenniaia politika tsarizma i russkoe obshchestvo na rubezhe novogo stoletiia' in A. P. Bazhova *et al.* (eds), *Istoriia SSSR*, pervaia seriia, vol. 4 (Moscow, 1967), pp. 56–8; I. A. Fedosov, 'Prosvechchennyi absoliutizm v Rossii', *Voprosy istorii*, no. 9 (1970), p. 38; N. Ia. Eidelman, *Gran vekov: Politicheskaia borba v Rossii, konets XVIII – nachalo XIX Stoletiia* (Moscow, 1981), pp. 73, 139, 160.

13. L. G. Beskrovnyi *et al.* (eds), *Istoriia SSSR*, pervaia seriia, vol. 3 (Moscow, 1967), pp. 7–11, 189–91, 584–5.

14. Marx to Weydemeyer, 5 March 1852, with his own emphases in Marx and Engels, *Selected Correspondence, 1846–1895* (London, 1943), p. 57; Adam Ferguson, *An Essay on the History of Civil Society, 1767* (Edinburgh, 1966), for example, from the Introduction by Duncan Forbes, pp. xxii–xxiv, xxxi–xxxviii.

15. I. de Madariaga argues against the use of the term 'autocracy' in 'Autocracy and Sovereignty', *Canadian-American Slavic Studies*, vol. 16 (1982). See also her criticism of 'neo-Marxist perspective' in the *Times Literary Supplement*, 21 June 1985, p. 700.

16. See I. Wallerstein, *The Modern World-System* (London, 1974).

17. See, for example, D. Parker, *The Making of French Absolutism* (London, 1983) and R. Bonney, 'What's in a Name?', *French History*, vol. 1 (1987).

18. G. Parker, *The Military Revolution, Military Innovation and the Rise of the West, 1500–1800* (Cambridge, 1988), p. 43, writes:

Warfare in early modern Europe was certainly transformed by three important, related developments – a new use of firepower, a new type of fortifications, and an increase in army size. But the timing of the transformation was far slower, and the impact less total, than was once thought. Most of the wars fought in Europe before the French Revolution were not brought to an end by a strategy of extermination, but. . . through a strategy of attrition, via the patient accumulation of minor victories and the slow erosion of the enemy's economic base.

19. See, for example, A. A. Preobrazhenskii, 'XVII stoletie i genezis kapitalisticheskikh otnoshenii v Rossii', *Novaia i noveishaia istoriia*, no. 3 (1989).

20. V. S. Rumiantseva, *Narodnoe antitserkovnoe dvizhenie v Rossii v XVII veke* (Moscow, 1986) and 'Tendentsiia razvitiia obshchestvennogo soznaniia i prosveshcheniia v Rossii XVII veka', *Voprosy istorii*, no. 2 (1988).

21. See E. D. Domar, 'The Causes of Slavery or Serfdom: A Hypothesis', *Journal of Economic History*, vol. 30 (1970); P. Dukes, 'Catherine's Enlightened Absolutism and the Problem of Serfdom', in W. E. Butler (ed.), *Russian Law: Historical and Political Perspectives* (Leyden, 1977); P. Kolchin, *Unfree Labor: American Slavery and Russian Serfdom* (Cambridge, MA, 1987).

22. P. Burke, 'Did Europe exist before 1700?', *History of European Ideas*,

vol. 1 (1980); H. D. Schmidt, 'The Establishment of Europe as a Political Expression' *Historical Journal,* vol. 9 (1966).

23. See in particular M. Raeff, *The Well-Ordered Police State: Social and Institutional Change through Law in the Germanies and Russia, 1600–1800* (New Haven, CT, 1983); C. Peterson, *Peter the Great's Administrative and Judicial Reforms: Swedish Antecedents and the Process of Reception* (Stockholm, 1979).

24. E. V. Anisimov, 'Petr I: rozhdenie imperii', *Voprosy istorii,* no. 7 (1989) writes:

The Petrine reforms led to the formation of the military-bureaucratic state with a strong centralised autocratic power, based on a serf economy, and a strong army (the size of which continued to grow after the war). That Peter's formidable ship of state set sail for India was a natural consequence of the internal development of the Empire. During Peter's reign, the foundations of Russia's imperial policy in the eighteenth and nineteenth century were laid. Imperial stereotypes began to take shape.

On Anisimov's earlier work, see C. B. Stevens (ed.), 'E. V. Anisimov on Petrine and post-Petrine Russia', *Soviet Studies in History,* vol. 28 (1989).

25. J. LeDonne, 'Ruling Families in the Russian Political Order, 1689–1825', *Cahiers du Monde russe et soviétique* vol. 28 (1987) argues for the continuity in the membership of the leading strata of the nobility. D. S. Likhachev, 'The Petrine Reforms and the Development of Russian Culture', *Canadian-American Slavic Studies,* vol. 13 (1979), pp. 230–2, warns us not to be tricked by Peter's 'gift of imbuing the transformations he effected with a vividly demonstrative character' into ignoring the fact that his reforms were the inevitable results of the whole development of Russian culture as the beginning of the transition from a medieval to a modern model. Inevitable, too, was the break with the whole medieval sign system by the culture produced by Peter. The transition which had previously proceeded at a subconscious level became, under Peter, a conscious process.

26. See, for example, R. Vierhaus, *Germany in the Age of Absolutism* (Cambridge, 1988).

27. O. A. Omelchenko, 'Konstitutsiia "prosveshchennogo absoliutizma" v Rossi (Neizvestnye zakonodatelnye proekty Ekateriny II)', *Sovetskoe gosudarstvo i pravo,* no. 8 (1989) gives some recognition to this fact.

28. In several versions, the *Nakaz* begins with an invocation, 'O Lord my God, hearken unto me, and instruct me; that I may administer Judgment unto thy People; as the sacred Laws direct to judge with Righteousness!'

29. See, for example, A. I. Aksenov, *Genealogiia moskovskogo kupechestva XVIIIv: iz istorii formirovaniia russkoi burzhuazii* (Moscow, 1988).

30. See B. N. Mironov, *Vnutrennii rynok Rossii vo vtoroi polovine XVIII – pervoi polovine XIXv* (Leningrad, 1981); *Khlebnye tseny v Rossii za dva stoletiia (XVIII–XIXvv.)* (Leningrad, 1985); 'Le mouvement des prix des céréales en Russie du XVIIIe siècle au début du XXe siècle', *Annales: economies, sociétés, civilisations,* vol. 41 (1986). For another interesting view, see I. Blanchard, *Russia's 'Age of Silver': Precious Metal Production*

and Economic Growth in the Eighteenth Century (London and New York, 1989).

31. P. N. Miliukov, *Ocherki po istorii russkoi kultury*, vol. 3 (Paris, 1937), pp. 403–4. See Chapter 5, note 57 above. And see also M. M. Gromyko, 'Kultura russkogo krestianstva XVIII–XIX vekov kak predmet istoricheskogo issledovaniia', *Istoriia SSSR*, no. 3 (1987).

32. P. Anderson, *Lineages of the Absolutist State* (London, 1974), p. 429.

33. M. Raeff, 'The Russian Nobility', in I. Banac and P. Bushkovich (eds), *The Nobility in Russia and Eastern Europe* (New Haven, CT, 1983), pp. 106–9; and, more generally, M. Raeff, *The Well-Ordered Police State: Social and Institutional Change through Law in the Germanies and Russia, 1600–1800* (New Haven, CT, 1983). For an interesting case study, see P. Petschauer, 'The Philosopher and the Reformer: Tsar Peter I, G. W. Leibniz and the College System', *Canadian-American Slavic Studies*, vol. 13 (1979). For a stimulating survey, see P. Kennedy, *The Rise and Fall of the Great Powers: Economic Change and Military Conflict from 1500 to 2000* (New York and London, 1988).

An interesting example of early Russian expansion towards the Balkans may be pursued through: J. A. Duran, 'Catherine II, Potemkin and Colonization Policy in Southern Russia', *Russian Review*, vol. 28 (1969); R. E. Jones, 'Opposition to War and Expansion in Late Eighteenth-Century Russia', *Jahrbücher für Geschichte Osteuropas*, vol. 32 (1984); H. Ragsdale, 'Evaluating the Traditions of Russian Aggression: Catherine II and the Greek Project', *Slavonic Review*, vol. 66 (1988). For a general survey, see M. S. Anderson, *The Eastern Question, 1774–1923* (London and New York, 1966). See also note 24 above.

34. See P. Dukes, *The Last Great Game: USA versus USSR: Events, Conjunctures, Structures* (London and New York, 1989), p. 143, and *passim*.

35. See, for example, S. White, *Political Culture and Soviet Politics* (London, 1979); A. H. Brown (ed.), *Political Culture and Communist Studies* (London, 1984).

Select Bibliography

Two useful aids are R. Bartlett and P. Clendenning (eds), *Eighteenth Century Russia: A Select Bibliography of Works Published since 1955* (Newtonville, MA, 1981) and P. A. Crowther, *A Bibliography of Works in English and Russian History to 1800* (Oxford and New York, 1969). L. A. J. Hughes produces 'Russian Studies: The Eighteenth Century', for *The Year's Work in Modern Language Studies* of the Modern Humanities Research Association. Further assistance regarding reading, as well as interesting descriptive analysis may be found in Robert Auty and Dimitri Obolensky (eds), *Companion to Russian Studies:* vol. 1, *An Introduction to Russian History* (Cambridge, 1976); vol. 2, *An Introduction to Russian Language and Literature* (Cambridge, 1977); vol. 3, *An Introduction to Russian Art and Architecture* (Cambridge, 1980).

Further introductions to the subject of this book are to be found in survey histories such as those by P. Dukes, M. T. Florinsky, L. Kochan and R. Abraham, and N. V. Riasanovsky. Of these, Florinsky gives the fullest account of the eighteenth century but is less complete on the seventeenth century, concerning which see V. O. Kliuchevsky (styled Klyuchevsky) translated by L. Archibald as *The Rise of the Romanovs* (London, 1970) and by N. Duddington as *Course in Russian History: The Seventeenth Century* (New York, 1968). See also G. V. Vernadsky, *The Tsardom of Muscovy, 1547–1682*, 2 vols (New Haven CT, and London, 1969). S. M. Soloviev's multi-volumed *History of Russia* is being brought out in translation (Gulf Breeze, FL, 1976), with several volumes either out or on their way for the seventeenth century and the eighteenth century up to the 1770s. Two less scholarly but still useful works are R. N. Bain, *The First Romanovs, 1613–1725: A History of Muscovite Civilisation and the Rise of Modern Russia under Peter the Great and his Forerunners* (London, 1905) and Z. Schakovskoy, *Precursors of Peter the Great: The Reign of Tsar Alexis, Peter the Great's Father, and the Young Peter's Struggle against the Regent*

Sophia for the Mastery of Russia (London, 1964). On the eighteenth century, see M. Raeff, *Imperial Russia, 1682–1825: The Coming of Age of Modern Russia* (New York, 1971) and A. Lentin, *Russia in the Eighteenth Century: From Peter the Great to Catherine the Great, 1696–1796* (London, 1973).

The periods covered in the book's six chapters may be most conveniently pursued as follows. Unfortunately, Chapter One, 1613–1645, still awaits full coverage. On Tsar Michael and his successors, a sound introduction is to be found in W. Lincoln, *The Romanovs: Autocrats of All the Russias* (New York, 1981). See also the Notes on pp. 28–9, especially the article on Filaret by J. L. H. Keep, and Kliuchevsky and Vernadsky as above. For Chapter Two, 1645–1689, P. Longworth, *Alexis: Tsar of All the Russias* (London, 1984) is basic. A full-scale study of the Regent Sophia is nearing completion by L. A. J. Hughes, whose preliminary sketch, 'Sophia, Regent of Russia', is to be found in *History Today* (July 1982). For other items, see Notes, pp. 62–4, and again, Kliuchevsky and Vernadsky as above. With Chapter Three, 1689–1725 we arrive in a period that has been more fully covered than its two predecessors. M. S. Anderson, *Peter the Great* (London, 1978) is the most reliable up-to-date study, although B. H. Sumner, *Peter the Great and the Emergence of Russia* (London, 1951) remains useful, as does M. Raeff (ed. and intro.), *Peter the Great: Reformer or Revolutionary?* (Boston, 1963). R. Wittram, Peter I, *Czar and Kaiser,* 2 vols (Gottingen, 1964) is a major biography, while Hans Bagger, *Peter den Stores. Reformer: En forskningsoversigt* (Copenhagen, 1979) has been translated into Russian as Khans Bagger, *Reformy Petra Velikogo: obzor issledovanii* (Moscow, 1985). It comprises a good summary account of the reforms and an excellent bibliography of works in Russian and other languages. See also pp. 109–11 above. Chapter Four, 1725–1761, like Chapters One and Two, contains large areas still to be fully investigated. Meehan-Waters, *Autocracy and Aristocracy: The Russian Service Elite of 1730* (New Brunswick, NJ, 1982) is a fundamental study with a wider relevance for the theme of this book than the subtitle might suggest. Soviet analysis was much advanced by S. M. Troitsky. For his work, that of E. V. Anisimov and others, see pp. 143–4 above. Isabel de Madariaga's *Russia in the Age of Catherine the Great* (London, 1981) is a central work for Chapter Five, 1761–1796. J. T. Alexander, *Catherine the Great: Life and Legend* (New York and Oxford, 1989) is the best biography. See generally for this well-covered period, pp. 188–92 above. Finally, Chapter Six, 1796–1801, may be most conveniently approached through H. Ragsdale (ed.), *Paul I: A Reassessment of his Life and Reign* (Pittsburgh, 1979). Or the articles in *Canadian-American Slavic Studies,* vol. 7 (1973). An outstanding Soviet work is N. Ia. Eidelman, *Gran vekov: politicheskaia borba v Rossii: konets XVIII – nachalo XIX stoletiia* (Moscow, 1981). A major biography by R. E. McGrew is nearing completion. For some of his analysis, and that of others, see pp. 220–3 above.

Among useful reference works are S. G. Pushkarev (comp.), *Dictionary of Russian Historical Terms from the Eleventh Century to 1917* (New Haven, CT, 1970) and J. L. Wieczynski (ed.), *The Modern Encyclopaedia of Russian and Soviet History* (Gulf Breeze, FL, 1976). Translations of significant documents may be found in G. V. Vernadsky *et al.* (eds), *A Source Book for Russian History from Early Times to 1917,* 3 vols (London and New Haven, CT, 1972); P. Dukes (ed.), *Russia under Catherine the Great,* 2 vols (Newtonville MA 1977–8); and G. L. Freeze (ed.), *From Supplication to Revolution: A Documentary Social History of Imperial Russia* (Oxford, 1988). A collaborative British–Soviet collection of documents on Russo-British relations during the reign of Peter the Great is to be published by Cambridge University Press. An introduction to the many interesting travel books is A. G. Cross, *Russia under Western Eyes, 1553–1815* (London, 1971). On British travel and other reactions, see M. S. Anderson, *Britain's Discovery of Russia, 1553–1815* (London, 1958). On Russians in Britain, see A. G. Cross, *'By the Banks of the Thames': Russians in Eighteenth Century Britain* (Newtonville MA, 1980). A second volume on Britons in Russia in the eighteenth century is forthcoming. On a different kind of contact, see A. G. Cross, *The Russian Theme in English Literature from the Sixteenth Century to 1980: An Introductory Survey and a Bibliography* (Oxford, 1985). On early Russian–US contacts, see N. N. Bashkina *et al.* (eds), *The United States and Russia: The Beginnings of Relations, 1765–1815* (Washington, DC, 1980); and N. N. Bolkhovitinov, *The Beginnings of Russian–American Relations, 1775–1815* (Cambridge, MA, 1975).

For those who read Russian, the best introduction is B. A. Rybakov and others (eds), *Istoriia SSSR,* first series, 6 Vol. (Moscow, 1967–70). Vol. 3 covers the period *c.* 1650–1795. A concise version of the overall Soviet interpretation may be found in *History of the USSR*, vol. 1 (Moscow, 1977), while Soviet articles may be found in translation in *Soviet Studies in History.* Other useful periodicals are *Russian Review, Slavic Review, Canadian-American Slavic Studies, Irish Slavonic Studies, Scottish Slavonic Review.* The leading Soviet journals are *Istoriia SSSR, Novaia i noveishaia istoriia* and *Voprosy istorii.*

On absolutism in general, see, for example, P. Anderson, *Lineages of the Absolutist State* (London, 1974), and T. Skocpol, *States and Social Revolutions: A Comparative Analysis of France, Russia and China* (Cambridge, 1979). The wider context may also be pursued in the *New Cambridge Modern History* and in various works on eighteenth-century Europe by M. S. Anderson, J. Black and others. A useful introduction to the earlier period is J. H. Shennan, *The Origins of the Modern European State, 1450–1727* (London, 1974).

The bibliography of the period 1613–1801 in Russian history is vast and continually expanding. There follows a summary list of publications, for the most part not included in the chapter Notes or in the Select Bibliography above:

M. P. Alekseev, *Russko–angliiskie sviazi (XVIII vek – pervaia polovina XIX veka* (Moscow, 1982).

T. V. Alekseeva (ed.), *Russkoe iskusstvo XVII veka* (Moscow, 1968, 1973).

P. Avrich, *Russian Rebels, 1600–1800* (London, 1973).

S. H. Baron, *Muscovite Russia: Collected Essays* (London, 1980).

L. G. Beskrovny and B. B. Kafengauz (eds), *Khrestomatiia po istorii SSSR: XVIII vek* (Moscow, 1963).

J. L. Black, *G. F. Müller and the Imperial Russian Academy* (Kingston and Montreal, 1986).

J. Blum, *Lord and Peasant in Russia from the Ninth to the Nineteenth Century* (Princeton, NJ, 1961).

V. I. Buganov, *Krestianskie voiny v Rossii XVII–XVIII vv.* (Moscow, 1976).

L. V. Cherepnin (ed.), *Krestianskie voiny v Rossii XVII–XVIII vekov: problemy, poiski, resheniia* (Moscow, 1974).

L. V. Cherepnin, *Zemskie sobory russkogo gosudarstva v XVI–XVII vv.* (Moscow, 1978).

M. Cherniavsky (ed.), *The Structure of Russian History: Interpretative Essays* (New York, 1970).

M. Cherniavsky, *Tsar and People: Studies in Russian Myths* (New Haven, CT, 1961).

M. Confino, *Domaines et seigneurs en Russie vers la fin du XVIIIe siècle: Etude de structures agraires et de mentalités économiques* (Paris, 1963).

M. Confino, *Systèmes agraires et progrès agricole: l'assolement triennal en Russie au XVIIIe–XIXe siècles* (Paris, 1969).

A. G. Cross (ed.), *Great Britain and Russia in the Eighteenth Century: Contacts and Comparisons* (Newtonville, MA, 1979).

A. G. Cross (ed.), *Russia and the West* (Newtonville, MA, 1983).

A. G. Cross, R. P. Bartlett and K. Rasmussen (eds), *Russia and the World of the Eighteenth Century* (Columbus, OH, 1988).

R. O. Crummey, *The Old Believers and the World of Antichrist; The Vyg Community and the Russian State, 1694–1855* (Madison, WI, 1970).

R. O. Crummey, 'Peter and the Boiar aristocracy, 1689–1700', *Canadian-American Slavic Studies*, Vol. 8 (1974).

R. O. Crummey, 'Russian absolutism and the nobility', *Journal of Modern History*, vol. 49 (1977).

E. Donnert, *La Russie au siècle des Lumières* (Leipzig, 1983).

C. Drage, *Russian Literature in the Eighteenth Century: The Solemn*

Ode, the Epic, other Poetic Genres, the Story, the Novel, Drama (London, 1978).

N. M. Druzhinin *et al.* (eds), *Absoliutizm v Rossii XVII–XVIII vv.* (Moscow, 1964).

C. Duffy, *Russia's Way to the West: Origins and Nature of Russia's Military Power, 1700–1800* (London, 1981).

A. S. Eleonskaia, *Russkaia publitsistika vtoroi poloviny XVII veka* (Moscow, 1978).

M. E. Falkus, *The Industrialization of Russia, 1700–1914* (London, 1972).

G. L. Freeze, *The Russian Levites: Parish Clergy in the Eighteenth Century* (Cambridge, MA, 1977).

J. G. Garrard (ed.), *The Eighteenth Century in Russia* (Oxford, 1973).

C. E. Gribble, *A Short Dictionary of Eighteenth-Century Russian* (Cambridge, MA, 1976).

G. H. Hamilton, *The Art and Architecture of Russia* (Harmondsworth, 1954).

R. Hellie, 'The Petrine army: continuity, change and impact', *Canadian-American Slavic Studies,* vol. 8 (1974).

R. Hudson, Jr, 'Urban estate engineering in eighteenth-century Russia: Catherine the Great and the elusive *meshchanstvo*', *Canadian-American Slavic Studies,* Vol. 18 (1984).

A. L. Kaganovich, *Arts of Russia: Seventeenth and Eighteenth Centuries* (Geneva, 1968).

A. Kahan, *The Plow, the Hammer and the Knout: An Economic History of Eighteenth-Century Russia* (Chicago and London, 1985).

J. L. H. Keep, *Soldiers of the Tsar: Army and Society in Russia, 1462–1874* (Oxford, 1985).

J. D. Klier, *Russia Gathers her Jews: The Origins of the 'Jewish Question' in Russia, 1772–1825* (DeKalb, IL, 1986).

A. V. Kokorev (ed.), *Khrestomatiia po russkoi literature XVIII veka* (Moscow, 1961).

B. I. Krasnobaev, *Russkaia kultura vtoroi poloviny XVIII–nachala XIXv.* (Moscow, 1983).

G. V. Lantzeff, *Siberia in the Seventeenth Century: A Study of the Colonial Administration,* University of California Publications in History, Vol. 30 (1943).

J. P. LeDonne, 'Ruling families in the Russian political order, 1689–1825', *Cahiers du monde russe et soviétique,* vol. 28 (1987).

G. A. Lensen (ed.), *Russia's Eastward Expansion* (Englewood Cliffs, NJ, 1964).

P. Longworth, *The Cossacks* (London and New York, 1969).

G. Marker, *Publishing, Printing and the Origins of Intellectual Life in Russia, 1700–1800* (Princeton, NJ, 1985).

D. McKay and H. M. Scott, *The Rise of the Great Powers, 1648–1815* (London, 1983).

R. L. Nichols and T. G. Stavrou (eds), *Russian Orthodoxy under the Old Regime* (New York, 1981).

S. A. Peshtich, *Russkaia istoriografiia XVIII veka*, 3 vols (Leningrad, 1961–71).

G. M. Phipps, *Britons in Seventeenth-Century Russia* (Ann Arbor, MI, 1972).

W. M. Pintner and D. K. Rowney (eds), *Russian Officialdom: The Bureaucratization of Russian Society from the Seventeenth to the Twentieth Century* (London, 1980).

W. M. Pintner, 'The burden of defense in Imperial Russia', *Russian Review*, vol. 43 (1984).

S. F. Platonov, *Russia and the West* (Hattiesburg, W. Va., 1972).

M. Raeff, *Understanding Imperial Russia: State and Society in the Old Regime* (New York, 1981).

M. Raeff, *The Well-Ordered Police State: Social and Institutional Change through Law in the Germanies and Russia, 1600–1800* (New Haven, CT, 1983).

M. Raeff (ed.), 'Kliuchevskii's Russia: critical studies', *Canadian-American Slavic Studies*, Vol. 20 (1986).

H. Rogger, *National Consciousness in Eighteenth-Century Russia* (Cambridge, MA, 1960).

A. Rothstein, *Peter the Great and Marlborough: Politics and Diplomacy in Converging Wars* (London, 1986).

M. Rywkin (ed.), *Russian Colonial Expansion to 1917* (London, 1988).

D. Saunders, *The Ukrainian Impact on Russian Culture, 1750–1850* (Edmonton, Alb, 1985).

G. R. Seaman, *History of Russian Music* (Oxford, 1967).

Y. N. Semyonov, *Siberia: Its Conquest and Development* (London, 1963).

R. E. F. Smith and D. Christian, *Bread and Salt; A Social and Economic History of Food and Drink* (Cambridge, 1984).

Y. M. Sokolov, *Russian Folklore* (New York, 1950).

S. M. Soloviev, *History of Russia*:

Vol. 14, *The Time of Troubles: Boris Godunov and Dmitry the Pretender*, G. E. Orchard (ed.)

Vol. 24, *The Character of Old Russia*, A. V. Muller (ed.).

Vol. 25. *Tsar Fedor Rebellion in Moscow, The Accession of Sofia and Her Policy* L. A. J. Hughes (ed.)

Vol. 29, *Peter the Great: The Grand Reforms Begin*. K. A. Papmehl (ed.).

Vol. 34, *Empress Anna: Favorites, Policies, Campaigns*, W. J. Gleason (ed.).

Vol. 35, *The Rule of Empress Anna*, R. Hantula (ed.).

Vol. 45, *The Rule of Catherine the Great, The Legislative Commission (1766–1768)*, W. H. Hill, (ed.) (Gulf Breeze, Fla, 1980, 1981, 1982, 1984, 1986).

O. Subtelny, *Domination of Eastern Europe: Sixteenth to Eighteenth Century Background* (Gloucester, MA, 1986).

E. C. Thaden, *Russia's Western Borderlands, 1710–1870* (Princeton, NJ, 1984).

H. J. Torke, 'Continuity and change in the relations between bureaucracy and society in Russia, 1613–1861', *Canadian-American Slavic Studies*, Vol. 5 (1971), with comment by J. L. H. Keep in Vol. 6 (1972).

S. M. Troitsky, *Finansovaia politika russkogo absoliutizma v XVIII veke* (Moscow, 1966).

S. M. Troitsky, *Russkii absoliutizm i dvorianstvo v XVIIIv: formirovanie biurokratii* (Moscow, 1974).

S. M. Troitsky, *Rossiia v XVIII veke: Sbornik statei i publikatsii* (Moscow, 1982).

G. Yaney, *The Systematization of Russian Government: Social Evolution in the Domestic Administration of Imperial Russia, 1711–1905* (Urbana, IL, 1973).

A. Yanov, *The Russian Challenge* (Oxford and New York, 1987).

A. A. Zimin (ed.), *Khrestomatiia po istorii SSSR, XVI–XVIIvv.* (Moscow, 1962).

V. A. Zoltarev *et al.* (eds) *Vo slavu otechestva: razvitie voennoi mysli i voennogo iskusstva v Rossii vo vtoroi polovine XVIIIv.* (Moscow, 1984).

Maps

URAL MOUNTAINS

Solikamsk

Perm

Kungur

R. Ufa

R. Kama

R. Viatka

Viatka

Kazan

Velikii Ustiug

R. Sukhona

R. Unzha

R. Dvina (Northern)

Archangel

Kholmogory

Kostroma

Suzdal

WHITE SEA

SOLOVETSKY I.

Kargopol

Vologda

Iaroslavl

Troitse Sergiev

Lake Onega

Tver

Bezhetsk

Staritsa

Lake Ladoga

Olonets

R. Neva

St Petersburg

Novgorod

North Cape

KARELIA

Vyborg

I.

KRONSTADT

Narva

Pskov

R. Narva

FINLAND

Dorpat

R. Dvina

Cape Gangut

Gulf of Finland

Revel

ESTONIA

LIVONIA

ALAND ISLANDS

Nystad

DAGO I.

OESEL I.

Riga

COURLAND

SWEDEN

Stockholm

BALTIC SEA

200 mls

200 kms

0

0

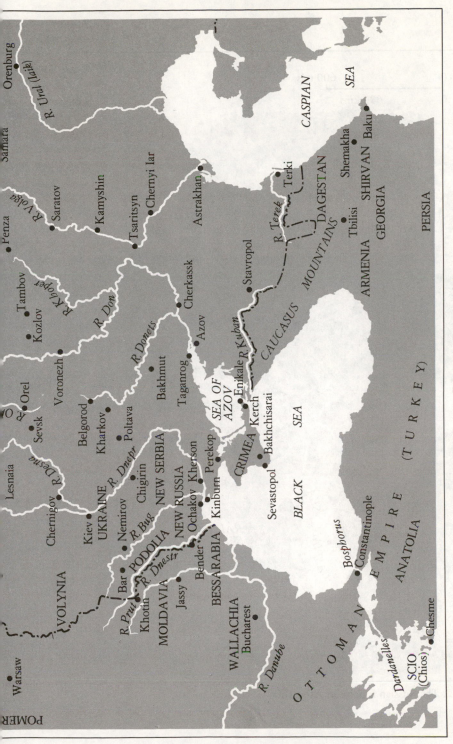

1. The Russian Empire in Europe, 1800

2. The Russian Empire in Asia, 1800

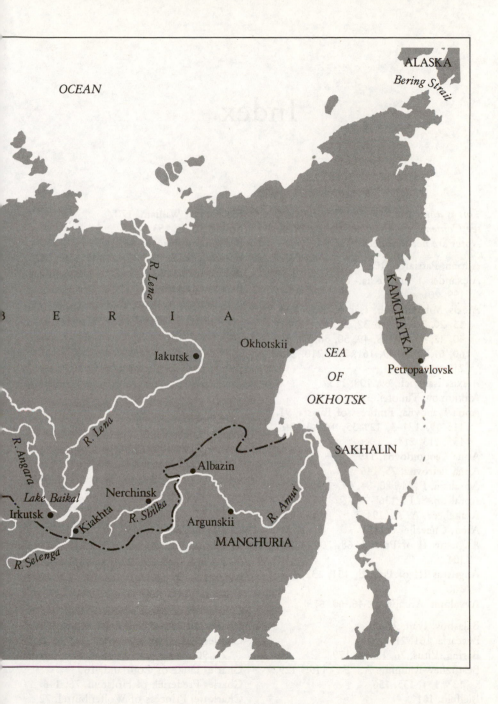

Index